ENEMIES OF GOD

ENEMIES OF GOD

The Witch-hunt in Scotland

CHRISTINA LARNER

With a Foreword by
NORMAN COHN

1981
CHATTO & WINDUS
LONDON

Published by
Chatto & Windus Ltd
40 William IV Street
London WC2N 4DF

★

Clarke Irwin & Co Ltd
Toronto

*British Library Cataloguing
in Publication Data*

Larner, Christina
Enemies of God.
1. Witchcraft–Scotland–History
I. Title
272'.8   BF1581
ISBN 0–7011–2424–5

Printed in Great Britain by
Ebenezer Baylis & Son Ltd,
The Trinity Press, Worcester, and London

For my parents
John *and* Nella Ross

'For all those that wold draw us from God (be they Kings or Quenes) being of the Devil's nature, are enemyis unto God, and therefore will God that in such cases we declare ourselves enemyis unto them.'

JOHN KNOX, 1564

'declarez deument attainctz et convaincuz d'avoir damnablement communiqué avec le diable, ennemy de la gloire de Dieu et du genre humain, s'estre donnez à luy et l'avoir adoré . . .'

Sentence passed in Gien, 1600

'Judges allow themselves too much liberty, in condemning such as are accused of this crime because they conclude they cannot be severe enough to the enemies of God; and Assizers are afraid to suffer such to escape as are remitted to them, lest they let loose an enraged Wizard in their neighbourhood. And thus poor Innocents die in multitudes by an unworthy martyredom, and Burning comes in fashion.'

SIR GEORGE MACKENZIE, 1672

CONTENTS

MAPS

The maps were prepared by the cartography section of the Department of Geography, University of Glasgow.

FOREWORD

As Christina Larner indicates in her Acknowledgements, I have some responsibility for the existence of this book.

For many years I was director of a research centre—the Columbus Centre—which was concerned with the comparative study of the dynamics of persecution and extermination. When the Centre first came into existence, in 1966, two specific historical problems were at the very core of its programme of research: the motivations behind what is commonly called the Holocaust—that is to say, the officially organized killing of millions of Jews in Continental Europe during the second world war; and the motivations behind what is commonly called the great witch-hunt—that is to say, the many thousands of officially organized trials and executions of suspected witches, in various parts of western and central Europe, during the sixteenth and seventeenth centuries.

Originally I intended to cope with the second of these problems single-handed. But a couple of years' work sufficed to convince me that the subject was too vast for any one scholar; so, having severely delimited my own contribution, I began to look around for someone who would be willing and able to make a detailed study of the actual operation of witch-hunting in a single area. By 1970 my enquiries had led me to a remarkable thesis on Scottish witchcraft beliefs in the sixteenth and seventeenth centuries, which some years earlier had brought its author the degree of Ph.D. at Edinburgh. I tried to persuade that author, Christina Larner, to resume research on the witch-hunt in Scotland; and fortunately I succeeded. *Enemies of God* embodies the results of her research. Although by this time the Columbus Centre has ceased to exist, the book thus represents, in a very real sense, a continuation of the Centre's work.

I find it deeply gratifying to have been associated with this book, however indirectly. Perhaps only one who has himself wrestled with the problems surrounding the great witch-hunt can fully appreciate what an achievement it is. It is true that during the past twenty years or so scholarly work in this field has reached an altogether new level of sophistication—but it is also true that until now nobody had produced convincing answers to a number of key questions. Why did the witch-hunt happen when it did—in the age of Shakespeare and Descartes, even of Newton—rather than in the crude and ignorant world of the early middle ages? To what extent, and in what sense, was witch-hunting directed specifically against women—and why? What, precisely, was the relationship between religious and political indoctrination in the early modern period—and what bearing did they have on witch-hunting? In my view, after the appearance of *Enemies of God* these questions will have to be debated in quite a different way from the way they have been debated in the past; if indeed they still need to be debated at all.

This book makes a truly original contribution not simply to historical knowledge but to historical understanding. The vast territory which we call the great witch-hunt has long awaited an explorer who would be equally learned, and equally gifted, as historian and as sociologist. In Christina Larner it has found that explorer. Where hitherto our view has been blocked by a seemingly impenetrable mass of undergrowth, a path has been hacked out. A wide vista stands revealed. From now on it can surely never be lost to view.

NORMAN COHN

ACKNOWLEDGEMENTS

My principal debts are to Norman Cohn, who originally suggested that I write this book, and whose advice, encouragement, and intellectual generosity were unfailing; and to John Eldridge who convinced me that research on seventeenth-century deviance could properly be carried out in a department mainly concerned with the sociology of modern industrial societies. The Social Science Research Council gave me a three-year award which made possible the systematic collection of cases on which this book is partly based, and I would also like to thank here my two research assistants, Christopher Hyde Lee and Hugh McLachlan, who collaborated with me in this project.* Some of the quotations in this book are from transcripts made by these two scholars.

Much of the book was drafted when the University of Glasgow gave me a sabbatical term and sent me as Snell Visitor to Balliol College, Oxford. To both of these institutions my thanks are due.

John Larner, Al Soman, J. M. Ross, and Simon Mitchell read and commented on the entire manuscript. Among the many other individuals who have commented on sections, or otherwise given advice, information, or criticism, are Ben Benson, Stuart Clark, Derek Corcoran, Tim Curtis, Jason Ditton, R. S. Downie, Hendrik Frandsen, Gilbert Geis, the late Alec Haddow, Gustav Henningsen, Jens Christian Johansen, Bruce Lenman, Brian Levack, Alan Macfarlane, Max Marwick, Erik Midelfort, Rosalind Mitchison, Ian Muirhead, Irene Nove, Geoffrey Parker, Catherine Ross, Malcolm Scott, Hans Sebald, Lesley Smith, Christopher Smout, A. E. Truckell, R. Walinski-Kiehl, Ian Whyte, and Jenny Wormald. I would also like to thank the many past students in the Department of Sociology who discussed the issues with me. Pru Larsen typed and retyped the manuscript. The errors and inadequacies are my own.

C.L.

Glasgow, March 1980

* *A Source-Book of Scottish Witchcraft*, Glasgow 1977.

ABBREVIATIONS

SBSW Christina Larner, Christopher Hyde Lee, and Hugh V. McLachlan, *A Source Book of Scottish Witchcraft*, Glasgow, 1977. It is referred to in the text as the *Source Book*.

APS *Acts of the Parliament of Scotland*, London 1914.

RPC *Register of the Privy Council of Scotland*, Edinburgh 1880.

SRO Manuscript material in the Scottish Record Office.

JC MS records of the Justiciary Court.

RCE MS Records of the Committee of Estates.

A number after the name of an accused witch in the footnotes indicates the number in *SBSW*.

SPELLING OF NAMES

Since there were no agreed rules of spelling in seventeenth-century Scotland both personal names and place names are frequently spelt different ways in the same manuscript. Where personal names are concerned one version has been arbitrarily selected. In the case of place names the modern version is used, except for those that have disappeared from the map.

QUOTATIONS

Quotations from the source material have normally been printed without alteration but where they seemed obscure to the modern eye they have been amended without acknowledgement. In some cases translations of words have been inserted in brackets.

INTRODUCTION

This book is about the crime of witchcraft in Scotland, and is therefore confined chronologically to the period from 1563, when it became an offence in statute law punishable by death, to 1736, when the crime became officially impossible. It is concerned with the relationship of witch-beliefs in Scotland to witch-beliefs in other cultures, with the relationship of the Scottish witch-hunt to the witch-hunt on the continent of Europe, with the way in which witch-hunting affected peasant life, and with the way in which it reflected the ideological battle current in seventeenth-century Scotland.

The book has three main themes. The first is that witch-hunting was an activity fostered by the ruling class; it was not a spontaneous movement on the part of the peasantry to which the ruling and administrative classes were obliged to respond. This involves some definitions. The term 'witch-hunting' is preferred to the more neutral 'prosecutions for witchcraft' because it emphasizes that witchcraft suspects were not obvious; they had to be searched for. It also reminds us of common features in the original European witch-hunt and the generally recurring process to which it has given its name: the process whereby the politically powerful pursue a group of persons selected for their beliefs or supposed attributes rather than for anything they have done. A minor disadvantage is that the use of this term draws attention away from the role of witchcraft as an integral part of a criminal code which included many other manifestations exotic to modern jurisprudence of the belief system lying behind it.

Another necessary definition is that of the term 'ruling class' which unfortunately evokes strong negative and positive emotional responses. It could be objected to rationally by fellow sociologists on the grounds that it is anachronistic to apply it to a pre-capitalist society, and by historians on the grounds that it ignores the actual complexity of stratification in seventeenth-century Scotland. To the first I would argue that there is no more convenient term to describe the powerful in relation to the powerless; to the second that, despite considerable gradations of rank among privy councillors, nobles, lairds, grand tenants, lawyers, ministers, and various petty administrators, between all these categories and the peasants from whom ninety-five per cent of witch suspects were drawn, there was a social, political, and economic gulf. The term 'peasant', which is currently the subject of controversy, is likewise used in its most basic sense to mean one who works on the land with family labour to provide no more than subsistence, rent, and other dues.

Witch-hunting was a ruling class activity also because any large scale pursuit and rounding up of categories of person requires official organization and administration. This does not actually conflict with the proposition that local pressures might have caused witch-hunting in particular areas nor preclude an examination of why certain areas produced suspects when others did not. It does imply, though, that local pressures would need to be felt by the local ruling class. Peasants left to themselves will identify individuals as witches and will resort to a variety of anti-witchcraft measures in self-defence; they cannot pursue these measures to the punishment, banishment, or official execution of even one witch, let alone a multiplicity of witches, without the administrative machinery and encouragement of their rulers. When encouragement is forthcoming, however, they can supply an almost unlimited number of suspects. The actual pattern of witch-hunting in Scotland reinforces this assumption of ruling class control in that witch-hunting crises were nearly always preceded by official expressions of anxiety about witchcraft, and were marked by the simultaneous increase in the supply of suspects from a variety of localities, not all of which are likely to have experienced intolerable internal pressures at the same time in the same way.

The second theme is that witchcraft is an idea, before it is a phenomenon. It is an idea of considerable social flexibility and range. Beyond the basic elements by which we recognize it across cultures—that witchcraft is in general the summation of all evil and in particular the capacity and intention to harm through non-natural means—it may include inversions of any of the positive values peculiar to a given society. Witch-beliefs may therefore encompass a variety of alleged activities, possible and impossible, probable and improbable, and attribute to the performers of these activities a variety of character-istics, all of which serve to highlight local social values.

This emphasis is not directly helpful in excluding or including particular interpretations which focus on the possibility or impossibility of certain types of behaviour most frequently categorized as witch-craft. We may decide that formal cursing, incantation, and the manipulation of objects are possible and well authenticated, that secret meetings are possible but badly authenticated, while the causing of misfortune through incantation and sexual intercourse with the Devil are impossible. This, however, is through the application of other criteria than the one that the evidence for witchcraft relates first and foremost to a set of beliefs rather than activities. The emphasis *is* helpful in analysing the role of witch-beliefs within a complex semi-literate culture. Since most historical evidence comes in literary form we have far more knowledge of the norms and values of past societies than we

do of actual behaviour. Historical knowledge is primarily the knowledge of past dominant values; past actions and behaviour emerge in
fragmented photographic stills through the distorting mirror of past
beliefs. If the idea of a secret, mainly female society is taken as an
example, it is not possible to say definitely that such a society could not
have occurred or that, although the evidence for it is fragile and based
entirely on confession, it did not occur. It is, however, possible to say
definitely that a secret society of women was both believed in and
feared during the period of the witch-hunt.

While it may be feasible to analyse some aspects of political and
military history on the basis of relating fragmented action-stills
directly to each other, it is not really possible to treat the witch-hunt in
this way. Neither an imperfect nor even a definitive list of executed
women has much interest apart from the meaning given to those
executions. To treat witch-hunting primarily as an expression of
beliefs, however, is to get caught up in general debates of considerable
philosophical sophistication which I have neither the space nor the
equipment to engage in. I do, however, suggest ways in which European witch-hunting is concerned with these debates. In particular,
because the Europe of the witch-hunt had features characteristic both
of primitive small-scale societies and of literate, stratified, large-scale
societies, there are problems concerning both the issue of relativism:
how the modern interpreter should view remote belief systems, and
the role of ideology in a stratified society. These again involve questions as to whether ideas have an autonomous life and influence social
development; whether they are to be regarded as social products
reflecting the socio-economic structure; or whether both these positions
can be partially true.

A third, and subordinate theme since the first two have bearing on
all types of persecution and all types of belief, is that of the extent to
which witch-hunting is to some degree a synonym for woman-hunting. This does not mean that simple overt sex war is treated as a satisfactory explanation for witch-hunting, or that the twenty per cent or
so of men who were accused are not to be taken into account. It means
that the fact that the accused were overwhelmingly female should form
a major part of any analysis. Recent explanations for this female
preponderance seem unsatisfactory. The suggestion that more women
than men belonged to the ranks of the defenceless poor seems inadequate; even if the proportion of impoverished females to males was
the same as that of accused witches it still explains nothing. The suggestion that the stereotype of a witch was always a woman seems
tautological.

The identification of the relationship of witch-hunting to woman-
hunting is intended to concentrate attention on such questions as why
women were criminalized on a large scale for the first time in this
period, and whether there is any significance in the simultaneous rise of

prosecutions for witchcraft (old women) and infanticide (young women); whether there was any change in the socio-economic position of women in this period; why a female secret society should seem particularly threatening at this juncture; and to what extent the popularization of Christianity, a patriarchal form of religion, was a factor.

These themes of class, ideology, and patriarchy, shape the nature of the questions which I think should be asked about the European witch-hunt in general and the Scottish hunt in particular. They cannot provide the answers; for the answers, if there be any, must be inferred from the surviving documentary and secondary material.

A general account of the Scottish witch-prosecutions is at one time both long overdue and distinctly premature. It is long overdue because, despite the ill fame of Scotland as a peculiarly hostile environment for those whose neighbours identified them as witches, an ill fame which has lasted from the sixteenth century to the present, there has been little research and no attempt at a synthesis this century. There has been extensive use of well-known Scottish material, two attempts at enumeration, and a steady supply of retold tales, but no new analysis. Such an analysis seems particularly overdue in that the present emphasis in European witchcraft research is on local studies, and the Scottish experience of witchcraft seems in many respects to occupy an interesting middle position between the English experience on the one hand and that of the European continent on the other. It is, however, premature for two reasons. It is premature first because of the existing state of scholarship on aspects of seventeenth-century Scotland important to an understanding of the witch-trials there. While politics and religion have been relatively well served, little work has been done on the social structure, and almost nothing on crime and the legal history of the period. Lenman and Parker[1] have now provided a hand list of sources for criminological research, but there is as yet no analysis of general rates for crime and misdemeanour against which those for witchcraft can be set. Anyone whose main concern was with Scottish history, rather than with one substantive theme for comparative purposes, would turn to one of these areas. It is premature in the second place because my research was concentrated on the central records. Detailed analysis of all the records local and central for one or more limited areas which might help to answer some of the questions posed in this book has yet to be done.

However, the reasons for publishing an overview at this stage seem more pressing than those for delay. The study of European witchcraft has recently received much stimulation from the work and ideas of Thomas[2] and Macfarlane[3] on English witchcraft and Cohn[4] on the development of the educated demonology behind the European prosecutions. Work is at present being concentrated on detailed local studies. Monographs on south-western Germany, north-west Germany, Switzerland, France, Luxembourg, Massachusetts, and Finland have been produced, and shorter pieces on Russia and Denmark. Further work is in progress on Bamberg and on the very earliest witch trials.[5] Any new overall synthesis of the great European persecution will have to wait until this phase of research has been completed, although it may be that such a synthesis will be overtaken by the developing study of pre-industrial criminology of which witchcraft prosecutions are but a part.

The present book is intended primarily as a contribution to this growing body of local witchcraft studies, and therefore its comparative context and the relationship of its themes to general theories of witchcraft is emphasized. For this reason too it is assumed that some readers may lack a background knowledge of Scottish history, and for their benefit a chronological table is included as an appendix.

The title of the book indicates its overall interpretive theme: the significance of ideology in the new post-Reformation regime; the importance attached in new regimes to conformity and discipline as symbols of their legitimacy; and the economy of using the witch figure in this general pattern of increased moral control as a personification of all forms of deviance and revolt. If there was one idea which dominated all others in seventeenth-century Scotland it was that of the godly state in which it was the duty of the secular arm to impose the will of God upon the people. This book is about the women and men (in a ratio of about four to one) who, during this period, were identified by their neighbours, their ministers and elders, their landlords, and the officials of their government, as enemies of God. For the European witch, unlike her* African or American-Indian counterpart, was a transfigured creature who began her career in the farmyard as an enemy of her neighbour, and ended it in the courts as a public person, an enemy of God and of the godly society.

* For convenience feminine pronouns embrace masculine in all references to suspected witches.

CHAPTER ONE

THE IDEA OF WITCHCRAFT

The idea of witchcraft is not universal in primitive or pre-industrial societies,[1] but it is widely distributed. If it is legitimate to use the term 'witchcraft' to refer to ideas and beliefs held in such a variety of cultures across time and space, there must be at least one universal element. The common element in all witch-beliefs is that witchcraft is a general evil power. Furthermore this power is distinguished from physical force or any other mechanism or natural phenomenon within the technological understanding of the society concerned. Witchcraft is supernatural evil. Individual witches are evil persons, and individual acts of witchcraft are specific evil acts which are performed through supernatural powers. The characteristic ingredients of an act of witchcraft are that the witch should feel malice towards an individual who has offended her, and that through cursing, incantation, sorcery, or the sheer force of her ill will, should cause illness or death to the livestock, family, or person of the individual concerned.

This is the common element which was drawn out by Thomas and Macfarlane in their works on English witchcraft in which they demonstrated for the first time that the English witch was not normally a randomly selected victim of the judiciary, but a person who had exhibited hatred and malice in the same way as the witches of the classic ethnographic texts of Africa, New Guinea, and America. It is becoming clear that on the continent of Europe too this belief in primary witchcraft continued to underlie the accretions and interpretations of Church and law, and the same is certainly true of Scotland. The mass witch-hunts of Europe may have brought into the legal process persons who had never been suspected of primary witchcraft, but this seems to have been because the supply of such persons had run dry. Primary witchcraft was known in the European texts as *maleficium*. In Scotland it was called 'malefice' and is so referred to throughout this book.

There is almost nothing else in the variety of witch-beliefs which can be found in all witch-believing societies. Even at this level it is necessary to make an exception. Evans-Pritchard's work on the Azande, which has been the greatest single influence on witchcraft studies, suggests that the Azande regarded witchcraft as an attribute of ordinary people rather than of special, totally evil people. Certain individuals may have an inheritable substance (witchcraft) in their stomachs which they may or may not choose to activate during their lives.[2] The Azande, however, although they regarded witchcraft as a widely diffused attribute, did share with other African societies a certain ambiguity about who the witch responsible for any particular misfortune might be. It is this ambiguity which gives the role of witch doctor such significance in Africa. On each occasion when witchcraft is suspected it is necessary to find out the identity of the witch. This contrasts with European societies in which there may be only one or two well known local witches whose reputation has been built up over the years, and who tend to be the first suspects for all local misfortunes. It could be that the more precise role differentiation of a complex and structured society accounts for the more permanent indentification of suspected witches among the European peasantry as compared with African tribesmen. Another variant, however, is to be found in European societies such as the Scottish Highlands[3] and contemporary Southern Italy.[4] In the Scottish Highlands witches, like the fairies, were often anonymous. In addition, known individuals, both there and in Southern Italy, are credited with possessing the evil eye which is regarded as distinct from witchcraft and can cause *unintended* harm to the person 'overlooked'. These beliefs can explain individual misfortune without anyone having to shoulder the blame.

The identification of witches in mass witch-hunts differs from the private quest for a culprit. In these mass hunts the similarities between European and tribal procedure are greater. The exercise is not that of seeking for a culprit for a specific malefice; it is a cleansing operation. It is a public act of ridding the land of witches and is associatied with coronations, new regimes, and ceremonial occasions.[5]

In the attempt to distinguish among witch-beliefs those which are fundamental, those which are extremely common, those which are occasional, and those which are peculiar to one society, it is necessary to make a further preliminary distribution. The witch-beliefs of simple and preliterate societies are likely to be homogeneous. The beliefs of any given society of this type such as the Azande, the Nyakusa, or the Navaho may be quite complex and they may be clearly differentiated in many significant details from other such societies, but they will be internally consistent and generally agreed.[6] In a peasant, semi-literate society, on the other hand, in which there are conflicts of economic interest and conflicting and rival interpretations of the meaning of the world they live in, no such homogeneity of witch-beliefs is to be expected, although there are likely to be interconnections between the strands of belief.

If we turn from the universal malefice to areas of diversity, the first point to be noticed is that most, though not all, witch-believing societies distinguish between black and white magic, and that this is related to the distinction between sorcery and witchcraft. This second distinction was first made explicit by Evans-Pritchard[7] and may therefore count as an observer's rather than a practitioner's view, but it does reflect the assumptions of many witch-believing societies. Sorcery is taken to mean the use of words and actions (incantation and the manipulation of objects, substances, or livestock) to generate supernatural power. Witchcraft is the generation of supernatural power with or without particular performances and is therefore an umbrella term. White witchcraft is concerned with the healing arts, with prophecy, with finding lost objects, with the supply of love potions, and with performances and rituals designed to counter black witchcraft. White witchcraft always involves manipulative sorcery. Black witchcraft or malefice may or may not involve sorcery, but some indication, whether articulate and precise cursing, gnomic utterance, or scarcely audible mumbling, is usually necessary to establish that the mobilization of powerful ill will has been attempted.

Most societies make this distinction. European Civil Law decreed that white witchcraft, though culpable, was not punishable by death, whereas black witchcraft was.[8] The distinction was eroded by Canon Law and the commentators specializing in demonology in that all supernatural power not emanating from the Church was deemed to be demonic. Those claiming to heal outside the context of the Church must have got their powers from the Devil. The abolition of the distinction did find an echo in peasant experience in that the healer as a person of power was potentially threatening. Power was neutral but could be used to harm as well as to heal, and it became a common feature of European witch-trials that the accused was said to have both laid on and taken off a disease. The most extreme position with regard to the conflation of black and white magic may well have been that taken in the Scottish Witchcraft Act of 1563 in which consulters of witches were said to be worthy of death in the same manner as practitioners.[9] Any acknowledgement of an unofficial source of power was to be suppressed. The attitude of a polity towards white witchcraft is an indication of the level of anxiety about non-conformity. England continued to tolerate cunning men and women (who were quite distinct from black witches) throughout the period of the prosecution. Major witch-hunts in Scotland and on the continent on the other hand tended to engulf the healer along with the curser.

So far as the maleficent witch is concerned, however, it is a truism of anthropology that witch-beliefs represent an inversion of the positive values of the society concerned.[10] It is not surprising therefore that there are large common areas in the stereotype of the witch and of witch behaviour. The witch is old, ugly, and female in most societies. The Lugbara of East Africa have a variant on this in that witches are said to be constantly smiling and over amiable in order to deceive.[11] The idea of the witch as old, ugly, or deformed does not require any special explanation and is extremely common. The idea of the witch as a woman is less universal. For the Azande, witches, who were unusual anyway in not being totally or permanently evil, could be of either sex;[12] so too for the Navaho of North America though they were more frequently male.[13] The Lugbara specifically excluded women from the practice of witchcraft; they were deemed to be capable only of manipulative sorcery. Witchcraft was part of the power struggle among men.[14] These cultures seem to be in a minority, however, and in many others the propensity of women towards witchcraft is remarked upon. Goody asked the women of the Gonja why this should be so and received the reply that women were more evil than men.[15] This echoes the explanations of all witch-believing societies in which the witch is stereotypically a woman. From Christian Europe to West Africa women are witches because they are more wanton, more weak, and more wicked than men.

So far as the behaviour and activities of witches are concerned there are first the acts of personal malefice. These are often very local in their application. In fishing villages witches frighten off the fish and sink ships. In agricultural areas they flatten crops, attract blight, and destroy livestock. The individual witch performing individual acts of malefice, however, represents private fears and explains particular misfortunes. Beliefs about the corporate acts of witches in secret night meetings represent public and social fears. Their meetings are an inversion of approved social life, and there is much variety in their activities. Frequently they rob graveyards and feast on corpses. The bodies of babies, sometimes specially killed for the purpose, are eaten. The Navaho believed that eating the bodies of those they had killed increased their own magical powers. Others used parts of corpses as elements in their sorcery. Sexual orgies with indiscriminate copulation appears in the witch-beliefs of parts of Europe including Scotland as well as in those of the Pondo and the Mbugwe.[16] Another widely distributed belief is that of the night-flying witch. Macfarlane has pointed out that this is necessary to explain how witches are able to strike so secretly at a distance and how they are able to meet together unobserved by respectable members of the community.[17] The night-flying witch was known in Germany as early as the eleventh century, in Scotland and other parts of Europe in the seventeenth century, and among the Cewa, the Nyakusa, and the Tallensi.[18] Sometimes she flew on birds and animals; sometimes on twigs and branches. An alternative to riding is transformation into either a bird or a swift-moving beast such as a hare in Scotland or a hyena in Africa.[19]

European witch-beliefs, which are the principal concern of this book, share in varying detail all these elements with other cultures. The only witch-beliefs which are peculiar to Christian Europe are the worship of the Christian Devil, the Black Mass or inverted Protestant celebrations, and the Demonic Pact. It could even be argued that the European witches' sabbath is in fact a variant of African beliefs in witches' meetings, and that the only feature which is uniquely European is the

Demonic Pact. In this the witch renounces her Christian baptism and in a ceremony which is usually private, dedicates her immortal soul to the Devil and is promised various earthly advantages in return. The Pact is normally consummated by the reception of the Devil's mark, inflicted by a nip or a bite, on the witch's person and by one or more acts of sexual intercourse. The Pact was not universal in European countries which prosecuted witches. It featured relatively insignificantly, for example, in England and not at all in Russia. But in those countries under the influence of Canon Law or within the jurisdiction of the *Constitutio Criminalis Carolina* instituted by the Emperor Charles V in 1532,[20] it became more important than accusations of malefice or sorcery in securing a conviction in a court of law.

It is this network of ideas, with its more or less compulsory and more or less optional elements, which is the centrepoint of discussions among philosophers, anthropologists, and sociologists on how the contemporary observer should view alien or remote systems of belief.[21] The questions at issue are whether such beliefs should be regarded as irrational, internally rational, or rational *per se*; and whether it is proper or improper to apply modern standards of scientific rationality to the beliefs of other cultures.

These discussions, however, have been concerned only with pre-literate (integrated) belief systems, and have ignored pre-industrial (inter-related) systems. This avoidance is partly because the origins of the debate lie in anthropology, but it has been continued for philosophical convenience, and latterly made more explicit. Gellner, for example, has pointed out that between the simple polarization of 'savage' and 'modern' systems of thought there is a middle ground that may be both extensive and interesting. He suggests that it is worth while to 'think away this enormous middle ground' for the sake of philosophical clarity.[22] No help either can be expected from students of European witchcraft, who have so far avoided direct consideration of the problem of relativism altogether. They have tended if anything to take for granted the special irrationality of witch-beliefs within the general context of sixteenth- and seventeenth-century beliefs and values.

Despite this lack of encouragement, however, it seems as desirable for students of witch-beliefs of the middle ground as for those of simple societies to consider the issues and adopt an explicit stance with regard to them. Unlike some philosophical problems these have direct bearing on the way in which the material is to be treated. The following brief suggestions, which run rather cavalierly over the subtleties of the debate, are intended first to adapt its structure so that investigators of the middle ground may be allowed to participate, and second to draw out the implications of participation for European witchcraft studies.

Two opposed positions in the debate on how the modern commentator should view alien belief systems are represented by Winch on the one hand and Gellner on the other. Winch argues a position of total relativism: that all ideas and practices embody values and are socially determined, and that therefore one should not judge those of an alien society in relation to the values of one's own society.[23] Gellner suggests on the contrary that 'it is intuitively repellent to suggest that the Azande's acceptance of witchcraft is as rational as our rejection of it'.[24] Behind both these positions is a strong moral imperative. Winch, depending on his assertion that all beliefs and practices stem from values, feels that it is improper for holders of one set of values to criticize holders of another. Gellner implies that it is treating savages with contempt to apply standards which we think inadequate for our own beliefs and practices.

The reason why it is difficult for researchers of the middle ground to join in this debate as it stands, is that in its terms the beliefs of both modern and simple societies are assumed to be internally homogeneous. That is to say those of modern societies are taken to be essentially scientific; those of simple societies essentially magical. For middle ground societies (whether seventeenth-century Europe or the twentieth-century Middle East) such an assumption is impossible. The conflict in these societies between traditional modes of thought and a developing technology is overt and conducted within the society itself. In Scotland in 1684, for example, the High Court of Justiciary in a witchcraft trial determined that the death of a woman was not the result of witchcraft. Surgeons had ascertained that there was enough arsenic in her to kill six people.[25] The debate on rationality and on relativism as at present constituted gives little help on how such material is to be regarded.

The assumed homogeneity of the belief systems of both simple and modern societies is a barrier to applying any discussion on them to middle ground societies. This homogeneity is however fictional. The simplest societies are capable of making a distinction between knowledge of how to make a cooking pot and knowledge about the influence of ancestors on next year's harvest. Indeed, they set aside certain people to take responsibility for the second as priests and witch doctors. The most technologically advanced societies for their part have extensive cultural dimensions which are unrelated to technological understanding. In fact it is quite possible to take any belief system at all, whether simple, middle ground, or modern, and distinguish 'technology' from 'speculation'. 'Technology' covers practical knowledge of how to make things work and irreversible knowledge as to why they work. 'Speculation' covers everything else from reversible explanations as to why things work to social values and spiritual beliefs.

This distinction makes it possible to adopt for any given culture a non-relativist stance with regard to technology and a relativist one with regard to speculation. The only real difficulty here is that of clearly separating these areas. The border line between technology and that area of speculation which bears directly on technology is impossible for any society, including our own, to draw for itself. Indeed the reason why witchcraft beliefs feature so strongly in the rationality debate is that they operate precisely on that boundary on which speculation is related to technology and metaphysical welded to practical knowledge. The position is therefore philosophically over simple. What is more it leaves out altogether the question of logical truth and the question of criteria for judging the relative social utility of different speculative systems. It is not however nonsense, and has particular advantages as an approach to partially literate pre-industrial societies.

The first advantage of this position then is that it allows the commentator to follow conceptual struggles within the society itself, to distinguish areas of technological expertise and (implicitly) to applaud successes, while remaining neutral with regard to areas of speculation and value. The second advantage is that those speculative areas themselves become more homogeneous. They are all equally areas of value. For the anthropologist the exotic nature of his total area of study is obvious. For the historical sociologist or the historian, however, there are linear cords binding present beliefs to those of the past. Those beliefs which have been least tenacious are singled out by the commentator as requiring special explanation. Because we may meet across the dinner table tomorrow educated members of our modern industrial society who believe in a trinitarian god, the resurrection of the body, and the life everlasting, these aspects of seventeenth-century belief are less culturally alien, and seem less speculative than those which have failed to survive among modern elites.

If we treat all non-technological areas of seventeenth-century culture as homogeneous then we can notionally cut those linear cords which make some aspects of belief a reserved area, and regard all the values of seventeenth-century Scotland, for example, as an alien belief system. Despite the areas of conflict within it which distinguish it from an integrated pre-literate system, it is still sufficiently inter-connected and has enough common assumptions to call it a system. On this understanding the key elements in the witch-belief—the Demonic Pact and the practice of effective malefice—are neither more nor less alien than non-tenacious elements in the positive religion: the Crown Rights of the Redeemer, the Covenanted State, prelapsarian predestination to eternal damnation. They are neither more nor less alien than the more tenacious elements of the trinitarian deity and eternal salvation. The inter-relation of all speculative areas becomes admissible. For this reason the chapters on the belief system in seventeenth-century Scotland consider not only the forms of witch-belief but also the way in which witch-beliefs related to official theology and the political significance of this relationship. Scottish seventeenth-century theological disputes and witch-beliefs were deflated partly by technological progress, partly by economic aspirations and political settlements, but most effectively by the eighteenth-century political dethronement of God.

CHAPTER TWO

EXPLANATIONS FOR THE EUROPEAN WITCH-HUNT[1]

While the debate as to how external observers should view witch-beliefs has been conducted by anthropologists and philosophers and concerned with pre-literate societies, the European witch-hunt has been largely the concern of historians. Mair, writing before Thomas and Macfarlane published on English witchcraft, pointed out that students of European witchcraft had concentrated on witch-hunting and elite attitudes to witchcraft to the neglect of the operation of witch-beliefs among the populace.[2] There are, however, good reasons for this. The first is that the European witch-hunt was a unique phenomenon. Although it was protracted over three centuries, and although it manifested itself spasmodically in certain restricted areas of Europe, it had a set of features which, taken together, had not been seen anywhere before the fifteenth century and were never seen again anywhere after the end of the seventeenth century except possibly in eighteenth-century Poland. Since these included the belief of a literate ruling class in the existence of witches and the need to annihilate them, and since there is still no satisfactory consensus on the explanation for this, it remains a problem. The second is that popular European witch-beliefs lie buried in the manuscripts under elite interpretation. They are the second layer that the researcher finds, not the first, and the historiography of European witchcraft reflects this. What is more there is much to suggest that popular witch-beliefs were themselves altered by elite witch-hunting, and were not quite the same in their operation as in periods and areas untouched by the hunt. Since nearly all the evidence for popular belief is a product of the hunt, however, this is inference drawn partly from primitive ethnography, and partly from areas of Europe such as England and Russia which were lightly touched by the witch-hunt. The purpose of this chapter, therefore, is to outline our present knowledge of the European hunt in order to set the Scottish hunt in that context, and to discuss recent interpretations and explanations of it.

A preliminary point, which will recur in the context of the Scottish hunt, is that the total number of executions, let alone the number of prosecutions, for witchcraft can never be known. In the first place far too many records have been lost or destroyed, and because of the highly episodic nature of witch-hunting the extrapolation of mathematical probabilities from the figures which do exist would be inappropriate. In the second, the surviving records demonstrate the indifference to formal and regular detail of a pre-bureaucratic age. Names are not always given. There are frequent references to 'many witches'. Verdicts are omitted. It is a positivist's nightmare. To make matters worse in the days when cliometrics were simply a form of competitive invention precise if rounded figures were liberally offered for the numbers executed for witchcraft. These figures run to hundreds of thousands and, although now regarded by those doing research in the criminal archives as considerable exaggerations, are well established in the witchcraft literature and difficult to eradicate.

Despite the permanent impossibility of producing definitive figures two points are clear. The first is that recent work has greatly improved our knowledge of figures for particular areas, and the second that the modification of figures for these areas does not eliminate the extraordinary nature of these prosecutions, which are legitimately termed 'the witch-craze' by Trevor-Roper.[3] The essential problem remains the same as it was for earlier scholars who worked on the basis of exaggerated figures. The major witch panics have always been regarded as aberrations from the time that they were happening until the present, even if the phenomenon to be accounted for consisted of the prevalence of witches rather than the irrationality or cruelty of their pursuers. The conspicuousness of witch-hunting is not modified by precise figures, and there is a sense in which failure to be appalled by the hunt on the grounds that we now know that on a particular day we are talking of twenty-seven witches rather than two hundred would be a distortion of its own.

The recent work, which has both improved our knowledge of the hunt and exposed the improbability of such knowledge ever being complete, is of two kinds: the general discussions of the background to the main witch-hunt by Cohn and Kieckhefer, and the local studies of Thomas, Macfarlane, Midelfort, Monter, Schormann, Dupont-Bouchat, Muchembled, and Soman.[4] The following account of the chronology and geography of the European hunt draws on them, but also partly on Trevor-Roper whose account of witch-hunting as a whole has not been replaced. Cohn, whose *Europe's Inner Demons* deals with the development of the witch fantasy, abandoned an original plan to write a second volume on the hunt itself on the grounds that a new synthesis was premature.[5] It may well be that current work on criminology in pre-industrial Europe[6] will set the witchcraft prosecutions in a more general criminal context and make a major new monograph on European witchcraft anachronistic.

Although there was not one continuous witch-hunt there was a continuous period during which witchcraft was a capital crime in most of Europe. During this period many areas never had a witch-hunt, others had one or more, some had many. Yet others prosecuted witches in ones or twos, but the vast majority of those convicted were tried in groups during epidemics of witch-hunting. What made the numbers soar was the official belief that witchcraft was a conspiracy and the use of torture to make suspects incriminate others.

Until recently it was thought that there were two principal waves of mass trials: the first in the fourteenth century in France and Italy: the second in the sixteenth and seventeenth centuries, concentrated in Germany, Eastern France, Switzerland, and Scotland. The single discovery which has most affected our view of the pattern of witch-hunting was Cohn's finding, published in 1975, that the mass trials of the fourteenth century never in fact occurred. The story of their existence was propagated by Soldan in 1843 and by the influential Hansen in 1900 and was based upon three forgeries of the fifteenth, sixteenth, and nineteenth centuries. This discovery eliminates the mass trials of Toulouse from 1335 to 1350 during which 400 persons are said to have been executed, and at Carcassonne in the same period where another 200 were said to have been accounted for.[7]

This completely alters our picture of the course of the European witch-hunt. The most recent coverage of the earliest period is by Kieckhefer who came to much the same conclusions as Cohn about the authenticity of these early trials, though by a slightly different route. He covers the period from 1300 to 1500 and, though his main purpose was to trace evidence for popular belief and distinguish it from educated belief, he provided a chronological analysis of the early stages of witch-hunting.[8] He argues that cases before 1300 were so rare that it is difficult to detect any pattern in them. The period 1300–1500 he divided into four stages. In the first, from 1300 to 1330, the rate of prosecution was very low. Trials occurred mostly in France, England, and Germany. Kieckhefer observes that the most remarkable feature of the early trials is their political character: these trials tended to involve prominent figures either as victim or suspect. The second period is from 1330 to 1375 during which political trials were almost unknown. With the elimination of the fabricated events at Toulouse and Carcassone these trials were similar in ideological content to the mainly political ones which had gone before in that they concentrated on charges of sorcery and only rarely featured diabolism (by which Kieckhefer means the Demonic Pact and witches' meetings). As before nearly all of them were in France and Germany with occasional cases in England and Italy. It was during the third period, from 1375 to 1435, that there was a steady increase both in the number of trials and in the proportion of them which involved diabolism. Kieckhefer suggests that though this increase may merely reflect an increase in surviving judicial records it probably was real. It could have been connected with the increased use of inquisitorial procedure in local courts, which removed responsibility from the accuser to the judicial authorities thus making accusation less dangerous and more attractive. It could also, he suggests, have been affected by social tensions and panic generated by the plague.[9] During this phase Switzerland and Italy began to provide cases in numbers comparable to those of France and Germany and it was in Italy that the only instances of diabolism appeared. Cohn and Kieckhefer's revised chronology suggests that diabolism first appeared in trials which were still largely about sorcery in late fourteenth and early fifteenth-century Italy, instead of first appearing fully developed in early fourteenth-century France.

In Kieckhefer's final period, that from 1435 to 1500, the majority of cases came from France, Germany, and Switzerland. The rate of prosecution was much higher than for the earlier periods. Kieckhefer suggests that the intense witch-hunting of this period anticipated the great outbreaks of the sixteenth and seventeenth centuries. There were more mass outbreaks, and more cases involving diabolism. Yet the trials with a diabolic content were still fewer than those for sorcery alone.[10]

During the first half of the sixteenth century it looked as though witch-hunting might have been dying out. There were outbreaks in Como in Italy, and in the Basque country, but very few elsewhere. France and Germany, which had been the centres of the witch-hunt in the late fifteenth century and were to be so again in the later sixteenth and seventeenth centuries, seemed almost to have forgotten witch-craft. Yet although prosecution was dormant the fundamental principles of the diabolic witch theory were increasingly widely accepted, and all Europe, including regions where trials had not previously taken place, was vulnerable to witch scares.

The prosecutions returned in the 1560s and increased to panic proportions at the end of the century. This time witch-hunting was not confined geographically principally to France and Germany in the way it had been in the fifteenth century. Certainly there were mass trials in Brandenburg, Württemberg, Baden, Bavaria, and Mecklenberg, and there was also a marked increase in prosecutions in France; but many other regions began prosecuting either for the first time or for the first time in large numbers.[11] Trials increased in England and in Switzerland, though in both countries they amounted to a few cases a year rather than mass outbreaks. The 1560s also saw cases in Transylvania and a few cases in Scotland.

The end of the century and the beginning of the seventeenth saw a further outbreak and geographical extension. The Rhineland and Bavaria had many trials; similar episodes occurred slightly later in Flanders. In 1600 witch-trials began again in the Franche-Comté.[12] Apart from the Basque area, however, the number of trials abated in the early years of the seventeenth century, and once again it might have looked at the time as though witch-hunting was on the decline. Yet the 1620s saw the worst of all prosecutions, described by Trevor-Roper as 'the climax of the European witch-craze'.[13] It was at its most intense in Würzburg, Bamberg, Franche-Comté, Alsace, and Scotland.

The number of prosecutions declined again in the 1630s but there were to be many more panics. Some of them because of improved records and the expansion of popular literature are particularly well known. In Franche-Comté there was a major hunt in 1657.[14] In England there was the outbreak in 1645 associated with the witch-finder, Matthew Hopkins. Sweden experienced witch panic for the first time with the Mora witches of 1669, and further hunts there included one in Stockholm in 1676.[15] The last major outbreaks were in Salem, Massachusetts (which can be regarded as an extension of the European hunt) in 1692[16] and in Paisley in Scotland in 1697. Eighteenth-century trials were rare and those leading to executions rarer still. They occurred in France, Germany, Scotland, Switzerland and Poland. (The Polish pattern was quite exceptional, with the greatest number of trials and executions occurring in the eighteenth century in conjunction with Jesuit evangelization.[17]) The last legal execution seems to have been in Switzerland in 1782.

When Mair was writing in 1969 she suggested that writers on European witchcraft were more concerned with witch-hunting than with witch-beliefs, and the claim then had some justice in it. It was also true that there was not very much interaction between writers from different disciplines. The theory of Murray[18] that a witch cult had existed and had been in fact a benign pre-Christian fertility religion was still maintaining its credibility among serious scholars. Most thought it necessary to consider it, and although Trevor-Roper felt able to dismiss it in a footnote, it was not finally dispatched until Cohn devoted a chapter to exposing her use of sources.[19]

Trevor-Roper's synthesis and interpretation of the witch-hunt summed up the work of non-Murrayist writers of previous decades and established witchcraft as a central rather than a peripheral problem of sixteenth- and seventeenth-century Europe. It was explicitly an essay on witch-hunting. Trevor-Roper identified Aristotelean modes of thought with the witch beliefs of the educated, and related the chronology of witch-hunting to the rise and fall of religious zeal; to conquest by Protestant forces, to reconquest by Counter-Reformation forces; to periods in which clergy were able to dominate the secular authorities; and to areas where there was already a tradition of intolerance and persecution on other issues than witchcraft.[20] While he gave prominence to social forces (periods of internal unrest provoked witch-hunting; external warfare and government by foreign forces dispelled it), he did not suggest that the levels of witch-hunting reflected the anxieties of peasants who might well have found rule by foreign forces as much a cause for anxiety as internal conflict; they reflected the interests and purposes of those in control. In order to understand the witch-hunt we must understand the minds and motivation of the ruling elite.

Some suggestions about the witch-hunt by sociologists had, however, already been made. Erikson had looked at the material on Salem, Massachusetts, from the point of view of deviance theory, and suggested that the purpose of the witch-hunt was to re-define the values of society.[21] In sociology the term 'deviance' covers an area both more inclusive and more shifting than that of crime, for it refers to the breaking not merely of formal laws but of social rules and norms. These rules and norms can vary from group to group within a society and therefore one group's deviance may be another's conformity, but despite the shifting character of this concept those of generally bad or eccentric reputation can be described as deviant in relation to a society as a whole. Erikson consciously extended Durkheim's theory that crime draws a community together by defining those who are outside it. Witchcraft had a special value as a crime in a theologically orientated community.[22] It not only defined the godly majority: it identified the enemies of society with the enemies of God.

An important essay by Currie from the stance of the sociology of law, 'The Control of Witchcraft in Renaissance Europe' published in 1968, has been curiously neglected by later writers.[23] He pointed to the difference between England and continental Europe in methods of social control as a result of the differences in their legal systems. He identified the continental system as inquisitional, and structurally designed for the 'systematic and massive production of confessed deviants'. The English accusatory principle operated in a context of external constraints on the legal system and resulted in fewer witches and fewer executions. He saw these two systems as two ends of a continuum along which different social control systems may be placed.

The most successful incursion into European witch studies from the social sciences so far, however, has come from anthropology. The work of Thomas on English witchcraft and that of Macfarlane on witchcraft accusations in the county of Essex[24] changed the focus of historical studies through the application of functionalist anthropological models. The subject of their work was not the witch-hunter but the witch in the community. The witch ceased to be an 'innocent' person randomly selected and was shown to be someone with particular social characteristics who had been accused of witchcraft by neighbours who also had particular social characteristics. English witches were old, poor, and female. Less obviously they were older and poorer than those who accused them. They were nearly always in a fairly close relationship to the accused; a relationship in which the accepted norms were those of love, neighbourliness, or charity. Quarrels and damaged relationships were nearly always part of the evidence recorded at English trials for witchcraft. Witch-beliefs can be seen in this light as performing a useful function. They could be a reason for terminating a relationship which had become intolerable or an excuse for ill treating or quarrelling with an inferior. Witchcraft further served as an explanatory model for specific misfortunes. Social guilt and inexplicable personal disasters were the factors most likely to provoke accusations.

Macfarlane showed that the uses of witch-beliefs in sixteenth- and seventeenth-century Essex were reflected in a variety of primitive cultures. In so doing he found a rich vein of sources for historical sociology, found in fact the historian's second layer, the direct voice of the peasant. He presented a portrait of the villagers of Essex disturbing each other's cows and pigs, making their green patches muddy, refusing the poor Godes-good, calling each other names, refusing to allow someone to nurse a child (effectively a refusal to hand out patronage) and not returning borrowed dishes.[25] Witchcraft accusations in England are a door to the peasant economy and the peasant experience, and, as will be seen, they are also in Scotland.

In functionalist theory, however, witch-beliefs are normally seen as filling not merely useful but necessary functions. It is a framework which is frequently illuminating, but it was developed in relation to fieldwork during which the seasons were the principal source of change, rather than to archives. Functionalist theory has never looked its strongest when applied to social change. The idea of the social strain gauge developed by Marwick,[26] according to which the level of witchcraft accusations reflects tension in the community, and which was intended to have only a synchronic application is stretched beyond its limits when it is made to explain why witch-hunting began in England in the mid-sixteenth century and ended in the mid-seventeenth. The argument runs that social strain was caused by specific social and economic change. The enclosure movement increased the numbers of the poor and furthered the trend towards a cash economy. At the same time the bureaucratization of poor relief under the Elizabethan Poor Laws divested the individual of responsibility for charity. This shift from a neighbourly to a commercial ethic, which was especially marked in the progressive agricultural area of East Anglia, caused social tension which manifested itself in accusations of witchcraft. Classic examples of this type of accusation occurred when the newly pauperized came begging and were turned away although cultural expectations were still that they should have been lodged and given soup. The rejected beggar would then curse the uncharitable householder who would in turn justify his action by accusing the cursing beggar of witchcraft. The decline of accusations in the mid-seventeenth century is accounted for by the acceptance of new commercial, less personal norms of behaviour. Macfarlane has now rejected the idea that there were important changes in social structure at the beginning of the period of the witch-hunt[27] but it has taken root in witchcraft analysis.

If this explanation is taken within a self-contained English context it has considerable plausibility. English witch accusations appeared most frequently in the most agriculturally advanced areas. What is more the contents of the accusations and the confessions only rarely included diabolism. The manifestations of English witch-beliefs in the sixteenth- and seventeenth-century trials both in the conditions which gave rise to them and the details of the beliefs closely resembled those of simple societies in the classic texts of ethnography. It therefore seemed reason-able to assume that as they seemed endemic in most pre-industrial societies they had remained unchanged from earlier periods of English history when communities were simply not sufficiently under stress to bring accusations to the surface.

Even within an English context, however, there are difficulties about the functionalist model of social strain taken on its own. Many of the accusations relate to human problems which may be expected to occur, if not universally, certainly more widely than just during the transition to a commercial ethic. Failure to return borrowed property, quarrels between neighbours of equal and unequal status, failures in charity, may be assumed to have occurred in fifteenth- as well as sixteenth-century England. Left out of the explanation, indeed deliberately eschewed, are the passing of the Witchcraft Acts of 1542 and 1563.[28] It is argued that previous legal arrangements were adequate to process accusations of witchcraft. Also ignored are the encroach-ments in England of what has been termed the 'judicial revolution'.[29] By this is meant the process by which over a considerable period of time (but coinciding with what in the marxist frame of reference is known as the transition from feudalism to capitalism) there was a change from restorative, inter-personal justice, to abstract, rational bureaucratic justice with repressive sanctions. It had the effect in many countries, including England, of shifting responsibility from the accuser to the court official, which in turn had the effect of making frivolous or vindictive accusation possible without fear of reper-cussions.

The problems which appear over the theory of social strain even in the context of a self-contained England become more acute when applied to prosecutions on the continent of Europe or in Scotland. Indeed, no one who has worked on continental witch-hunting could apply the theory convincingly. This is partly because when the witch-hunt is looked at as a whole it is clear that what England experienced was a faint ripple from the continental cataclysm. In like manner Russia, also on the fringe of Europe and also outside the sphere of influence of Roman law, experienced a moderate witch-hunt without diabolic content following a change in the law in 1552. Zguta in his article on Russian witchcraft, in which he draws on a collection of documents published by Novombergskii in 1906,[30] suggests that Russian witchcraft does substantiate the social strain theory in that early Russian witch-trials were nearly always connected with outbreaks of famine or disease. Witches were frequently accused of causing such mass misfortunes.[31] He seems here, however, to be confusing witch-beliefs seen as explanation, in which the connection with witchcraft is direct, with the more general theory of social strain in which accusations of witchcraft are seen as displacement for deeper and wider social troubles than isolated disasters.

The principal factor which makes the social strain explanation unsatisfactory when applied to the continental witch-hunt, however, and raises further questions about the English one, is the conspicuous and unequivocal way in which the ruling elite controlled and manipulated the demand for and the supply of witchcraft suspects. The behaviour and motivation of that elite, therefore, seems more important in explaining witch-hunting, as opposed to understanding the operation of witch-beliefs, than the experiences of the peasantry. A further contrast between England and the continent is seen in the demonological element which featured so prominently on the continent and in Scotland, and is almost completely absent from the English and the Russian trials.

In spite of the special nature of the witch-hunt in England and the inapplicability of functional explanation to the witch-hunt as a whole the work of Thomas and Macfarlane has left a permanent mark on continental studies. There are two aspects to this: in the first place the importance of popular belief has been acknowledged and explored, and in the second the social categories of those who reached the courts has been more carefully examined. A third possible line of enquiry of the type demanded by Mair and most fully explored by Macfarlane on Essex: micro studies of relationships, networks, and the operation of witch-beliefs in daily life has not really yet been taken up, although Muchembled has shown that the material exists.[32]

The first issue, where the English studies have been most influential, is in the shift of emphasis to popular beliefs. Because these, rather than the beliefs of the magistrates who prosecuted them, were so clearly exposed and delineated in the work on England, it became clear that they were at the very least a significant factor in underpinning, supporting, and manning the production line of the human fodder for witchcraft trials. Recent work has therefore attempted to isolate popular belief as a factor in the European hunt.

Cohn's *Europe's Inner Demons* is a study of the origins and the ingredients of the whole witch fantasy. He traces the development of the ideas of the dehumanized individual given over to evil, of the orgy, the cannibalization of infants, and the night-flying witch. Cohn distinguished these from the belief in sorcery and suggested that these two types of belief 'inspired two very different kinds of witch-trial; but they could also be combined, and this is what commonly happened at the height of the great witch-hunt'.[33] Cohn made clear that these two types of belief could not always be conveniently categorized into popular and educated. On the one hand the belief in the night-flying witch has been popularly held. On the other sorcery has been the occupation and the resource of princes as well as peasants. Nor is it entirely clear how the demonological fantasy grew. The diabolical content of the witch-trials seems to have increased at the same time as printed demonological works were being produced rather than as a clear consequence of them.

Kieckhefer, in his *European Witch Trials*, does attempt to distinguish sharply between popular and educated beliefs. He argues that he has discovered a reliable methodology for distinguishing popular from learned beliefs.[34] The early trials which he covers record the accusations of neighbours in the vernacular; the final verdict of the court is in Latin. In this way one can identify two discrete sets of beliefs without any tautological pre-assumptions about what the content of these might be. He found that the vernacular *ipsissima verba* of the accusers were exclusively concerned with sorcery. He admits that by 1500 educated ideas might have infiltrated the peasantry but thinks that up to this date the separation might hold.

This method of procedure takes us further forward, and it is one which can be followed in later centuries where both accusations and final verdict are in the vernacular. It is still possible to distinguish at least the alleged *ipsissima verba* of the peasantry from the court proceedings, which tend in any case to follow a common form. The problem is that so do many of the accusations, which suggests that they were processed for the courts, or had learned from the courts. Although it seems clear that throughout the prosecutions the interests of the peasantry lay in sorcery and in malefice, while the officials of the courts were more concerned with diabolism, the distinction cannot be made too firmly. The indications are that there was more than one level of popular belief. Everyday belief was concerned with malefice, but peasants could share with their rulers and indeed transmitted to them communal fantasies of secret meetings and the night-flying witch. Popular belief could vary from region to region, and popular belief like educated belief was not necessarily static. Where there is more than one cultural level these are likely to interact.

All the other studies which have appeared recently are regional, and there seems to be a consensus that this is the way forward for the time being. The principal impetus of all this research has been towards the improvement of the detailed picture of witch-hunting. The authors of these studies also offer analyses which seem appropriate to their area of Europe and consider how far these may be generally applicable. Midelfort in his study of south-western Germany laid particular emphasis on the nocturnal sabbath as the essential ingredient in a mass trial, by which he meant more than thirty or so cases a year. He makes the important point though that the idea of witchcraft was not 'rigid and monolithic, but flexible and varied'. He also noted that even when the mass trials were occurring they were outnumbered by small trials involving one or two people in which accusations were likely to be for sorcery.[35] The traditional trials therefore continued right through the period of diabolic trials. Monter found few mass trials, and identified what he called small-scale panics involving six or seven individuals as most typical of Franche-Comté and Switzerland.[36] Soman confirms this in his work on French trials and has extended the range of the discussion by placing the witchcraft trials in a general criminal context. In particular he relates witchcraft to arson which he sees as sharing elements of revenge and blackmail and being similarly difficult to prove.[37]

There now seems to be a consensus that there were a number of factors behind the witch-hunt. Changes in the law were of considerable importance. The development of printing, religious strife, demographic disasters, social stress, may have played their part. The most recent analyses have laid the emphasis on the struggle for the minds of the peasantry which was a feature of the late medieval and early modern period.

Delumeau has argued that the peasantry of Europe were Christianized for the first time during the Reformation and Counter Reformation. Both these movements emphasized the importance of lay personal religion in a way previously unknown. In pre-Reformation Europe religious belief and practice were matters for the professionals; lay religion was optional. The idea that individuals were responsible for their own salvation transformed the belief structure. The Reformation and Counter Reformation brought religion, including a sense of sin, to the peasant through preaching and pastoral care. Delumeau relates this to witch-hunting by arguing that the various scourges of famine and disease which afflicted the peasantry began to be seen as the punishment of a just God. The responsibility for sin was seen to lie with the witches. Delumeau also argues that there is a basic antipathy between what he calls 'true religion' and magic, and that the witch-hunt was the product of an assault upon the animist mentality of the partly Christianized peasant. Hunting ceased when 'true religion' had been well established at parish level.[38]

This interpretation may underestimate the extent to which official religion propagated rather than opposed a belief in the physical power of demonic forces, but it does stress the significance of ideological conformity at the individual level. The whole concept of the Demonic Pact is dependent on the idea of personal responsibility.

The argument that Christianization was an important element in the witch-hunt is set in a wider framework by Muchembled who sees both as a product of the intensified control by the rulers of newly emergent and shifting political entities. He argues that this involved the imposition of urban values onto the countryside, and suggests that the most persistent witch-hunts took place in border areas where social control was most precarious.[39] Certainly it was a period when the new ruling classes demanded that official ideologies should receive assent from the populace. Collisions between these ideologies and rebellious individuals produced persecutions.

All recent writers, while concentrating with good reason on the mainsprings of the persecution since these are still not entirely clear, have responded to the introduction of social scientific ideas. This has largely taken the form of analysing the social status of those accused rather than studying the operation of witch-belief at village level. So although the significance of popular belief and some sociological discussion has been incorporated into the analysis no one has attempted to replicate Macfarlane's microscopic treatment of the interplay of relationships behind accusations of sorcery.

This neglect may have been partly because the wider aspects of functionalist explanation seemed inadequate in relation to the European witch-hunt. Moreover the dominance of diabolic witchcraft meant that large areas of belief were not so obviously amenable to social anthropological analysis. Indeed Monter goes so far as to argue that the kind of witchcraft which he was examining in Franche-Comté and Switzerland and which focused on the Demonic Pact was a totally different phenomenon from English sorcery.[40]

It is clear that in the mass witch-hunts persons brought in as suspects were not confined to those whose neighbours accused them of sorcery. Names were often extracted by torturing other accused witches and these names inevitably included those who had no existing reputation for witchcraft. European hunts of this type were clearly in a different category from English cases. It has nevertheless been shown by Cohn, Kieckhefer, Midelfort, Soman, and others that trials for sorcery alone continued to be quite common throughout even the most intense period of diabolic prosecutions, and that in many other trials the charge of diabolism was superimposed upon charges of sorcery. This suggests that the material for a microscopic analysis of peasant life as mirrored by witch-belief does exist for the continent as for Essex. It certainly exists for Scotland where the pattern of witch-hunting was on the continental model.

There are good reasons for the neglect of this line of enquiry so far. The English witchcraft statutes laid down different penalties for particular degrees and frequency of sorcery offences. The details of the malefice were therefore the very substance of the prosecution itself. The material for anthropological enquiry lay in what I have called the first layer of research. In diabolic trials, where the central offence was not so much specific acts of witchcraft as simply being a witch, the first layer met by the researcher is the court decision on that central issue. Earlier accusations of sorcery may exist alongside this material or they may lie in the records of lower courts. The top layer of material for European trials has by no means been fully explored, and to continue attempts to establish the macro-patterns more firmly does seem a reasonable way to proceed. It could be argued that the two could proceed alongside each other and, while this is undoubtedly so, it is also worth suggesting that too much should not be expected from such micro-studies so far as the witch-hunt is concerned. If, as seems to be the case, peasant life in areas of the continent which experienced witch-hunting was not substantially different so far as economic and social structures are concerned from those which did not, then micro studies of witchcraft accusations will be a rewarding way of exploring the details of these structures. It will not necessarily illuminate the problem of the rise, distribution, and decline of witch-beliefs and accusations.

It would indeed be possible to reverse Mair's complaint about European studies and suggest that despite evidence in the ethnographic literature of the episodic and idiosyncratic nature of much African and American witch beliefs and accusations explanations are normally restricted to microscopic functional analysis when politico-historical analysis might also be enlightening. Nor has much synthetic comparative analysis been done of structural differences between primitive societies which have witch-beliefs and those which do not. In both these areas anthropological material might be directly helpful to European research.

There are two other recent interpretations derived not from local research but from specialized view points: the feminist and the marxist. The feminist position will be considered later in the context of the sociological portrait of the witch. The marxist or radical position has been used both to identify the ruling class and to identify the peasantry as the source of witch-hunting. For Harris witchcraft was a cynical device of the ruling class to distract the peasantry from their revolutionary purpose by focussing their dissatisfactions and hatreds on their neighbours.[41] Harris's thesis is unsatisfactory in that the evidence for ruling class cynicism is slender and incidental. Their sincerity in the pursuit of witches as witches, however, does not detract from the obvious utility of witch-hunting as a means of social control. Elites do not need to be cynical in pursuit of their interests. They certainly feared witchcraft and the conspiratorial cells of witches.

Le Roy Ladurie sees diabolic witch-beliefs as the mythical counterpart of agrarian revolt. Popular uprisings are social sabbats. The witches' sabbat is a diabolical attempt to escape the reality of the failure of the social sabbats. In his vision the source of the beliefs appears to be peasant rather than elite, though the forces of order 'led the hunt for witches and the repression of the uprisings with equal energy'.[42] The specific psychological utility of demonic beliefs is clear in this account though the sources of it are hazy. While the applicability of radical theories to parts of France and Germany where peasant consciousness was high is clear, they are less obvious in relation to the urban witch-hunting of some German towns and of rural areas with low levels of peasant unrest.

This in brief is the present position in interpretations of the European hunt. The place of Scottish witch-hunting in the European pattern is chronologically within the second stage, that of the mid-sixteenth to late seventeenth century. The first phase of the Scottish hunt followed the mid-sixteenth-century flare-up, and after sharing the general lull of the early seventeenth century it revived again with the main upsurge of the 1620s. Scotland shared the decline in prosecutions which followed the peak of 1628 to 1630, but for the rest of the century witch-hunts there had an idiosyncratic course. The ending of the prosecutions, while markedly later than in England, was similar in timing to many other parts of Europe.

An analysis of the Scottish witch-hunt cannot therefore help to explain the origins of the European hunt which lay in Italy, France, and Germany. Much of the problem, however, lies not in the origins of the hunt but in the selectiveness of its diffusion, in the conditions which nurtured it, and in the variety of its forms. It is in the exploration of these areas that the Scottish experience has something to offer.

CHAPTER THREE

THE SOURCES FOR
A STUDY OF SCOTTISH WITCHCRAFT

It is customary in positivist historical writing to make a distinction between primary and secondary sources and list them separately in the bibliography. Primary sources are products of the period under discussion, and preferably not produced in order to illuminate the particular problem under discussion but for some other purpose. Secondary sources are later syntheses of primary material and usually intended to convert the reader to a particular view of the problem or period. Primary sources are more unselfconscious than secondary sources. They are the chief support for the totally blank mind with which it is deemed proper to approach an archive.

It is easy to mock at this attitude. How does the totally blank mind select one archive rather than another; one collection of documents within the archive rather than another? The strength of the positivist case really lies at a slightly later stage of the research process. If the researcher has approached the archive with a mind full of conceptual litter he may find the documents are unable to furnish the answers to his questions and may, by containing information which was not expected, provoke a reformulation of hypotheses. This positivist case is much stronger in relation to documentary research where the available material is more fixed and finite than it is in relation to survey research where the data is actually generated in response to hypotheses and limited by the range of these hypotheses.

That being said there are nevertheless serious problems inherent in the traditional approach to sources. We do not have empty minds about the ground to be explored, the aspects of it which are interesting, or the nature of the evidence. Our view of any historical problem is coloured by the views of our predecessors and the evidence produced in support of those views. So likewise were their views. Whether our reaction to the ideas of previous writers is favourable, cautious, or negative, we are dependent on their selection of material for our initial formulation of hypotheses.

From the sixteenth to the twentieth century the selection and presentation of Scottish witchcraft cases to the interested readership has always reflected prevailing ideas about the nature and place of witch-beliefs and witch-hunting. It is these ideas which have controlled the publication of primary material. The logical approach to the sources, therefore, is to take them not in the order in which they were written,

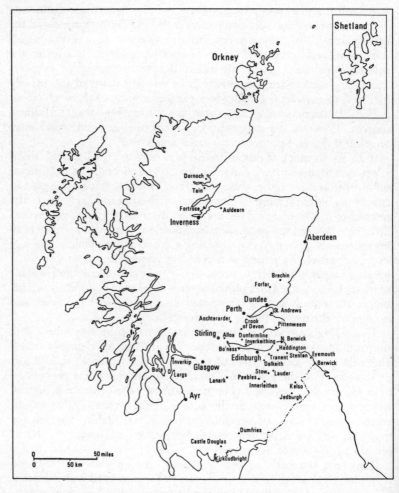

PRINCIPAL PLACES MENTIONED IN TEXT

but in the order in which they were published, for this was the way in which our current picture of Scottish witch-beliefs has been built up.

A further problem is that when we turn to the primary sources themselves there is no bedrock. The most basic sources are the manuscripts of trials for witchcraft. These are uncontaminated by ideas only in the sense that they are unselected, and in the sense that they list decisions and occurrences: acquittals, banishments, and executions. In other ways, like published discussions of witchcraft, they exhibit and present the prevailing understanding of the meaning of witch-trials. The common form of the indictments and verdicts, the processing of the accusations and confessions, are all interpretations of the process. Perhaps the most primary of primary sources are economic: the detailed accounts of the cost of trying and executing a witch. It is because the subject under discussion is the influence of an idea that a clear distinction between primary and secondary sources is particularly difficult to make.

The literature of Scottish witchcraft can be divided into that published during the period of witch-hunting, the Enlightenment reaction, the nineteenth-century romantic and rationalist approaches, and the varied themes of the twentieth century.

The most marked feature of the late sixteenth- and seventeenth-century material is its scarcity.[1] Until very late in this period Scotland did not have a yellow press. There was hardly any counterpart to the rich English popular literature of chapbook, almanac, and horror story.[2] But Scotland, as an exotic and alien culture, did provide the English presses with raw material. Indeed the very first work on Scottish witchcraft, *Newes from Scotland*, was published in 1591 in London.[3] Although the title page carries the legend 'according to the Scottish copie' there is no known Scottish copy, and the orthography is English. It is a classic sixteenth-century English pamphlet and it set the pattern for the next three centuries in which Scotland was (correctly) represented in England as a place in which witch-beliefs were maintained and accused witches pursued with a ferocity unknown south of the border.

The only other sixteenth-century work was James VI's *Daemonologie*, published in Edinburgh in 1597 in the middle of a particularly severe witch-hunt, though possibly written earlier. It justified his own witch-hunting activities and attacked the sceptical works of Weyer and Scot. It had some influence in Scotland in the following century in that it was frequently referred to in indictments for witchcraft in the courts and in governmental exhortations to implement the laws against witchcraft with more severity. After James moved to England it was reprinted with anglicized spelling together with his other Edinburgh publications and contributed to his reputation as a demonologist there despite the fact that his interest in the subject had flagged once he had crossed the border.[4]

The first half of the seventeenth century saw almost nothing in the way of publications other than a tract dealing with the prosecution of the Irvine witches who were accused of storm raising in 1618.[5] The tract is undated and may not be contemporary. It is the sole example from this period of the kind of tract very common in England in which the trial proceedings and confessions of the witches were laid out.

The real flow of material came after the main witch-hunt was over. The latter half of the seventeenth century saw not only the cautious writings of Sir George Mackenzie, the Lord Advocate, but also a variety of tracts containing narratives of particular cases. Mackenzie's writings (*Pleadings in some Remarkable Cases* (1672) and *Laws and Customs of Scotland in Matters Criminal* (1678))[6] were as sceptical as they could be without laying the author open to the charge of atheism, or 'sadducism' as the contemporary jargon had it. They coincided with a sharp decline in prosecutions and convictions.

The pamphleteering of this period was led by George Sinclair, Professor of Natural Philosophy at the University of Glasgow and famous for his diving bell. His visits to England on scientific matters had made him think that there was money to be made from the occult. He accordingly published in 1685 a collection of plagiarized English stories and an assortment of Scottish narratives of witches, spirit possessions, and apparitions, and in February of that year successfully petitioned the Privy Council for the sole rights of publication.[7] He misjudged his market, however, for *Satan's Invisible World Discovered*[8] initially sold badly and he died a poor man. Ironically his book became popular and ran through several editions in the following centuries.[9] It was said frequently to have been the second book in a peasant's library of two.

In the 1690s and early eighteenth century several pamphlets were published dealing with an outbreak of witch-hunting in Renfrewshire, with apparitions in Galloway, and with a lynching in the Fife fishing port of Pittenweem. Some were republished in England with different titles.[10] There were also published two or three general demonological treatises by anonymous ministers attempting to sustain belief in the Devil and his servants.[11] This sudden late surge in published accounts of witchcraft is largely accounted for by the general rise in the level of publication and an expansion of literacy. It may also be that with the decline of the prosecutions and the recession of the real fear of witchcraft the reading population were more able to regard it as a subject for entertainment and titillation.

In the eighteenth century the focus of the educated Scot was directed outwards to the wide issues of philosophy and science, and to the generation of a sociological form of historical writing. Their own immediate past was interesting mainly for comparative purposes. Yet the last witch was executed as late as 1727, and the death penalty for witchcraft abolished only in 1735. Up to that date no one in any work published in Scotland objected to the existing statute and its repeal was entirely the work of Englishmen. A lawyer, William Forbes, writing as close to its repeal as 1730,[12] simply plagiarized Mackenzie's *Laws and Customs* on the subject of witchcraft, and then added a rather curious appendix refusing to take responsibility for his own published opinions. Soon after the 1563 statute was repealed, however, lawyers and others felt free to denounce the superstition and cruelty of a barbarous and irrational age. Erskine, Arnot, and Hume (the lawyer) in the latter half of the eighteenth century wrote in this vein,[13] and Arnot was the first to publish, in 1775, a collection of criminal trials which included several for witchcraft.[14]

The main publication of narratives and trial materials took place in the nineteenth century. The earliest rather haphazard collections mainly concerned the Paisley trials[15] but later the Scottish historical clubs of this period selected, transcribed, and published a great quantity of source material of the sixteenth, seventeenth, and eighteenth centuries. Their precursors in this exercise were the eighteenth-century historian Wodrow and the archivist and printer Ruddiman who, while their Enlightened colleagues had deliberately rejected the choking dust of the archives, collected and transcribed manuscript material.

Alongside the work of the historical clubs and Pitcairn's collection of criminal trials,[16] the subject of witchcraft was taken up by romantic and rationalist historians. Sharpe wrote an introduction to Law's *Memorialls* (a seventeenth-century collection of witchcraft cases and occult happenings published in 1818) which he afterwards published separately as a *History of the Belief in Witchcraft in Scotland*.[17] Dalyell published his *Darker Superstitions of Scotland* in 1834.[18] He drew partly on the unpublished archives of Orkney and is the only writer ever to have attempted a monograph analysing Scottish witchcraft based on such research. Since Dalyell there have been numerous general works on witchcraft in which Scotland is included, there has been further production of source material, there have been articles dealing with specialized aspects of the witch-hunt and a great many popular works, but no other critical survey of the hunt as a whole. Dalyell's work is itself ahistorical, dealing with themes and concentrating on classifying the beliefs rather than charting the rise and fall of prosecutions. Both he and Sharpe have the nineteenth-century rationalist interest in ancient superstition. Scott's *Letters on Demonology and Witchcraft*, while sharing Dalyell and Sharpe's assumptions comments only in passing on Scottish cases, but several of his Scottish novels, in particular *Redgauntlet*, *The Bride of Lammermoor*, and *Heart of Midlothian*, draw on his wide research into witchcraft and demonology.[19] Scott was also responsible for the publication in 1815 of Kirk's *The Secret Commonwealth*,[20] a remarkable mixture of neo-Platonic science, Highland mythology and fantasy which focused on fairyland and bore only a slight relationship to the material coming up in the criminal courts.

Both Mackay and Lecky in their works on popular superstition dealt with Scottish witchcraft,[21] and Lecky lashed himself into paroxysms of rationalist rage while so dealing.[22] Buckle in his *History of Civilization in England*[23] was also very severe on Scottish witch mania. The nineteenth century closed with an article by Legge, a scientific journalist, in *The Scottish Review* for 1891 in which he suggested that the numbers executed had been greatly exaggerated and were unlikely to have exceeded 3,400,[24] and with a bibliographical account of the witchcraft literature of Scotland by the collector Ferguson, which was published in 1899.[25]

In the twentieth century comment on the Scottish witch-hunt took a new direction. Murray supported her theory that there was an organized witch cult which was an ancient fertility religion by drawing heavily on Scottish sources.[26] She pointed out that the accounts of meetings were quite credible and suggested that the confessions were made without torture. As already noted, Cohn has now demonstrated that she selected her material in these confessions to eliminate those elements in them which were palpably impossible.[27] She was no doubt herself misled by the fact that some confession documents specified that no torture had been used. This did not mean that no torture had been used at any point in the proceedings or that other forms of pressure such as sleep deprivation, threats, or promises had not been used.

Between Murray's first exposition of her theory in 1921 and Cohn's final disposal of it in 1975, however, it took a firm hold, especially on writers on Scottish witchcraft. Keiller attempted to juggle the known names of those who were prosecuted in Aberdeenshire in 1597 into groups of thirteen with one man to represent the fertility god or devil and twelve women.[28] McPherson's survey of popular belief in northeast Scotland published in 1929 accepted the witch cult theory without question.[29] It appeared ambiguously in Stafford's discussion of James VI's witch-hunt of 1590–91,[30] and continues to be received wisdom in the numerous popular accounts of Scottish witchcraft.[31]

Other writings, and in particular the collection of trial transcripts and the *Calendar of Cases of Witchcraft* by Black,[32] continued to reflect nineteenth-century rationalism. Black's collection of cases published in 1938 gives brief extracts in roughly chronological order from all the cases he could find in printed sources, and was the first serious attempt at a comprehensive coverage. Since then we have had only recent articles by Clark and the present writer on aspects of James VI's concern with witchcraft.[33] What has been missing this century is in the first place any monograph equivalent to the works of Kittredge, Ewen, or Notestein on English witchcraft, quite apart from the work of Thomas and Macfarlane,[34] and in the second place any discussion of the witch-hunt in the standard political histories. This latter omission is slightly odd because the extensiveness of the witch-hunt and the role of the government has always been well known. The explanation may be that Scottish historical writing has been closely modelled on the Oxford History of England, and since witch-hunts were not a part of English political life they were not included in a Scottish analysis. This cannot be a total explanation since other features peculiar to Scotland have received detailed political analysis. Some attempt to remedy the omission have been made in the recent work of Mitchison and Smout[35] but they have been hampered by the lack, already mentioned, of serious monographs.

It would be wrong entirely to dismiss the very large numbers of popular works on witchcraft in Scotland. Although the majority of them propagate the baseless view that a formal witch cult did exist, they have also reproduced much contemporary material verbatim, and they together with certain fictional literature maintain a level of general interest in the subject from which the serious researcher undoubtedly benefits.[36]

Apart from this extensive popular and semi-popular literature, the available material on Scotland during the revival of serious research in European witchcraft in the early seventies consisted of a few articles on particular cases, a great deal of printed, but very scattered, source material, and Black's Calendar of Witchcraft Cases. The available source material, though extensive, reflected a nineteenth-century view that the most significant cases were the most colourful and exotic ones. What was lacking was the kind of detailed coverage offered by Macfarlane for Essex from which one could satisfy a social scientific interest in the 'normal' or average case. This social scientific concern is partly to establish reliable figures; partly to be in a better position to distinguish typical from atypical manifestations. This is the principal difference between the contemporary approach to records and that of previous historians. In so far as the quest for total rather than random coverage is successful it is this which is likely to provide a lasting contribution long after such operating concepts as class, patriarchy, and ideology have gone the way of those of progress and rationality.

It was to fill this Scottish gap in the growing body of archival work on European and English cases, that, in collaboration with Lee and McLachlan, I attempted to cover the court records for criminal cases of witchcraft. Witchcraft was an offence against statute law punishable by death from 1563 to 1735. There were a variety of ways in which a witch could be prosecuted, and this is one of the factors which makes the researcher's task a difficult one. The treason-by-witchcraft trials of 1590–91 were conducted in special courts of justiciary frequently presided over by the king. The trials, which took place mainly in Aberdeenshire, Fife, and the Lothians from 1591 to 1597, were conducted in local courts under the general Commission for trying witches issued by the Privy Council in 1591,[37] and their records are either lost or contained in family papers. When the general commission was withdrawn in 1597 the Privy Council reserved for itself the right to consider each application for a commission to try a witch.[38] In the confused and flexible system of criminal justice which operated this does not mean that the control of the Privy Council over witch-trials was total. It means that Privy Council commissions to local landowners and officials became the commonest single way of trying a witch. The second commonest was through the Court of Justiciary and its circuit courts, and the least common was through commissions of Parliament. During the second half of 1649, however, the Committee of Estates issued commissions for one hundred and fifty-seven trials. All these ways were more or less legal: legality itself was an elusive concept closely related to power struggles between various courts and organs of government. There are, however, quite apart from the period 1590 to 1597, enough references in local histories and other printed material to executions of witches whose cases never reached the central authorities to raise queries about the proportion of dubiously legal to official executions, and about the validity of any figures and projections for the total numbers of witches tried and executed.

There are three main groups of sources for the central government prosecutions for witchcraft. The first is that for the Court of Justiciary; primarily the Books of Adjournal, which are the manuscript minutes of trials in that court. These are held in the Scottish Record Office in Edinburgh. There are gaps from July 1650 to October 1652 and from July 1655 to June 1661, but the National Library of Scotland has abridged Books of Adjournal which cover some of these gaps. In addition there are, in the Record Office, unindexed boxes of pre-trial material. Some, but not all, of these boxes have a dittay roll within them with a list of crimes, but these refer to crimes which the official concerned wanted tried, and do not always relate to material in the box. Sample examination has produced papers which refer to witchcraft cases which never came to trial. There may well be more in these boxes. There are also the Circuit Court minutes; the records of the travelling justiciary. These are sometimes bound up with the Books of Adjournal, but it is not clear to what extent these records are complete, and some witchcraft trials of the circuit courts may have been lost to us. Some of this High Court material is available in print; notably in Pitcairn, *Criminal Trials in Scotland*; Black, *Some Unpublished Witchcraft Trials*, and R. Scott-Moncrieff's edition of an abstract of the Books of Adjournal.[39]

The second main source, containing the largest number of cases, is the Privy Council. The Privy Council minutes are available in print up to 1691 and in typescript thereafter. They are complete in so far as they include all the cases discussed. Some of the accounts may be truncated, but a sample examination of witchcraft cases in manuscript suggests that these are usually printed entire. But as in the case of the Justiciary Records there is unindexed material which was left unexplored.

The third main group of central sources is the Parliamentary records and those associated with them. In fact only a few witchcraft cases were processed through Parliamentary commissions, and these can be found in the printed *Acts of the Parliament of Scotland*. The manuscript records of the Committee of Estates, whose witch-processing activities in 1649 have been referred to, are also available in the Scottish Record Office.

The defects of the material lie partly in what is actually missing. There are hardly any records for the extensive witch-hunt of 1590–97. There are the gaps in the Justiciary records which have been mentioned, and clearly many of the background process papers have been lost. One of the deficiencies is that there is no feedback on the fate of the witches for whose trial Privy Council commissions were granted, except in the rare cases of appeal procedures. It is an understatement to say that Scotland was not a fully bureaucratized society in this period, and the horseman from the Burgh of Ayr, having extracted his commission for a local trial, had no motive to ride back again and report the results. Such records as survive for these trials by local landowners (which were by far the commonest type of trial), are likely to be found in private family papers and sheriff court records, which until 1745 were likewise the private property of hereditary sheriffs.[40]

The material which does survive is also defective in terms of the type of information presented. The fate of the witch is often unreported, and likewise his or her marital and social status. Never, even in the processes, do we get an account of the type of questions asked, and the way in which confessions are extracted has to be inferred.[41] In these respects the Scottish records are very often much less complete and informative than continental or English records. Record-keeping itself, even at central governmental level, seems to have been an under-systematized and under-valued activity compared with contemporary standards elsewhere.

In theory, however, these central records, even if they do not tell us much about them, should have yielded all the witches who were put on trial. The local records should have contained only the early procedures against these witches, plus the proceedings against those who were dealt with by the Kirk sessions through minor punishments or not proceeded against at all. In fact it is clear that an unknown number of witches were executed without going through the 'legitimate' channels. Black's *Calendar* refers to some of these, and other researchers on Moray, Fife, Galloway and Dalkeith[42] have uncovered more cases of this nature. In addition there is the problem of Orkney which had devolved administrative powers and operated rather like a separate kingdom during this period. There is also the problem of the regalities. These were petty kingdoms which could try all crimes except treason and witchcraft, but do in fact seem to have tried occasional cases of witchcraft.

The net result of the coverage of these sources was a list of cases, with their primary source or sources where known, printed from camera-ready copy in 1977 as *A Source Book of Scottish Witchcraft*. Many of the 3,069 items were anonymous cases, some of them multiple. References to 'many witches' are quite common. The cases were arranged chronologically under the courts in which they were brought up, and therefore some of the named witches occur more than once under different courts. The duplications are not always very easy to identify since the spelling is varied. The nature of the *lacunae*: the sparseness of the records for the cases from 1590 to 1597, the difficulties of matching entries for anonymous witches with those already named, and the strongly episodic nature of witch-hunting, makes any statistical work from this list unreliable and potentially misleading. Despite these caveats, however, the major patterns of witch-hunting: the rise and fall of prosecutions, the timing of the mass hunts, the places most widely affected, and approximate numbers in relation to prosecutions in other parts of Europe can be established with reasonable confidence.

When we turn from quantitative to qualitative analysis the source material is rich enough. It is not necessary to have precise numbers to establish what is common form in a legal document and what is individual and eccentric. The trial documents provide many examples of pretrial material: the signed accusations of local witnesses with regard to malefice, the confession of the accused herself, and the final indictment and verdict.

In addition to the trial material itself there are the ecclesiastical records of Kirk session, synod, and presbytery. Not many witchcraft cases came to the higher church courts of synod and presbytery but the Kirk session records are a rich source for social life in general. They deal with parish misdemeanour at its most elemental level: slander, gossip, marital quarrels, sexual offences from pre-nuptial fornication to quadrilapses into adultery, neighbours' brawls, drunkenness, disorder, failure to attend the Kirk, and the original accusations of sorcery and witchcraft. These records, which have survived erratically, were not systematically explored for the *Source Book* because of the central administration of the crime, because it looked as though it would not be cost-effective except for the panic years, and because these records should really be analysed as a whole to put witch-hunting in the context of the wider role of the session in social control. A useful future exercise would be the analysis of records which are reasonably complete for particular panic years in order to match cases at the local level with those that came up in the central courts. There is a sub-stantial piece of work to be done collating local and central records for the years 1649, 1661, and 1662, for example. So far as other years go, however, it would be possible to read a kirk session register extending over a period of some years and find less than half a dozen cases which had any connection with witchcraft or charming. It would be interesting to compare social control in these relatively calm periods with its operation in the panic years.

In addition to official records there are numerous contemporary accounts of witchcraft cases in journals and letters many of which were published in the nineteenth century either by the Historical Clubs or by an independent editor.[43] Furthermore few of the local histories which proliferated in the nineteenth and early twentieth centuries were complete without their reference to witches in the area.[44] Many of the untraceable anonymous witches noted in Black's *Calendar* and in the *Source Book* originate in this kind of material.

When the details offered in these various sources are taken together it is possible to build up a picture of what is typical and what is atypical in patterns of witch-hunting and witch-belief and compare them with patterns in other areas of Europe and elsewhere. To what extent do the elaborate and detailed confessions of the famous witches of Forfar, Auldearn, and the Crook of Devon represent the tip of an iceberg? How important are the various elements of malefice, Pact, and witches' meeting in obtaining a conviction? What kind of people were accused of witchcraft? What were the mechanisms by which a witch was brought to trial and by what springs were these mechanisms activated? Did the mass hunts start by spontaneous popular combustion or through external ruling class pressure? How did the witch-beliefs relate to other aspects of religious belief? To what extent was the Scottish experience similar to that of other parts of Europe? The material described here, while frustrating by virtue of the *lacunae* common in historical material, is adequate for at least provisional arguments and suggestions towards the answering of these and other questions.

CHAPTER FOUR

SOCIAL STRUCTURE
AND SOCIAL CONTROL

There is some difficulty in writing a synthetic account, however brief, of the social structure of seventeenth-century Scotland, in that very little primary research has been done. Those familiar with recent scholarship on seventeenth-century England would be surprised by the contrast. The political and religious struggles have been well rehearsed,[1] but left relatively unexplored are the formal and informal systems of social stratification, the extent of upward and downward social mobility, the numbers and social origins of the ministers who, together with the lawyers, were the 'new men' of post-Reformation Scotland, the social origins of dissident religious groups in the later seventeenth century, the beliefs and culture of the peasantry, the formal powers of criminal jurisdiction and their application in practice, the relative importance of different crimes and the number of cases. Even the lines of live historical controversy have scarcely been laid down. It has not been asked whether the gentry were or were not rising, or whether the poor had any collective consciousness. Only recently has it been suggested by Stevenson that if there *was* a 'general crisis' in seventeenth-century Europe Scotland might have been involved in it,[2] and by Foster that Scotland raises peculiar problems for those committed to a Marxist–Leninist interpretation of history.[3] One does not need to share Foster's teleological assumptions about what ought to have been happening, or agree with his assertions about the weakness and short-lived nature of feudalism in Scotland, in order to be grateful for his raising questions about the economic and social structure and the development of capitalism.

No one in particular is to blame for this state of affairs. It is due in part to the relatively small number of people involved in Scottish historical research, in part to the internal tradition of treating Scottish history as local and private, and in part to the habit of emphasizing the known, rather than raising questions about the unknown. It does mean, in practice, that what can be said about social structure and social mobility, and, above all, about the state of law and legal organization in the period is impressionistic, though the situation has been much improved by the recent work of Whyte on agriculture and rural society in this period.[4]

With that proviso there are three main hypotheses to be made in the first part of this chapter. First, non-Gaelic-speaking Scotland can be described as having a peasant economy throughout the period of witch-prosecutions; second, that the social structure was feudal, in that essential relationships were vertical and based on land, payments in kind, and services, including military services; third, this social and economic structure was relatively unchanged for a period a great deal longer at both ends than that covered by the witch-prosecutions, relative, that is to say, to England and parts of the continent. If these suggestions hold, then it follows that the outbursts of witch prosecuting cannot be explained in terms of changes in the basic structure of society, unless it is argued that the very small changes which may have occurred in some of the agriculturally most advanced counties such as Fife, Morayshire, and the Lothians,[5] were sufficient in relative terms to cause the same kind of social stress which is said to have been caused by the enclosure movement in England.

This does not mean that social and economic organization was of no importance. Obviously the way in which the hunts developed and the selection of the people who were hunted were affected by the social order. It merely means that the changes in this aspect of Scottish life prior to and during the period of witch-prosecution were not sufficient in themselves to explain the hunt. There were, however, two major changes in the nature of Scottish society which, while not affecting either the stratification or the economic system except to reinforce them strongly, may have been important factors in the development of a witch-hunt. They followed from the break from Rome and the attempt to develop a nation-state. The first was the strenuous imposition of an entirely new ideology, Calvinist Christianity, on the populace, and the second, closely connected, was the development of a new system of social control by which the behaviour and geographical mobility of large sections of the populace were closely monitored. The new regime asserted its legitimacy by redefining conformity and orthodoxy, and by providing a machinery for the enforcement of orthodoxy and the punishment of deviance which is discussed in the second part of this chapter.

Social and Economic Structure

Seventeenth-century Scotland fits well into the category described by Daniel Thorner as a 'peasant economy'.[6] He uses the term to describe total economies as opposed to individual household units, and while he reserves his exposition for large-scale kingdoms or empires he does not exclude small-nation peasant economies, and specifically includes pre-Union Scotland in his examples of these. For Thorner, there are five criteria for determining whether the total economy of a given country is to be taken as a peasant economy, all of which must be satisfied. Roughly half the total population must be agricultural, and more than half the working population must be engaged in agriculture. There must exist a state power and a ruling hierarchy in which the 'kinship' or 'clan' order has weakened sufficiently to give way to a territorial state. His fourth criterion is the urban-rural separation, the fulfilment of which demands a 'significant number of towns with a definite pattern of urban life quite different from that of the countryside'. The economy therefore, must not be purely agricultural. There must be a fairly marked degree of division of labour in society and 'a distinct urban concentration of artisans or other industrial and intellectual workers of various skills'. Peasants in a peasant economy are a lesser order than townsmen, and are there to be exploited. Agriculture must be sufficiently advanced to feed 'not only the peasants and the governing hierarchies, but also the townspeople'.[7] His fifth criterion, which he regards as most fundamental, is that of the unit of production. In the peasant economy the typical unit of production is the peasant family household: 'a socio-economic unit which grows crops primarily by the physical efforts of the members of the family'.[8] The household may engage in other activities, and there may be hired or non-family members of the household helping, but their contribution must be less than that of family members.

Scotland east and south of the Highland line had fitted most of these criteria for some time before the Reformation, and continued to fit it until the late eighteenth century. Thorner's first two categories concerned the proportion of the population engaged in agriculture. According to Smout roughly three-quarters of the population were peasants,[9] which is more than enough though it is not clear whether it is too many for the model. The third category of a territorial state power and a ruling hierarchy certainly existed from the times of James VI, and some might want to argue that it was established well before that. The urban-rural separation had more certainly existed for some time. The burghs were well developed by the fourteenth century. By the seventeenth they had all the specialist features required by Thorner's model, but it is not clear whether they had enough dominance (though the refusal to allow crafts to be practised outside them suggests that they did) or whether the numerical balance between town and country was adequate.[10] The urban-rural relationship is as complex in Scotland as elsewhere. It may have been of some importance in witch prosecuting. Thorner's fifth category, the peasant family as the unit of production, almost certainly existed in the form required, although very little is so far known about the details of family economic organization. What is not in doubt is that the land was cultivated in small family groups, though there may have been considerable co-operation between groups.[11] It was not cultivated by the large-scale use of hired labour which is the essence of capitalist agriculture.

Having suggested that Scotland had all the essential features of a peasant economy it is difficult to discuss her economic condition further without a consideration of the social structure with which it was intimately connected. To define a society as peasant does not tell you, and Thorner points this out, 'whether the peasants are serfs, semi-free, or free'.[12] The typical seventeenth-century Scottish peasant appears to have been a semi-free tenant farmer, and the social order within which he operated strongly feudal.

Both the term 'peasant' and the term 'feudal' have been invented by external observers as opposed to being used by participants. For this reason they require redefinition every time they are used. Thorner's peasant model has been used to identify the economy. It is not of course incompatible with the marxist economic model of the feudal mode of production which posits an exploitative relationship between lord and peasant. It is however more developed and less deterministic and with its emphasis on the towns relates to the late feudal or 'transitional' part of the marxist model.

It should be said that the marxist model of the transition from feudalism to capitalism is not as such an important point of reference in this book despite the fact that the witch-hunt is interpreted in terms of ruling class concerns. The reason for this is partly that while the marxist 'transition' may be illuminating and has certainly proved so for Carter's analysis of nineteenth-century north-eastern Scotland,[13] in the period under scrutiny here there were no more than the most elementary forms of capitalist development in trade and agriculture. More fundamentally, while it may well be true that 'feudalism' and 'capitalism' represent pure types of economic structure, one requires a better word than 'transition' to describe a period which lasted from three to five centuries and had some well defined characteristics of its own. The fact that these characteristics were not economic and existed in conjunction with static as well as changing economies suggests that political, religious, and social changes may have a greater degree of autonomy than is normally allowed for them in marxist analyses.

The other principal use of the term 'feudal' is that developed by legal historians to describe a set of formal vertical relationships between men. The legal obligation to give military service to feudal superiors is normally regarded as the most essential element in this, but there is a network of other arrangements dependent on the feudal relationship in relation to tenure of land, attendance at law courts, non-military services, and payment in kind. J. Foster's reflections on the weakness of feudalism in Scotland relates in part to the non-development of a manorial system.[14] Wormald's suggestion that feudalism is already an inappropriate term to use about fifteenth-century Scotland is related to the observation that the direct connection between land and service was being replaced by a different type of contract in which the economic aspects were more important than personal service.[15] A further factor

was the development of feuferme, the selling of land for fixed payment without the previous responsibility for law and order.

The retention of the term feudal to describe the social order of
seventeenth-century Scotland is meant to indicate that it was based on
land, that significant relationships were vertical or based on kin rather
than horizontal and based on common economic interests, that there is
some evidence that contracts between males reached their apogee in
the late sixteenth century and involved formal arrangements about
services: agricultural, legal, and military, about use and tenure of land,
and about payment in kind.[16] However much these were modified in
detail during the seventeenth century it was not until after 1747 that
their structure was radically altered. It is precisely because Scotland
differed from much of Europe and from England in her retention and
in some aspects strengthening of these structures, it seems worth
while retaining the word feudal to describe them.

The use of this observer's term and the suggestion that the landed
with their kin and adherents constituted a ruling class is imposed upon a
system which contained within both the landed and non-landed
sections a considerable degree of stratification and rank consciousness.
The table attempts to set out the mid-seventeenth-century social order
as perceived at the time.

This is, of course, like most attempts to clarify the confused, somewhat misleading. As suggested, most people, three-quarters or more of
the population, were countrymen, and social and economic organization was dependent on land. In the first group are the landowners, and
then, as now in Scotland, very large areas of land were owned by a
small number of people. There were probably not more than about
five thousand landowners, excluding the 'bonnet-lairds' of the south
west.[17] The largest areas were those infertile lands owned by the
Highland chiefs and used mainly for pasture. Next were the great
estates of the nobles. In the most fertile areas the divisions were smaller
and there might be as many as three or four estates in one parish. The
owners of these smaller estates were not members of the nobility; they
were landed gentry, and were known as 'lairds', or 'barons'. These
were descriptions, not titles, and the laird indicated his landed status by
adding his land to his name. Not all lairds were barons. The baron held
a charter. He could hold feudal courts (known as baron courts) and
summon tenants to appear in them and serve in them. Most of their
holdings were of a fair size and supported large numbers of tenants
and sub-tenants. The exceptions to this general pattern were the
'bonnet-lairds' already mentioned. These were so called because they
were economically and socially indistinguishable from a poor tenant or
sub-tenant. Indeed, although they were land owners they might in terms
of stratification have less status and less wealth than many tenant farmers.
They were not very common except in the south-west, and their in-
clusion in the first group is one of the misleading aspects of this chart.

Social stratification in seventeenth-century Scotland

RURAL	URBAN	
LANDOWNERS	BURGESSES (Freemen)	NON BURGESSES
Nobility		
Highland Chiefs	Merchants	Advocates
Barons		Writers
Lairds	CRAFTSMEN	Notaries
	Maltsters	
Wadsetters	Cordiners	
Portioners Ministers	Weavers	
Bonnet-lairds	Bakers	
(mainly Galloway	Hammermen	
and West)	Coopers	
	Skinners	
NON-LANDOWNERS	Wrights	
	Fleshers	UNFREEMEN
	Masons	Chamberlains
TENANTS	Bonnetmakers	Respectable widows
Tacksmen	Dyers	Clarks
(Highland	Surgeons	
grand tenants)	Apothecaries	*(stratification not*
Baillies & Factors	Skippers	*clear)*
Tenants		Journeymen
Kindly tenants		Servants
Sub tenants		Common labourers
Crofters Teachers		Drovers
Cottars		Carters
Grassmen		Coalmen
		Alesellers
LANDLESS		Milk vendors
Taskers		Fishermen
Landless labourers		Seamen
Indoor farm		
servants		
		Prostitutes
Vagabonds		Thieves
Beggars		Vagabonds

It is difficult to describe the remaining groupings without a further look at the land-holding system. Land-holding took two forms, wardship and feuferme. All land was ultimately held in feudal relationship to the crown, and landowning, throughout the whole period of the persecutions, involved a network of personal obligations. Those whose tenure was the older form of wardhold were obliged to provide military service, to hold courts and be responsible for law and order in their territories, and to attend the King's court when required. Wardship involved payments (casualties) every time the property changed hands on the death of the owner, to the feudal superior. If the new owner was a minor the feudal superior administered the property and took the rents; if there was no heir then the property reverted. This had the effect of nullifying improvements on the estate, and may well have been one of the reasons for the static condition of agriculture. At the same time it kept much of the country in a state of readiness for the local mobilization of troops until its abolition in 1748.

Feuferme was a development of the fifteenth and sixteenth centuries and was a system peculiar to Scotland. It was a 'fixed and heritable tenure granted in return for a fixed rent and for certain fixed casualties'.[18] Feuing was about cash. It was a way of realizing money from land without having to wait for a convenient death. It involved no obligations to provide military service, and, more important from the point of view of this study, no responsibility for law and order. The extent of feuferme land-holding by the end of the witch-prosecuting period is quite unclear. According to Smout, wardholding had died out everywhere except the Highlands by 1690.[19] According to Grant, writing forty years earlier and quoting the contemporary lawyer, Lord Stair, wardholding was still normal in 1690.[20] In fact there was clearly a considerable transition from wardholding even if the extent of it is not clear, and this had some influence in extending the ownership of land, and in the establishment of more secure tenancies. The Scottish peasant, however, was not normally a landowner even on the smallest scale, and was a different sort of creature from the English yeoman farmer, and from many European peasants of the period. His tenure of land was frequently very insecure and was dependent on his fulfilment of obligations to the landlord or his intermediary.

Next in the table were non-landowners who were nevertheless people of substance with very often a middle position between tenant and landlord. Portioners were those who had been leased portions of an estate for life or two generations. They could be described as quasi-landlords. Wadsetters were creditors of their landlords who had been given land in lieu of the debt. Once the debt was paid off the former debtor became absolute owner of the land again. In fact wadset was very often indefinite in duration and could probably be heritable. Tacksmen were a type of grand tenant, and were commonest in the highlands. They were often younger sons of the land holders who were leased large portions of land to administer and from which they could receive rents and sometimes services.

The second group in the table include the tenants and sub-tenants. Some tenants were fairly substantial people: an eight-oxen man might have a considerable number of sub-tenants under him. Kindly tenants are a slightly obscure group; nobody knows quite what their legal status was, but they appear to have had a particularly strong moral security of tenure, and right to pass their tenancy on to kin. At least one case of witch prosecution in 1662 covered the attempt of a Highland land owner to dispossess a group of kindly tenants who were inconveniently in possession of his land.

Crofters and cottars were forms of sub-tenants. They received enough land for their own subsistence or more in return for labour and rents in kind. The humblest form of sub-tenancy appears to be that of the tasker. He performed various tasks in return for food and a cottage with kailyard and ground. The kailyard would be much what is suggested: adequate to grow the odd vegetable, but not enough to provide a subsistence. He was not expected to be self-sufficient. In general only the very humblest, the landless labourers and the indoor farm servants, received wages in cash in the countryside.[21] They were a class who in times of dearth merged with the army of vagabonds.

The urban list is not a simple vertical stratification scale. The basic distinction was between freemen (the burgesses), and unfreemen or indwellers, but the term unfreemen would not normally be applied to the grander members of the non-burgess class, some of whom might be socially superior to many of the burgesses who were the members of the merchant and craft guilds. There was a fairly rigid and formal rank distinction between these two classes of burgesses. Lawyers, ministers, and some bureaucrats, were the ambiguous members of the community. They had status; an advocate or even the chamberlain of a grand household would certainly rank above an apothecary or a bonnet-maker, though without the formal political position of a burgess. The urban group normally associated with the terms unfreemen and indwellers was an assortment of wage labourers and self-employed persons whose stratification is not clear. It is not even clear whether there existed a permanent separate criminal class of prostitutes, thieves, and vagabonds quite distinct from the virtuous urban poor.

The most dubious aspect of the table, however, may well be the rural-urban division. As suggested, this is the most questionable part of Thorner's model in terms of its applicability to seventeenth-century Scotland. Scotland was at this time an almost completely rural community. The towns except for Edinburgh were extremely small: Donaldson has suggested that less than one-fifth of the population lived in the burghs;[22] and the country was on everyone's doorstep. The towns were markets, they were ports, they were centres of administration, and trade. The division into urban and rural, although real, was not as absolute as it appears here, especially at the top and bottom of the scale. Landowners took part in trade: they owned portions of ships like the great merchants, and they owned town houses. Those who failed to do this were the ones who ended up in the hands of their wadsetters. Great merchants on the other hand, bought themselves land and set up as lairds as soon as they could afford it. At the bottom of the scale too the traffic between town and country would be considerable, for anyone who sold their labour for cash might do it seasonally in town and country. Craftsmen and lawyers were the most urban of Scotsmen. Craftsmen in particular were formally restricted to an urban practice: burghs simply disallowed crafts to be practised outside their precincts.[23] The existence of this kind of ruling lends support to the idea that in a peasant economy the towns are the dominating force, but here the case still seems to be non-proven. The mere fact of being parasitic on the countryside for basic food does not necessarily classify the towns as exploitative. Other indicators suggest the continuing dominance of the landowner and the basically rural social structure of the country. The prestige of the lawyer in the town probably lay less in his skills than in the fact that he was likely to be a younger son of a laird or even of a noble. More significant may be that the sheriff courts, most of which were still hereditary jurisdictions until 1652, had dominance over the burgh courts.[24]

Compared with social stratification, the details of economic and agricultural organization have been well covered, especially by Lythe,[25] Hamilton,[26] and Smout.[27] There is no doubt whatever that in relation to much of England and to much of northern Europe the Scottish economy was in an exceedingly backward state, and at no point prior to or during our period did any important change occur. The basic economy was subsistence agriculture. While some specialization in relation to the suitability of certain crops did occur in different parts of the country, the normal mode of production was for the individual tenant farmer to be self sufficient for his family and dependents, with enough surplus for his rents. The inefficient infield-outfield system, a method of land use which involved the regular manuring of the better land, the infield, and the recurrent cultivation without fertilization of the outfield, prevailed everywhere.

Only a small, still unknown, proportion of tenant farmers were able to cultivate their land on their own. These were men substantial enough to own their own team of eight oxen. Much more common was the small collective farm, the 'farm-toun', a hamlet based upon a piece of land which would be divided among four or more families—which would co-operate over the use of oxen and in some sharing of labour. The land would be divided according to the run-rig system of strips of land, so that each family would have some infield, some outfield, and in some cases these strips would be redistributed each year thus rendering careful husbandry even less rewarding. Crops were mainly oats and barley, though wheat was grown in the richer agricultural areas.

These small hamlets based on a unit of land were much commoner than the English type of nucleated village. A parish was a group of farm touns with the Kirk-toun as the central one. Only round the coast were fishing villages similar to English villages to be found. This is a feature which makes the exact location of an accused witch and her relation to other local witches hard to establish, because some of the place names have either disappeared or are too frequently replicated to be identifiable. The place name often given for a witch is in fact that of the parish which could cover a wide area.

More ambiguous are questions which lie behind any stratification chart or model of an economy: questions of social mobility, of the extent of economic change, of rank and class consciousness, and of the role and status of women in the community. Social mobility in particular is a notoriously elusive concept. There has to be some arbitrary answer given to the question of how much mobility is required to turn a static society into a mobile one, before there is even much point in quantification. There is little, therefore, that can be said about this here, but it is clear that large-scale downward mobility occurred in times of famine, that is to say in the 1620s, 1640, and especially during the 'seven lean years' of the 1690s.[28] During the seventeenth century there was considerable population expansion, and there is evidence that the land, under the primitive methods of agriculture then operating, could not always support the population. There was large-scale emigration, and almost literally armies of Scotsmen found a livelihood in fighting as mercenaries on the continent. Not everyone was able to emigrate, however, and in times of dearth the hard core of vagabonds, gypsies, and others who spent their lives on the road, were augmented by wage labourers who migrated in search of work, and by dispossessed sub-tenants. Upward social mobility is even harder to estimate. The extension of feuferme landholding may well have increased mobility, but there is not yet enough evidence on this. The ministers and the lawyers, both new post-Reformation groups, tended to come originally from the landed gentry or the nobility, thus providing the outlet for younger sons that ecclesiastical posts have traditionally provided in feudal societies. Later in the seventeenth century there was a tendency for them to be self-perpetuating classes.

On rank or class consciousness there has been almost no research although Logue has published recently on the late eighteenth and early nineteenth century.[29] What evidence there is suggests that in the seventeenth century, while rank consciousness was sharp, militant class consciousness was at a remarkably low level or very well concealed.

Johnson in his *History of the Working Classes in Scotland* found about
two seventeenth-century examples, though with Red Clyde optimism
he did not draw the conclusion just drawn here;[30] Hill on the other
hand makes passing references to travelling Scotsmen who were
amazed at the level of aggression to be found among the poorer
sections of society in England.[31] It may be that research may uncover
signs of collective social unrest: the occasional references to 'riot' in the
High Court of Justiciary may lead somewhere, but the comments of
Smout on riot suggest that the urban mob in the seventeenth century
had not been politicized.[32] In the absence of new discoveries the
problem to be considered, and this is also true of much later Scottish
history, is the relative lack of social discontent and either urban or
peasant unrest.

This lack cannot really be explained in the terms suggested by
Gordon Donaldson that the level of agriculture was good by the
standards of the time, and 'the typical Scot was concerned mainly with
the provision of the needs of his own household' and was essentially
content.[33] A different view is given by Lythe who notes that 'foreign
observers almost unanimously damned Scottish arable farming'[34] and
suggests that the landowners' rents, payable in kind or money, 'often
absorbed up to a third of the value of the product of the land'.[35] While
this admittedly was a small proportion compared with the system of
mezzadria in rural Italy up till the 1950s in which dues were half the
value of the product, it should still have been enough to generate a
certain amount of discontent. Whyte's work provides further
evidence of a classic exploitative relationship including the obligation
for the producers to grow wheat which they themselves might not
use.[36]

Even if the system as described amounts to something more complex
than a simple dichotomous model of class exploitation, objective
reasons for social and economic discontent clearly existed in Scotland
as elsewhere. The lack of any manifestation of this, and the fact that
most visible peasant aggression in the seventeenth century was lined up
behind ruling class cleavages on political and religious issues, can
perhaps be explained in terms of the strength of feudal bonds and
feudal control, greatly reinforced, especially at the local level, by the
organization of the post-Reformation church, by the dispersed nature
of Scottish rural society with the consequent lack of gathering places
other than the church, and by the lack of large towns where the
equivalent of the English 'masterless men' might congregate. It has also
been suggested that the level of preoccupation with religious issues
lowered interest in economic and social ones.[37] The likeliest cause is
perhaps the exceptional insecurity of the Scottish peasant. He did not
own his land and he could not reliably pass on his tenancy to his
children. This is an excellent structural recipe for docility and deference. It is suggested by Donaldson that in the sixteenth century the

sub-tenant class in practice not only had security but were normally able to pass their tenancy on to their kin.[38] This practical security may have been modified in the seventeenth century by the rise in population and the localized move towards larger units noted by Whyte, but it was in any case entirely dependent on the tenant's good behaviour and continued exploitability. It stood for nothing when the time came for evictions.

The personal vertical relationships of the pre-Reformation period were only strengthened by the Reformation ideology and organization. It is often assumed that Scottish Calvinism had democratic implications. In spiritual terms it may have had such implications, but in practice the integration of the land-owning laity into the formal organization of the Church did nothing to modify the social structure, though it may have assisted the upward mobility of those who acquired land after the Reformation. It has recently become fashionable to use the term 'revolution' in connection with certain plateaus in the faction fighting of the seventeenth century, but it is doubtful whether anything worthy of that name has ever affected the socio-economic structure of rural Scotland. Certainly there were no permanent radical changes between the Reformation and the post 1745 settlement. Nor does it appear that the people took up arms before the late eighteenth century for any reason other than kingship, kinship, or religion.

There remains the question of the position of women. Women are beginning to emerge from the historical record, rather as the working classes did a generation or so ago, in response to changes in levels of consciousness among historians and social scientists. They have not, however, emerged very far. In many parts of Europe including Scotland they appear as individuals in the historical record for the first time as witches. The witch prosecutions are certainly the first time that women appear as criminals in any large numbers. Cases of infanticide, the other main female crime, only occur when there is a punitive attitude to illegitimacy, and seem to appear either later than or contemporaneously with witch prosecuting. The position of women is at present a very dark area.

In criminal law women did not exist. Their status was the same as children and convicted felons and they were not admitted as witnesses in courts of law. It was necessary to pass a special act in 1591 in order to allow their testimony in witchcraft cases. In civil law the position is more obscure. Most feudal contracts appear to have been made between men, but on the other hand women appear to have retained a considerable amount of independence on marriage, and the fact that they did not take on their husband's name may have been symbolic of such independence. Marriage was agnatic and women remained members of their original families.[39] They appear to have retained control over their dowries, and they may have been able to inherit property and possibly even tenancies of land. Certainly the records of the quarrels behind witchcraft accusations reveal instances in which women were shown as (recalcitrant) payers of rents, and as owners of 'gear' (livestock), even when married. It is not clear from the record, however, whether this was a formal ownership or merely a conventional attribution because they were in fact doing the actual work of finding grazing for the animals and dealing with the rent collector. It may be worth posing the question of whether the appearance of women in the criminal records coincides with some change in their social and economic status, even though it seems inherently improbable that such a change occurred simultaneously in those parts of Europe in which witches were prosecuted.

The general social and economic picture presented here is a static one. It is static in comparison with parts of England and parts of the continent, where we can see considerable agricultural change, the growth of substantial cities, the growth of industries, and extensive trade; it is static too in its own terms in that the changes to be perceived over a three-hundred-year period are fairly small, and confined to a small area; the richer agricultural lands. It has been suggested that here a certain amount of change did take place,[40] that there was a movement from collective farming to single ownership of a unit of land, and that to the extent that this was happening there was social and economic dislocation. The question is whether this represents sufficient change to generate witchcraft accusations if indeed these are symptomatic of unusual social strain. This could only be shown by the sort of detailed anthropological area-research which has not yet been done, demonstrating that those individuals who were accused were those who had been displaced or were about to be displaced, and that their accusers were the new single unit owners.

There were also some developments in industry in these areas. The extraction of coal and salt in Fife and the Lothians was during the seventeenth century involving legislation which enserfed the workers in these industries. But although the salt pans and the coal mines were in witch-prosecuting districts their workers do not seem to have featured prominently in the accusations. There was also clearly some development of trade during the seventeenth century, but again whether any of this amounts to the type of change which would cause peculiar social tensions not previously present is very doubtful.

The initiation and decline of witch prosecuting then were contained well within the limits of a period of little change in economic and social organization. A consideration of the basic components of economic and social structure therefore cannot logically contribute to explanations of why the prosecutions started in the first place: it does, however, help towards an understanding of some of the forms which witch-hunting took. Yet there were real changes in some aspects of social life, which may have been causal factors, and the most notable of these were in the organization and enforcement of religious worship, in the control of geographical mobility, and in the central and local application of the criminal law.

Social Control

If the social structure was static, the methods for controlling it were not. In one sense the Reformation can be described as the biggest reinforcement the feudal system in Scotland ever had, for in the ministers and elders of the Reformed Church the land-owning classes were provided with a police force and civil service.

The term 'social control' in this section is used in a sense narrower than the whole social system, but wider than the formal legal system. It refers to the formal and informal mechanisms for creating and enforcing rules, though in practice when dealing with a past society the formal mechanisms are inevitably more visible than the informal. This section deals briefly with the organization of criminal law, and with the activities of the local Kirk sessions as controllers of both crime and lesser misdemeanours, and considers the place of witch prosecution in the general pattern of control.

The larger part of the seventeenth-century machinery for both criminal and civil jurisdictions was a chaotic inheritance from pre-Reformation times. It was observed by Hugo Arnot, the eighteenth-century Edinburgh lawyer and historian that 'there is no determined system of criminal jurisprudence in Scotland. It is a matter of doubt what is a crime in the eye of her law, and what is not, also what is the punishment annexed'.[41] If this was true of the eighteenth century it was even more true of the seventeenth. Although some firm statements have been ventured both about seventeenth-century jurisprudence and about the status of the different criminal courts,[42] it is still a largely unknown and unresearched area.[43] In practice judicial outcomes seem often to have reflected the relative power of participants and their capacity to convince. It is not without significance that early legal writers wrote 'Practicks' rather than 'Institutes'.

The organization of criminal justice was complex and overlapping and the areas of competence often ill-defined. The types of jurisdictions can be divided into royal, baronial, and ecclesiastical, though in fact the category of 'royal' is a particularly confusing one. It includes not only central government institutions: Parliament, Privy Council, and the Court of Justiciary, plus their local extensions, the hereditary sheriff-doms and the royal burghs, all of which undeniably represented King's law; but also the regalities, which in a sense represented the abandon-ment of royal control. The regalities were areas where the King's writ was administered by the lord's officials rather than those of the King himself.

The King's writ itself as centrally administered dealt principally with treason and the 'four pleas of the crown': robbery, rape, murder, and arson. Witchcraft was added to these after 1597. The principal central bodies involved in criminal justice during the seventeenth century were the Justiciary Court (reconstituted as the High Court of Justiciary after 1672) and its travelling courts, the Justice Ayres (later the Circuit Courts), the Privy Council and those who received its commissions, and Parliament and its committees. King's justice was extended through the system of sheriffdoms, although since these were normally hereditary and part of the feudal arrangements the distinction between royal and feudal jurisdictions here is not very clear. Sheriff Courts had rights of jurisdiction over their whole area other than any burghs contained within it. Their rights did not include treason or the four pleas of the crown; nor could they try crimes for which the punishment was transportation. These included lease-making, adultery, and forgery. They could, however, try murder 'red hand', that is to say 'if the murderer were taken immediately upon the fact', provided that justice was summary. The case had to be tried and the sentence carried out within twenty-four hours of the act being committed.

Regality courts could in theory overthrow the judgement of sheriff courts. They could also try any crime including the four pleas of the crown, but excluding treason, and after 1597, witchcraft. Regalities made obvious sense in areas such as Argyll where it would have been troublesome to take accused persons to Edinburgh, but in practice their geographical distribution was somewhat random. Stewartry courts were basically regality courts for lands which had been appropriated by the monarch.

The baron courts were the lowest secular courts and they did not try many cases of serious crime. Their main function was to deal with cases relating to 'the weill of the tenandis and keiping of gude nichtburheid',[44] and to a certain extent this function was taken over and more energetically pursued in the seventeenth century by the kirk sessions. Some baron courts were entitled to try cases of theft 'red hand' and 'slaughter red hand' (i.e. a killing when there was no 'forethocht felony', the result, for example, of a brawl), but they could impose the death penalty only if the right of 'pit and gallow' was included in the baron's charter. Sheriff courts could overturn their judgements if it was not too late to do so.

The status of burgh courts is more obscure. Burghs were given a good deal of independence, but the court of a royal burgh was not allowed, unlike the hereditary regalities, to try the Four Pleas of the Crown. It is not clear whether a regality burgh court really had any greater powers than an ordinary burgh, a burgh of barony:[45] both appear to have been subordinate on appeal to the sheriff court. Over the whole system of courts in general absolute demarcation lines were not drawn.

This combination of overlapping feudal jurisdictions was the pre-Reformation inheritance; it was an area in which king, noble, baron, and city burgher struggled to keep or increase their area of control, and in which outcomes did little to create precedents. Yet despite the continuance of these structures until after the 1745 rebellion (with breaks for the Cromwellian rule) there were considerable changes in the organization of criminal justice after the Reformation. The principal developments were the expansion of statute law to include among other items pre-Reformation ecclesiastical crimes, the attempts by both James VI and Charles I to develop the role of the king's courts over against that of local feudal justice, the debatable and unresearched reception of Roman law, the growth of the legal profession, and the reform of the high court in 1672.

It would be misleading to suggest that any of this had the effect of improving legal procedures according to some concept of justice, although such concepts did concern lawyers of the period. From the point of view of the accused party justice remained rough, and outcomes could depend, whether at feudal or at central level, on relative power positions. So far as the central courts were concerned it was the opinion of Hugo Arnot that in the seventeenth century the Court of Justiciary was very submissive to government: 'its decrees were engines of oppression, the court used often to remit the jury, ordering them to amend their verdict'. If that did not work, 'the Privy Council, a most tyrannical court, used to interfere with the sentence of Justiciary'.[46] The relationship between these courts affected sentencing policy in all those crimes which were centrally controlled.

Yet social control did not end with the formal civil legal provisions. Ecclesiastical law after the Reformation was far more drastically changed than civil law. As in England several ecclesiastical offences were incorporated into statute law, but the greatest change was in organization. Although it took some time for pre-Reformation organizations to be phased out, they were gradually replaced by an entirely different structure.

The Kirk sessions, which by the mid-seventeenth century covered most of non-Highland Scotland and had penetrated Argyll and Inverness-shire, consisted of the minister and his elders. They met to arrange not only everything to do with public worship, but also to monitor all the disciplinary aspects of public life. They were the body through which the doctrine that even sinners and the ungodly should be forced to glorify God in their lives was enforced. More prosaically this was identified with suppressing scandalous sexual liaisons, drunkenness, brawling, sabbath-breaking, and backbiting, and with the transference of more serious offences to presbyteries or the secular courts. The penalties open to Kirk sessions were not clearly defined. They could not excommunicate, but in practice they could impose various 'degradation rituals',[47] ranging from mere appearance before the session to wearing sackcloth in front of the congregation, and they could fine. On the basis of these fines they supported the poor of the parish,[48] and since fornication was always a major item of business it would be fair to say that the equilibrium of the godly parish was maintained by the lascivious regularly providing for the needy.

The Kirk session, it was suggested, was a new intermediary organ of control in the social structure. Although the session took over the functions of the old Commissary Courts it was new in the level of its activity. It was intermediary by virtue of the social status of its members, and it monitored peasant life far more closely and in more detail than the baron and burgh courts which still operated and whose interests often overlapped with the Kirk session. What is more, the laird or noble did not have to control their tenants directly any longer; the Kirk session, as suggested, acted as a police force on their behalf. The minister was appointed and his stipend paid directly by the heritors—the landlords who owned land in the parish; and much of the stipend was paid in kind and often in arrears. The ministers came themselves from the landed or grand tenant class, but by the end of the seventeenth century, and probably earlier, they were almost a self-perpetuating class of their own. The elders were the most substantial tenants in the parish. W. R. Foster describes the elders of Stow as being one quarter village craftsmen and millers and the rest tenant farmers and small proprietors; the elders of Craigmillar were tenants of the laird of Craigmillar.[49] The flock were the permanent peasantry of the parish. The session therefore, as the new intermediary force between them and their landlords, provided a strong reinforcement of the feudal system. They were a new feudal weapon of social control in that they reinforced local justice. Landlords might attend Kirk services; but they were, despite the ideology of democracy under God which caused such annoyance to James VI, more or less immune from its discipline except during the periods of covenanting dominance. In 1649, for example, heritors were being summoned for adultery, but this was distinctly unusual.

The contrast with England is quite strong. Manning cites Sir Thomas Aston who argued in 1641 against the thesis that Presbyterianism could provide a means of strengthening the power of the nobility over the people and made a comparison with Scotland. There, Aston said, 'the peasants are more dependent on their lords than in England so the lords are able to dominate the Presbyterian system and through it keep control of the church and the monarchy.'[50] The implication was that in England the people were more powerful and would be able to use the Presbyterian system as a democratizing force. But in Scotland it strengthened the ascendant lairds.

Apart from the landowners, the other group which were outside the discipline of the session were the landless labourer and vagabond class. For in addition to controlling behaviour the session also controlled mobility. Not only was it essential for tenant farmers to accept behavioural control, it was an offence for them to take strangers under their roof without permission, and they could not themselves move their domicile and settle elsewhere without a certificate of good conduct from the session to take with them to their new parish. Any unfortunate episodes would be recorded on this certificate, and Janet Anderson in 1650, for example, had to take with her to her new parish the information that she had been suspected of witchcraft nine years previously.[51] This tight control over the mobility of peasants, which was established at this time, may well have been a response to a rising population; it may also have had some influence in holding back industrial growth, and in the high rate of emigration and steady supply of mercenary soldiers to the battlefields of Europe. If those without certificates of godliness were not allowed to settle within Scotland they were perhaps driven outside.

We have then in seventeenth-century Scotland a society which was economically and socially relatively static. There was a considerable degree of stratification with consciousness of rank at all social levels, and it is reasonable to impose on this self-perceived hierarchy a fairly sharp distinction between the ruling class and the rest of the populace. The ruling class proper consisted of the landed and the merchants, but it seems right to include those more marginal groups who ad-ministered on their behalf: ministers, lawyers, baillies, and factors. Makey has estimated that a minister would have an income ten times the size of his parishioners,[52] and so it seems likely that there was an economic as well as a social and educational gulf between them.

There was an absence of the peasant unrest seen in parts of France and Germany and of the urban disturbances of the 'masterless men' seen in England. Yet of course there was change and turbulence. The Reforma-tion of 1560 had replaced an elite which was tied to France with one which fought among itself for dominance and spoils in the building up of an independent nation state. The absence of the court in the next century intensified the faction conflict, and the increase of centraliza-tion, bureaucracy, and feuferme landholding without the right to hold courts, made central rather than local power more attractive. These changes together with the new Reformation ideology can be said to have constituted a social revolution in that the lives of the populace were greatly affected by them. It is in this area that the rise of witch-hunting must be sought.

The content of the new ideology will be discussed in the chapters on the belief system, but it should be noted here that the pre-Reformation church had left little mark on the beliefs and practices of the peasantry, and that for many the preaching of the Reformed clergy was their first contact with Christianity. After the Reformation many former priests who were regarded as too uneducated to be allowed to preach, were given the title of reader and made to lead their congregation from a prayer book until a qualified minister became available. But not only was it the first serious encounter with official religion; this was also very thoroughly and systematically taught. In both these aspects Scotland was unlike England. There were no absentee clergy. As the Kirk session system extended itself there were resident educated ministers, preaching every Sunday to a captive parish, there was a literacy drive which appears to have been moderately successful; and the ministers were in constant touch with each other; comparing their successes and failures, preaching at each others' fasts and special occasions, constantly reinforcing each other in their presbytery meetings. It was a very powerful, systematic and effective piece of indoctrination for which parallels can be found in twentieth-century societies which have experienced left-wing revolutions. It was also similar in kind to the religious and moral revivals to be found in other parts of Europe at the same time and with which some witchcraft outbreaks appear to be associated.

It has been observed by Morris that moral and ideological revolutions are a necessary accompaniment of new states and new rulers.[53] The new ideology legitimizes the new regime, and the moral cleansing demonstrates its effectiveness. The pursuit of the witch as a totally evil person, a totally committed enemy to the values of the new society however identified, is, of course, a highly economical way of effecting the moral cleansing of a society.

For post-Reformation Scotland the identification and abolition of witchcraft was only a part of the new pattern of moral endeavour, in which it was the acknowledged duty of the secular arm to ensure that the 'crown rights of the Redeemer' were demonstrated in the every-day behaviour of his subjects, yet the drive against witchcraft was in fact a most central crusade. It was not for nothing that witchcraft came to be set beside treason as the two crimes which could not be alienated to regalities. They represented enmity in its purest form to the two swords of God: the secular and the ecclesiastical.

While it is clear that it was possible to prosecute a witch under the old machinery and that from time to time such prosecutions did occur, it is also clear that the witch-prosecutions of the seventeenth century were conducted throughout under those parts of the machinery of social control which were entirely new: the statute of 1563 which made it a civil offence punishable by death, the Order in Council of 1597 which centralized its administration and extended the use of the Privy Council commission, and the Kirk session where many of the proceedings began and much of the evidence was collected. It was a process which took responsibility from the accusing individual and gave it to the highest powers in the land: the Lords of Privy Council and the Lord Advocate. It was supported by a newly received legal doctrine for which the authority was Canon Law. It was these elements in a socially and economically conservative revolution which nurtured the attack on deviance of which witchcraft was the supreme example.

CHAPTER FIVE

THE PATTERN OF WITCH-HUNTING
I NUMBERS AND ORIGINS

The main outline of witch-hunting in Scotland is fairly clear. Although witchcraft was a statutory criminal offence punishable by death from 1563 until 1735 the bulk of the prosecutions were concentrated in the seventy-two years from 1590 until 1662. The Scottish witch-hunt was part of the second wave of European prosecutions which began in the mid-sixteenth century. As on the continent of Europe, however, there was not one continuous witch-hunt. There were considerable fluctuations in the annual rate of prosecutions. There were lulls in which there were almost no cases, there were periods in which there was a regular small supply, and there were five peaks of intensive prosecution: in 1590–91, when James VI conducted an investigation into treasonable sorcery; in 1597 coinciding with the publication of his *Daemonologie*; in 1629–30 coinciding with the peak of the continental witch panic; in 1649 at the peak of Covenanting influence on political life; and from 1661–62 at the Restoration. The outbreaks of the 1590s seem to have been peaks in a period of continuous witch-hunting; that of 1629–30 was the culmination of a gradual build-up of judicial activity during the twenties; those of 1649 and 1661–62 were contained within a period (1640–1662) of fairly continuous witch-hunting with occasional lulls. From 1662 onwards prosecutions declined steadily, apart from an outbreak in East Lothian from 1678–79 and the late Renfrewshire trials of 1692. The eighteenth century saw only a few isolated prosecutions.[1]

The political events with which the witch-hunting peaks have been briefly associated here are intended as pegs rather than explanations in themselves, but the purpose of this and the following chapter is primarily to discuss the chronology of witch-hunting in relation to the most obvious immediate causal factor: the rise and fall of the level of official interest in the apprehension and conviction of this particular type of criminal. Exploration of the sources and spasmodic nature of this kind of social control, explanations for both the stable and changing elements in the geographical distribution of the hunt and consideration of the role of the peasantry, depend on the prior analysis of this most visible factor.

In the first place it is necessary, taking into account all the difficulties which make a witch-hunt a nightmare for those of a statistical

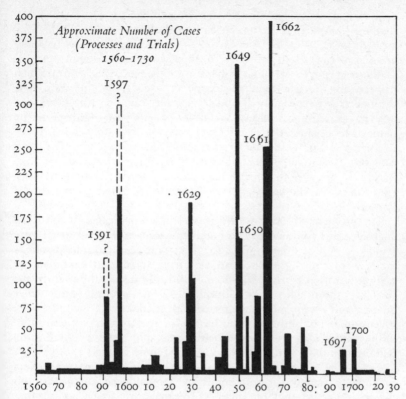

inclination, to make some estimate of the numbers which were involved in order to be able to make useful comparisons with the witch-hunts of other parts of Europe. Midelfort has suggested that in south-western Germany a large hunt was one which involved more than twenty suspects;[2] Monter, that the 'small panic' involving six or seven suspects was most typical of Switzerland.[3]

The Scottish hunts fall naturally into four categories. There were first the national hunts. These are the ones already mentioned as peaks of witch-hunting in which cases came from all over the non-Gaelic-speaking areas and even occasionally from the Gaelic areas of Invernesshire and Ross-shire. Other years, especially in the 1640s, and 1658 and 1659, could almost be counted national hunts, but were nearer to the localized large hunts which were of the second type and more like those described by Midelfort. Examples of these were the Inverkeithing hunt in 1623 when twenty-one women and one man were accused, and the hunt in Paiston in East Lothian in 1678 when seventeen women and two men were accused. Most of the local large hunts, however, were incorporated in the national hunts. The third type of hunt was similar to Monter's 'small panics'. The large Inver-keithing hunt of 1623 was preceded by a small one in 1621 in which six women were accused. One of these was a relative of one of those accused in 1623. This category of 'small panic' should really include all those, even if the group is as small as mother and daughter, in which suspects are thought to have conspired to commit witchcraft. The distinction between a small and large panic cannot really be drawn with any precision because we can never be certain that we have all the names and because the distinction is in any case only a matter of degree. The line could be drawn somewhere about ten. The final category is the isolated witch deemed to have acted alone and pursued locally for her malefice rather than officially for her ideological non-conformity. All the last three types were incorporated in the national hunts.

The problem of exact numbers which was indicated in the third chapter is not confined to the numbers executed. Behind that figure would be needed other figures for those who had committed suicide while in prison, those who had died from torture, ill treatment, or neglect in prison (if they could be confidently distinguished from the suicides), those who had committed suicide or fled before their arrest, those who had been acquitted at their trial, those who had been given minor punishments, banishment, or merely admonished, those whose cases had been dropped before trial, and those whose ill fame had brought them before the Kirk session but no further.

Even if we do confine ourselves to the limited problem of numbers of those executed for witchcraft in Scotland we are already in difficulties. We know from other sources than the criminal records that large numbers were tried for treasonable witchcraft during the winter of 1590–91. We have about seventy names and we do not know the fate of all of them.[4] Similarly we know from a variety of sources that the continuing witch-hunt after this crisis rose to another peak in the year 1597,[5] but since this was a decentralized witch-hunt we have very few records of individual cases. Local barons and sheriffs were entitled to make their own arrangements, and the details of executions are mostly lost for ever or scattered through such private family papers as survive from this period. How many then were executed? The other national hunts were those in 1629–30, 1649, and 1661–62. We have more reliable figures for these, and if the 1597 hunt was of the same order (which it may or may not have been) then it may have accounted for between 200 and 300 witches.

From 1597 onwards the problems are of a different order. From then it was illegal to try and execute a witch without an individual com-mission from the Privy Council or Parliament or a trial at the Court of Justiciary. A trial at the Court of Justiciary involved a journey to Edinburgh unless one of the Circuit Courts was travelling near by. A commission was normally granted to a local court of named individuals, usually landowners and their most substantial tenants and legal officers. This became the commonest method of processing an accused witch. It might be thought from this that a search of these central sources might yield a complete and reliable list of all executions but this is not the case. Our search produced 2,208 named and anonymous references to cases, of which only 599 are to named individuals whose execution is recorded.[6]

Starting from this basic figure a further list of 861 references from secondary sources include another 300 references to executions. Many of these are anonymous: they refer to 'many witches' or 'certain witches', and some of them clearly match with named cases, though not always. Named cases in this category which cannot be matched with cases in the criminal records add another 43. To get a reasonable figure, a major addition must be made from the Privy Council cases. Neither the level of bureaucratic development nor local funds for sending messengers to Edinburgh encouraged the reporting back of results of trials, and therefore a high proportion of commissioned cases have properly to be recorded as of unknown outcome. Nevertheless the probability is that although the acquittal rate in the Court of Justiciary was over fifty per cent, for Privy Council Commissions it was very low. Local authorities greatly preferred to get a local commission if they could; it was cheaper and the result was in their own hands. Most commissions were 'for trying and burning' which does not suggest a high level of acquittal. The basic figure included 128 Privy Council executions out of a total of 191 known outcomes. If the same percentage were extended to the 866 unknown outcomes and to the 267 unknown outcomes of the Parliamentary and Committee of Estates Commissions that would give us another 780 executions. Together with 200 cases allowed for the period up to 1597, and perhaps another 100 for dubiously legal cases in regalities and other local courts, we have a total of 1,337 executions with a possible margin of error of about 300 either way, though the figure seems more likely to be an overestimate. Black's guess, which was based on the assumption that acquittals were a rarity, was 4,400. The most modest estimate so far has been Legge who estimated 3,400 executions.[7] About one third of this figure, something over a thousand, would seem most likely.

Other figures, for minor penalties, banishments, acquittals, suicides, deaths in prison, abscondments, and Kirk session reprimands, would be, in varying degrees, even less reliable and beneath such figures would lurk, in positivist terminology, the 'dark figure' of informally identified witches against whom no formal complaint had ever been raised.

The problem of a 'dark figure' for witchcraft has some bearing on conventional criminology where it is a commonly used cover for unsatisfactory data. In so far as a 'dark figure' refers to a certain number of prosecutions or convictions for which the record has been or may have been lost this is an acceptable convention. In so far as it refers to the number of times that the crime or crimes in question have been committed this is quite another matter. It gives an objective status to certain actions as crimes which they do not actually have. Individual actions can only be defined as crimes by courts of law.

Until recently the historical study of crime was kept distinct from the study of witchcraft and its subject was assumed to have a reality which witchcraft did not have. Thus while positivist students of witchcraft were perfectly clear that the accused were innocent, that there was no 'dark figure' of malefice or of the number of pacts made with the Devil, and that the prosecution rate reflected judicial anxiety, not human behaviour, they were unable to apply this insight to other forms of judicial practice. It is only recently that it has been applied with any force by Ditton, who argues that 'crime waves' should be called 'control waves' as they reflect police activity; not criminal behaviour.[8] It could be argued that murder, for example, has an objective reality compared with witchcraft, and that the number of convicted murderers cannot exceed the number of slain corpses, but on the one hand a killing can only be identified as a murder in a court of law, and on the other nearly every convicted witch was associated with a trail of corpses: stillborn babies, mad cows, and apoplectic men.

Another related problem born of the separate treatment of witch-craft and other forms of crime is that while commentators on witch-craft were generally clear that a witch-hunt was related to ruling class behaviour and therefore had to be explained in terms of ruling class pathology, commentators on crime waves tended to explain them in terms of a pathology of the underworld. Ditton's understanding of crime as reflecting ruling class activity has been balanced by an opposite movement among witchcraft scholars, inspired by the con-servative, functionalist school of anthropologists, towards a view of witch-hunting as a spontaneous reaction of the peasantry to social and economic forces. A greater integration of criminal and witchcraft studies should serve to bring these issues into sharper focus.

If however we abandon the quest for a dark figure of peasant behaviour, and concentrate on the most visible aspects of judicial activity, the figures are sufficiently reliable to locate the times and places of greatest activity and to make reasonable comparisons with England and the continent. Witch-hunting was the most public form of social control ever devised because the identification of the witch was dependent on the public status (ill fame) of the accused, and con-viction was normally dependent on the reinforcement of her con-fession by witnesses to her malefices. Large scale witch-hunts were highly visible and remarked on by contemporaries, and although new caches of documents may reveal new cases or even new large local hunts it seems unlikely that national hunts previously unknown will emerge. While the figure for those executed in Scotland is considerably smaller than any previous estimates (which have ranged from 3,400 to 30,000), there are factors which justify old long-term reputations for very intensive witch-hunting. One obvious comparison, and the one which helped generate Scotland's reputation, is with England where the most extensive hunt ended in 17 hanged and where it is unlikely that more than 500 were executed over the same period in a very much larger population.[9] The main Scottish hunts, some of them confined to small areas, must have been similar in their impact to major hunts on the continent in Europe. Two hundred and fifty commissions 'for tryal and burning' were issued to the small county of East Lothian in one year, 1649, and most of these probably resulted in burning.[10] If one compares this with the recently compiled figures for parts of the continent in the local studies discussed in Chapter Two it is clear that the Scottish experience in certain areas was more repetitively traumatic than that of all but the most afflicted German towns and villages.

Although the beginning of witch-hunting in 1590 is unambiguous and the discontinuity with the previous era clear cut, witch prosecutions were not completely unknown before this date. The earliest suggested prosecution for witchcraft in Scotland was in 1479, when trouble arose between the King, James III, and his brother, leader of a large faction, the Earl of Mar. The Earl died in mysterious circumstances, and his death was followed by the execution of several witches and warlocks for conspiracy to cause the King's death by witchcraft.[11] No details are known about this case, for which there is no contemporary evidence and it may be mythical. It is interesting that both Cohn and Kieckhefer found that this type of politically motivated witch-hunt was most common in the earliest period of witch prosecuting on the continent.

Apart from this case very few have reached the records in the period prior to 1563; indeed only three named witches are known up to this date. We know from the instructions for regulating proceedings at the Justice Ayre of Jedburgh in 1510, however, that witchcraft and sorcery were among matters to be considered,[12] and from a St Andrews source in 1542 that the ecclesiastical machinery for trying witches and handing them over to the secular arm for burning existed, and was occasionally used. This included a commission 'for the accusing and summoning of witches and soothsayers and the proceeding against them to their condemnation and the handing over of them to the power of the secular judiciary'. There was clearly to be no question of their acquittal, and indeed we have confirmation from a second separate source that three unnamed women were burnt at the stake for witchcraft on October 10th 1542 in St Andrews. It is by no means obvious from the writ whether this trial was an unusual one or not. On the one hand the phraseology of the commission is common form, and the subject matter consists mainly of arrangements for the trial and pious references to the heinousness of the crimes: on the other there is the fact that not only were four leading churchmen appointed to try them, but they were to summon as assessors all the doctors, licentiates, and bachelors of theology they could get hold of. Furthermore these witches were transported from Edinburgh and Dunfermline (at a cost of thirty three shillings and fourpence) in order to face this tribunal.[13]

The legal basis for this pre-Reformation trial was Canon Law, but the responsibility for prosecution was clarified by the passing of the Witchcraft Act in 1563 in that for the first time witchcraft became a criminal offence in statute law. This secularization of the control of witchcraft seems to have been a factor in promoting prosecutions in Russia, Denmark, Imperial Europe, England and other areas,[14] and while it did not precipitate a witch-hunt in Scotland it certainly eased matters for the authorities nearly thirty years later. The Witchcraft Act became an essential point of reference in the following century.

The timing of the Witchcraft Act suggests a simple connection between the introduction of Calvinism, the passing of the Act, and subsequent prosecutions; but it was not made law because a literal interpretation of the Bible demanded the operation of Exodus, 12.11: 'Thou shalt not suffer a witch to live'. Nor was it made law because John Knox had learned to hunt witches in Calvin's Geneva for Calvin's interest in the subject seems to have been limited.[15] It seems rather that in the period following the initial successes of the Reformation movement, that is to say from 1560 to 1563, there was a power vacuum in the area of social control previously covered by ecclesiastical courts. The General Assembly of the new Church, therefore, sent a request to the Privy Council that they either allow the Assembly to take over these former ecclesiastical jurisdictions with the addition of such new offences as mass-mongering, or that the Privy Council take them over itself.[16] The list of suggested offences did not in fact include witchcraft, but when Parliament incorporated these offences into the criminal law, the drafter included a witchcraft act between those against adultery and bestiality.[17] It does not therefore seem to have been the Calvinist clergy who were initiators of the witchcraft legislation. Their application to the Privy Council was concerned with social control generally, and was the beginning of a long struggle for dominance between ecclesiastical and secular authorities.

The statute itself was as sceptical in its wording as the Witchcraft Act of 1735 which repealed it. It spoke of 'the heavy and abominable superstition used by divers of the lieges of this Realm by using of Witchcraft . . . and credence given thereto in time bygone . . . and for avoiding and away putting of all such vain superstition in times to come'; and states that 'no persons shall take upon hand in any times hereafter to use any manner of Witchcraft Sorcery or Necromancy nor give themselves forth to have any such craft or knowledge thereof,

there through abusing the people'.[18] What is more, given that it was
superstition in general, not merely the exploitation of superstition,
which was being legislated against, there was a certain logic about
consulters being as severely treated in the Act as practitioners. Death
was to be the penalty for all such activities.

The passing of the Act did not result in a great increase in witch
prosecutions, but once the Act was on the statute book the General
Assembly treated witchcraft as one of the contentious issues between
them and the secular authorities. John Knox initially applauded the
passing of these assorted 'morality' statutes as a sign that they were
moving towards a truly godly state,[19] but he did not remain satisfied.
Two years after the Act was passed witchcraft was included in a list of
'horrible crimes' to be suppressed, which was presented to the Queen
by the General Assembly, and from then on accusations of moral
slackness by the body of clergy to the civil powers were commonplace.
On the whole, however, the accounts of the proceedings of the General
Assembly throughout this early period suggest that their dominating
anxieties were about political power, finance, and the suppression of
ideologically unsound practices, principally the Roman mass. General
morality at this time came a bad fourth, and in this field witchcraft
ranked very much lower than sexual offences.[20]

Nevertheless even though the passing of the 1563 Witchcraft Act
was neither the result of nor the cause of an immediate witch fever, it
was a pre-condition of the witch-hunts of the 1590s and the seventeenth
century. It brought witchcraft formally into the criminal law at a time
when the law and legal practice were about to develop rapidly, and
despite its brevity and its sceptical wording the witch-hunters of the
1590s and the lawyers of the seventeenth century found it more than
adequate to their purposes. Indeed in 1649 the Act was ratified and
confirmed as it stood.

In the intervening years between the early post-Reformation legal
reconstruction and the trials of 1590–91 witch prosecutions appear to
have been building up, but the evidence is scanty. There was a slow
increase but it is not certain that this does not reflect an increase in the
number of records surviving. What is more, the cases that we do have
are all of a traditional type. There were murder cases: 'slaughteris
committit be witchcraft', and lesser types of malefice: there was the
straight invocation of spirits, and the healing arts. A high proportion
of individuals involved were of some social standing; this again may
reflect the survival of the type of records. But apart from one or two
isolated cases in which demonic or fairy figures appear it is hard to say
that there was much development in beliefs about witchcraft.

More significant was the developing relationship between church and
state, and the way in which moral issues continued to stand between
them. In 1567 Parliament was required to consider 'how witchcraft sal
be puneist and inquisition takin thereof'.[21] There is no record as to

whether any action was taken about this, but in February 1573 the Privy Council were also interesting themselves in witchcraft, and were for the first time deciding to treat it as a special case: the *crimen exceptum* principle already familiar on the continent.[22] Witchcraft was to be exempted from the benefit of pacification,[23] an amnesty for various offences; and in December of the same year witchcraft was exempted from remissions,[24] the process whereby escheated moveable goods were returned. The General Assembly, however, was not satisfied with the state of affairs, and in 1575 it set out articles to be presented to the Regent which included the claim 'That the Kirk hath power to cognosce and decerne upon heresies, blasphemie, witchcraft, and violation of the Sabbath day without prejudice always of the civill punishment'.[25] This appears to have been a further attempt to reserve to themselves powers of definition in the area of crimes related to religion. Civil punishments, however, did not apparently follow hard enough upon the Church's definitions, for ten years later, in 1583, among articles of the General Assembly to be presented to the king, there was the complaint, 'That there is no punishment for incest, adulterie, witchcraft, murthers, abominable and horrible oaths, in such sort that daylie sinne increaseth, and provoketh the wrath of God against the whole countrie'.[26] There was still no indication at this stage that witchcraft was regarded by the ruling classes as a particularly serious menace among other crimes and misdemeanours, and there was remarkably little to prepare people, church, or civil authorities for the revelations of the North Berwick witches, whose trials began in the November of 1590.

CHAPTER SIX

THE PATTERN OF WITCH-HUNTING
II CHRONOLOGY

The North Berwick witch-trials and the role of King James VI have
already been discussed in the recent secondary literature in some
detail.[1] The trials are significant in three respects. In the first place as
well as being the first mass trial since witchcraft was incorporated into
the criminal law they were also the last of the old type of political
witch-trial, known in England and other parts of Europe as well as in
Scotland, in which the accusation of witchcraft was a prop to the main
political purpose. Secondly, the continental witch theory which had
previously been unknown in Scotland was introduced, and thirdly, the
trials stimulated what may have been the most extensive general
witch-hunt of the whole period of witchcraft prosecution there, that
from 1591 until 1597. In the immediate aftermath the number of trials
may have diminished, but they increased again and reached a peak in
1597 when the action of the King brought them to an abrupt end.
Although the specific purpose of the treason trials (to incriminate the
Earl of Bothwell and establish that James was the Devil's prime
enemy) had passed, the role of the government in the control of
witchcraft remained important. For the King reminding the populace
of the dangers of witchcraft, and taking responsibility for rooting it
out, served to justify the recent episode and demonstrate his concern
for the safety of the realm.

Certainly James continued his personal efforts to root out witchcraft. The following winter he instructed his ambassador to urge
Elizabeth to hand over witches who had escaped into England, and
implied that she as monarch was equally threatened:

> Ye shall signifye to our darrest sister that efter deip consideratioun
> and serche made we have found out the ground and roote of these
> so cruell enterpryses to come from the bloodye counsellis of the
> enemyis to God, his trew Religion and to all Monarchies
> professing the same.[2]

Three years later, in 1595, the English ambassador Robert Bowes
received a letter mentioning that three witches who were said to have
dealt with Bothwell had been banished from Caithness which suggests
that the Bothwell issue was being kept alive,[3] and in July of 1597

Bowes wrote to Lord Burghley about 'the King's proceedings at
St. Andrews against the preachers and witches. Many witches
executed; their service to the devil'.[4] In another letter of 15th August he
reported that 'the King much pestered with witches, who swarm in
thousands' and refers to 'their confession of practices against the life of
the King and the young Prince'.[5] The political significance of witchcraft was thus sustained.

The most decisive instrument however, in the maintenance of
prosecutions, was not James' continued attempts to justify himself
which culminated six years later in his publication of *Daemonologie*, but
the Privy Council's general commission for examining witches passed
in October 1591. This commission handed out power to six individuals: two lawyers, two ministers, and two Edinburgh burgesses
including the Provost, to examine all cases of witchcraft pending, and,
more significantly, 'that heireftir salbe accused and dilaitit' and, after
reporting to the King and Council, to send them for trial at a local
assize. Most important of all the commission specifically encouraged
the use of torture: 'the personis wilfull or refuseand to declair the
veritie to putt to tortour, or sic uthir punishment to use can caus be
usit, as may move thame to utter the treuth'.[6]

This document was the licence for an indiscriminate witch-hunt.
What is more because of the nature of the licence: to send witches for
local trial, and because there are no records of the proceedings of this
commission, the full extent of the hunt can never be known. It is
difficult to suggest totally convincing explanations for the initiation of
any of the major outbreaks, but for the 1597 one there is particularly
little detailed evidence. It appears to have been well advanced by the
time James' *Daemonologie* was published, but its publication may have
helped to accelerate it. A major factor, or at least one which helped to
bring things to a crisis acknowledged to be such by the authorities in
the late summer of 1597, was the activities of a woman known as 'the
great witch of Balweary'. Margaret Atkin was accused of witchcraft
and asked to name her accomplices. When this list of accomplices was
well received she declared that she had a special ability to detect
witches, 'that they had a secret mark all of that sort, in their eyes,
whereby she could surely tell, how soon she looked upon any, whether
they were witches or not'.[7]

According to Archbishop Spottiswode she was so readily believed
that

> . . . she was carried from town to town to make discoveries in that
> kind. Many were brought in question by her dilations, especially
> at Glasgow where divers innocent women, through the credulity
> of the minister, Mr. John Cowper, were condemned and put to
> death. In the end she was found to be a mere deceiver (for the
> same persons that the one day she had declared guilty, the next

day being presented in another habit she cleansed) and sent back to Fife where first she was apprehended. At her trial she affirmed all to be false that she had confessed, either of herself or others, and persisted in this to her death.[8]

Spottiswode believed that it was this case which inspired the King to recall the standing commissions against witches;[9] and certainly the proclamation of August 1597 referred to the extensive complaints, and the number of innocent persons being accused.

During this year there seems to have been some tension between secular and ecclesiastical authorities over the prosecution of witches. In March the General Assembly complained that the civil magistrates were setting at liberty people who had been formally convicted of witchcraft, and demanded that presbyteries should severely censor any local magistrates who did this.[10] On the civil side the King had been noted as proceeding against preachers as well as witches in July; further the credulity of the Glasgow minister was particularly observed in the case of Margaret Atkin.[11] The Order of Council of August 12th specifically restored to the King powers which he had delegated in 1591, with a view to reducing the number of 'innocent' persons who were accused and convicted. The Order in Council gives a long list of the kind of people to whom standing commissions had been granted: 'sindrie noblemen, baronis, schireffis, stewartis, baillies, provestis and baillies of burrowis and townis and uthiris particulair personis', and pointed out that these commissions had been abused by individuals who had grudges against other individuals. The Order reiterated the heinousness of the crime of witchcraft and the intention of the King to stamp it out. It also reiterated the equal wickedness of consulters with witches, and stipulated that those who had been given commissions for the trial of witchcraft should also hand in the names of consulters to the Privy Council or forfeit their goods. The main purpose of the Order, however, was to ensure that all those wanting to try witches locally should seek for commissions anew, and that these should be granted to groups of three or four at a minimum in order to prevent individuals settling old scores. Anyone proceeding against witches by virtue of the old commissions 'to the execution of personis to the deid or melling (meddling) with thair guidis or geir (property), that the samin salbe repute slauchteris upoun foirthocht fellounie and spuilyie (removal of moveables illegally) respective . . .'[12] They would, in other words, become criminals themselves.

The immediate effect of the Order was that the supply of witch suspects dried up and cases were reduced to isolated incidents. The long term effect was that witchcraft became a centrally managed crime and was formally put on the same level as treason. These were the only crimes which were not allowed to be dealt with in regalities (regions to which the legal powers of the crown had been delegated). It is because of this official centralization that the role of the state in the prosecution of witchcraft continued to be of significance after James himself had departed for England.

In the aftermath of the 1597 outbreak, however, witchcraft was mainly important as an issue between the ecclesiastical and secular authorities. This was a struggle which was to continue throughout the next century, and was not entirely symbolized by attitudes to witchcraft alone. When the General Assembly wished to berate the Privy Council they accused them of slackness in dealing with moral issues. When the secular authorities wanted to demonstrate their claims to be a godly state they encouraged prosecutions of those crimes which most interested the church. In 1597, however, there was a clear feeling, reflected in the Order in Council, that matters had been allowed to get out of control and that the clergy were partly to blame. The Presbytery of Glasgow during the November of 1597 were suggesting that 'divers persons wha traduces and slanders the ministry of the city, as the authors of putting to death the persons lately execute for witchcraft' should be 'put in the branks (scold's bridle) at the judge's will'.[13] Again this emphasized the relationship between the two polities of a godly state. But in the following year the General Assembly had lower expectations of the secular arm: 'magistrats quho set Witches frie, being convict of witchcraft, to be severlie proceided against with the highest censures of the Kirk'.[14]

The efforts of the church to keep the operation against witches going seem to have been ineffective. In 1603 the Presbytery of Aberdeen ordered that all ministers should take oaths from all their parishioners 'quhat they knew of wiches and consulteris with thame',[15] but this does not seem to have produced much response. From 1597 until about 1621 when the numbers began to build up again, cases of witchcraft were scarce. There were a few each year, some of them of considerable interest in demonstrating the variety of ways in which witchcraft cases were handled, but nothing that could be described as a witch-hunt. As in the rest of Europe (apart from the Basque country and cases reaching the Parlement of Paris) there was a lull during the early part of the seventeenth century which was broken in the 1620s when prosecutions began to build up again. In August 1628, immediately following two small panics (six cases in Dumfries and nine cases in Prestonpans) and a number of single cases,[16] the Privy Council took a positive interest in the crime again by ordering that 'witches, sorcerers, necromancers and seekers of answers or helps at Thame' be proceeded against by justices and commissioners 'within thair severall circuits'.[17] This was not simply an attack on witchcraft but was incorporated in a general call to tighten up control on law and order: the injunction covered a page of other crimes that they wanted to be dealt with. It is not yet known to what extent figures for prosecutions for other crimes went up following this injunction, but figures for witchcraft showed a dramatic increase.

That is to say, instead of the dozen or so cases annually during the early 1620s about 350 suspects were tried between the last months of 1628 and 1630.[18]

For no very clear reason the numbers fell sharply again in 1631 to about the level before the 1628 Privy Council general attack on crime. Throughout the 1630s the numbers fell again to a small handful a year. The next main outbreak was in 1643 coinciding with the Solemn League and Covenant and the setting up of the Committee of Estates. For the next twenty years witchcraft was never to be very far from the consciousness of the populace although witch-hunting in general, and prosecutions in particular, rose to peaks in the years 1649 and 1661 to 1662. There were slight lulls from 1645 to 1648 and again from 1652 to 1657.

The period as a whole coincides with another time of tension between church and state over the boundaries of their areas of interest, and over the extent to which the church was entitled to define how the godly state should operate its mechanisms of social control. This expressed itself as it had done in the sixteenth century through a series of interchanges on a range of moral and criminal issues.

In 1640 the General Assembly advised ministers to be on the watch for witches, and in 1641 they presented a request to Parliament that 'the acts against charmeres, soizcereres, etc. be renewed and put in execution'.[19] Clearly they considered that not enough was being done. Parliament at this point was quite unresponsive and made a point of ignoring the request. In 1642 the General Assembly tried again. They re-emphasized their warning about witchcraft, and demanded that magistrates should co-operate in finding witches because 'witchcraft, charming and such like proceeds many times from ignorance'.[20] The following year, 1643, the General Assembly redefined the ecclesiastical view of witchcraft as a heresy, and demanded the establishment of a new standing Commission from the Privy Council.[21] This was rejected. An attempt to increase the powers of Kirk sessions and presbyteries was thwarted at local level by the parishes wanting the concurrence of the civil magistrates, many of whom were also elders of the parish. An attempt to find a standard punishment for consulting with witches failed; so did an attempt to get charming (uttering spells) listed as an offence.[22]

Despite these continued snubs by the civil authorities on the question of witchcraft, 1643 was a peak year for individual commissions. It is difficult to establish the precise relationship between the large increase in the number of cases at this time and the efforts of the General Assembly to stimulate interest, but they undoubtedly coincided. Although Parliament rejected in 1644 the request for a Standing Commission, it did set up a Committee to report first to the next General Assembly and then to Parliament, and in the meantime 'the estates (of Parliament) oredeanes the Lords of Secruit Counsell to grant

Commissiones for trying and executing of witches According to these former customs'.[23]

There is no record of the work of this Committee but in 1646 the General Assembly requested Parliament to make an addition to the 1563 Act regarding charming.[24] Reaction seems to have been slow, but in 1649 Parliament issued what was in a sense another rebuff in that it reasserted the traditional methods of witchcraft control. It stated that prosecution was to depend on the 1563 Witchcraft Act as it stood, with the exception that consultors were no longer to be liable to the death penalty. The possibility of introducing severer methods of control such as a standing commission or joint committees was rejected.[25] 1649, however, was the year which may have seen the greatest number of executions in the whole history of Scottish witch-hunting. Privy Council and Parliament issued commissions for trials freely; and during the summer recess of Parliament the Committee of Estates issued over 350 separate commissions for trials, nearly all in the area of East Lothian and Berwickshire.[26]

The background to the fencing match being played between church and state on this issue was that of the Solemn League and Covenant and the ascendancy in the government of the Covenanting party. The government appear to have been demonstrating on the one hand by their careful consideration and rejection of their propositions their independence of the ecclesiastical powers. They showed on the other, by their readiness to pursue individual cases of witchcraft, their concern that wickedness should be put down and that the state should demonstrate the righteousness of God. Where the state was blatantly worldly the clergy could claim to speak for divine issues. In a 'covenanted state' the clergy, perversely, lost power in their own special province because secular officials claimed to be acting directly on behalf of the divinity.

Witchcraft was again, as it had been in the late sixteenth century, only one of a number of issues which the church was concerned with. The year 1649 was also one of the few periods in which landowners were put on trial for adultery. In more normal times the morals of the gentry were regarded as being outside the control of the Kirk session. The heritors (those owning land in the parish), after all, appointed the ministers and were therefore most unlikely to fall under Kirk censure. But 1649 was a year for moral crusade, for it was necessary to demonstrate that the state was a covenanted state. On June 19, for example, Parliament granted a commission 'to try and execute certain persons', and prefaced this with the statement that 'the Estaites of Parliament finds unanimouslie the sinne of witchcraft daylie increaseth in this land',[27] thus blurring the distinction between 'sin' and 'crime' which had coincided before the Reformation with ecclesiastical and secular responsibilities.

In 1650 Parliament did finally appoint a special committee to handle witchcraft cases with powers to try cases and order executions. They were also asked 'to think upon a constant way of procedure in the processing of witches in tyme coming',[28] which suggests a degree of concern about the random nature of the existing procedure. It does not appear, however, that this committee was ever very effective although it received papers from presbyteries for consideration. Cases, which were anyway much fewer in 1650, tended to come direct to Parliament, and in November Parliament dissolved the special committee without it having apparently put forward any proposals at all. Instead it ordered the Committee of Bills to 'take in consideration papers given in concerning witches'.[29]

The new machinery was hardly put in use, however, before Cromwell's rule in Scotland began. It has frequently been observed that during the interregnum Cromwell's administrators set the witches free and eradicated witch-hunting. English good sense prevailed over Scottish superstition. There is a good deal of evidence to support this, illustrating, in particular, the more sceptical stage which English public opinion had reached. The Cromwellian Commissioners for the Administration of Justice in Scotland, in 1652, had sixty men and women before them accused of witchcraft, 'but they found so much Malice and so little proof against them that none were condemned'.[30] Later in the year they dealt with cases which had been pending at the time the armies came into Scotland. They were horrified by the descriptions of torture, and it was stated that 'The judges are resolved to enquire into the business, and have appointed the sheriff, ministers, and tormentors to be found out, and to have an account of the ground of this cruelty'.[31] A further account describes 'another woman that was suspected, according to their thoughts, to be a witch, was twenty-eight days and nights with bread and water, being stript stark naked, and laid upon a cold stone, with only a hair cloth over her. Others had hair shirts dipp'd in vinegar put on them to fetch off the skin. It's probable there will be more discoveries shortly of this kind of Amboyne usage (a reference to the treatment handed out by the Dutch to English settlers on the island of Amboyna (Molucca) in 1623); but here is enough for reasonable men to lament on.'[32]

The suspension of the normal machinery for processing witches—the Privy Council and the local commissions which it set up—together with the scepticism of the English judges initially reduced the flow of cases to a trickle. In 1657 however, application for trials began to build up again, and though the Court of Justiciary and its Circuit Courts which were still under English military control over a hundred cases were processed in 1658 and 1659. The dismissal and acquittal rate was slightly higher than was normal for that court, but there were during these two years at least forty executions.[33] It is not clear whether the English judges had been there long enough to have 'gone native' and been affected by the prevailing beliefs or whether local pressures, almost entirely from Alloa, Ayr, Stenton, and Tranent, were strong enough to require some response from the authorities.

This series of trials came to an abrupt end with the end of the Protectorate on 6th May 1659. At this point the judicial machinery ground to a halt and its absence soon generated in the ruling class a high level of anxiety about law and order. For some the freedom given to witches was particularly disturbing. 'Because the laws ar now silent this sin [of witchcraft] becomes daylie more frequent', observed the Earl of Haddington early in 1661.[34] He was the first to approach the newly constituted Privy Council in April of that year in connection with the long suspected Elspet Tailzeor, Margaret Bartilman, Marean Quheitt, and Jonet Carfrae. The hunt spread, and between April 1661 and the autumn of 1662 there were over 600 cases and approximately 300 executions.[35] The hunt died down six months after the Privy Council first became anxious about the frequency and validity of torture. They ordered that

> no one should arrest persons suspected of witchcraft except such as had warrant from the council, the Lord Justice General, sheriffs and other persons in authority and that there should be no pricking, torture, or other illegal means imployed to extort confessions or guilt.[36]

This edict meant a considerable change in the rights of local authorities. Under previous edicts it was illegal to try any individual suspect without a commission from the Privy Council to named persons, but nothing was laid down about how the information, preferably including a confession, which was laid before the Privy Council was to be obtained in the first place. There was nothing particularly illegal about arresting and detaining suspects. Imprisonment was not a punishment; it was an administrative convenience. By restricting the ability of local officers to apprehend and torture they inhibited the pretrial stages of pursuing a suspect. The objection to torture had been made before during the Protectorate, but this time it was confirmed and made official by the permanent rulers. It had to be made again, but the formal rejection of torture was a move a long way from the positive recommendation to it made by James VI, and from the common form of earlier witch-hunts.

The Privy Council then denounced several witch prickers: John Kincaid, Paterson, John Ramsey and John Dickson, as frauds. Kincaid, who had also been practising in East Lothian during the 1649 hunt made a confession that he had used tricks in his tests for witchcraft. At the same time the supply of 'rank witches': those who had a long-standing reputation, began to dry up, and so did the supply of witnesses prepared to testify to their malefices. Counter-accusations of slander began to rise. By the end of 1662 the hunt was over, and there was never again any witch-hunting on a scale which was more than local. During the later 1660s there were several cases in ones and twos, a group of seven or eight in Dumfries in 1671 (two of which are given detailed analysis in Chapter Ten), and a few cases later in the 1670s. During this period imprisoned witches regularly made successful application to be freed in the absence of any charges being proffered against them. The case of Marie Somervail of Jedburgh is typical:

> The which day anent ane petitione presented to his majesties justices be Marie Somervail prisoner within the tolbuith of Jedburgh Make and mention that wher the petitioner being caleit befor them at Jedburgh for the crym of witchcraft aleadyit comitted be her, wherupon she was incarcerat and put in prison and lyen ever since in ane sterving conditione. Notwithstanding that there was no information given in against her nor persone compeiring to insist against her and that she was content to apear before them whenever she should be calet. The justices having considered the foresaid petitione grants the desyre thereof and ordains the petitioner to be put at libertie.[37]

In 1678 there was a large outbreak in Edinburgh and in East Lothian, and the Privy Council again had to issue a reinforcing decree that inferior judges

> might not use any torture by pricking, or by with-holding them from sleep, but reserved all that to themselves, and the justices, and those who acted by commissions from them.[38]

Mackenzie, by this time Lord Advocate, was at this point a key figure in stemming witch-hunting. The cases coming into the High Court of Justiciary from 1678 to 1680 show a steady series of acquittals, minor penalties, and admonitions, although executions still occurred. Mackenzie was instrumental in advising accused witches how to make successful appeals, as a number of them were presented to him. The steady stream of acquittals must have been a factor in reducing the number of cases brought to court. No officials were going to take trouble to process cases which were likely to be dismissed or ultimately unsuccessful. By the 1690s the number of cases coming up were so few that the local outbreak in Renfrewshire in 1697 when a laird's eleven-year-old accused a number of her father's servants and tenants and tenants' children of bewitching her caused widespread reverberations, comment, and disquiet, and made this case one of the best documented of all Scottish cases. Seven out of twenty accused were executed in 1697 but other cases arising out of it were still pending in 1699. In that year Mary Morrison complained that she had suffered from frequent adjournments of her case 'to the great loss of their poor family and hazard of her life being very tender and infirme', and that she had been

> nowayes tainted with any public guilt or malefice to her neigh-
> bours either in their goods or goodname untill the forsaid possest
> persones in their fitts of torment did alleadge that the devil
> represented her as one of their tormenters. All which they now
> after their recovery to health again doe utterly dissoun.[39]

Mary Morrison was released, but she was not the last to be in trouble. There was an outbreak in Ross-shire in the same year, and Lachland and George Rattray were executed in Inverness in 1706.[40] These seem to have been the last legal executions and are certainly the last to appear in surviving central records. They went through the by then usual defence procedure of complaining of their imprisonment and asking for the issue to be resolved one way or the other. They were in this case ill advised. A small number of other eighteenth-century cases are mentioned only in secondary sources. *The Old Statistical Account of Scotland*, for example, alleges that 'many witches' were executed in Spott in 1705. It can only be concluded either that the central sources are unreliable, or that with an unsympathetic central judiciary there was a last ditch resort to illegal local trials. This second hypothesis seems the more likely, and certainly the last execution of all, in which the con-fused and senile Janet Horne is said to have thought the fire they built at Dornoch in 1727 was lit in order to warm her, was of this nature.[41] Outright lynchings, as a reaction to judicial inaction, seem to have been almost unknown. The only one recorded is of Janet Cornfoot who was returned free from Edinburgh in 1705 to Pittenweem and stoned to death by her neighbours.[42] Lynching is, however, both vague as a concept and as an activity intrinsically unlikely to be recorded, except when the authorities are investigating abuses. If one included in a list of lynchings all those who died under torture during the main witch-hunting period the number would be substantial.

The repeal of the 1563 Witchcraft Act came eight years after the death of Janet Horne in Dornoch and was not the result of any initiative from Scotland. Three burghers from the south of England proposed the repeal of the English Witchcraft Acts and the Scottish Act was included through a House of Lords amendment. They were replaced by the Witchcraft Act 1735 which admitted only the crime of pretended witchcraft and which prescribed for a conviction a maxi-mum of a year's imprisonment and pillorying on quarter days. No-one appears ever to have been prosecuted under its provisions in Scotland. They were indeed inapplicable there since there were as yet no prisons other than pre-trial residences such as tolbooths, no pillories, and no quarter days. Between 1680 and 1735 the witch-belief disappeared almost without comment from the cognitive map of the ruling class, and retired to the secret, uncharted areas of peasant exchange. Only the occasional summons at Kirk sessions for superstitious practices gave evidence of its continued vitality.

CHAPTER SEVEN

THE PATTERN OF WITCH-HUNTING
III GEOGRAPHICAL DISTRIBUTION
AND LOCAL RESPONSIBILITY

While the level of governmental interest is an obvious factor in the overall numbers of cases at any one time, it has no such bearing on the geographical distribution of these cases. Despite the central organization of witch-hunting, certain areas provided far more suspects than others, and some small towns and villages consistently produced them throughout the period. The witch-hunt of 1590–91 started in East Lothian, Ross-shire and Aberdeenshire. The peak of 1597 spread over the eastern seaboard and as far west as Glasgow. The 1629–30 outbreak was widespread over Fife, the Lothians, Peebles and the Borders, Lanarkshire, and Stirling. There were also four cases at Caithness. The 1649 outbreak was almost entirely confined to Fife, the Lothians, and the Borders, with a few cases in Aberdeenshire, Kincardineshire, and Stirling. The 1661–62 hunt began and was maintained in these tradi-tional areas, but became more widespread. Auldearn, Perthshire, the Crook of Devon, the Ayrshire seaboard, Inverness-shire, Bute, Glas-gow, Lanarkshire and Renfrewshire all supplied cases. The sporadic cases after 1662 tended to come from the areas that had traditionally supplied them.

Some areas saw very little witch-hunting. In the Highlands, especi-ally those parts outside the Kirk sessions, system and within the domi-nion of the clans there was no witch-hunting, or none that reached the records. Gaelic-speaking areas in general provided very few cases although Tain in Ross-shire was an exception to this. There were cases from Tain as early as 1590 and as late as 1699. Towards the end of the 1661–62 hunt there were several cases in Strathglass in which the land-lord used accusations of witchcraft as a means of evicting some un-wanted tenants. On the whole, though, Gaelic patronymic names such as those of Mary Nein Goune Baike of Strathglass and Marion Nein Gollimichaell of Tain are rare in lists of suspects.[1] Possibly because of ease of access to Edinburgh, Fife and the Lothians feature most promi-nently throughout. The relative ease of networks within the area also seems to have promoted the diffusion of witch-hunting in that minis-ters from different parishes were able to meet frequently and attend each others' solemn fasts at executions. Within these general areas there were certain small towns and villages which appear again and again.

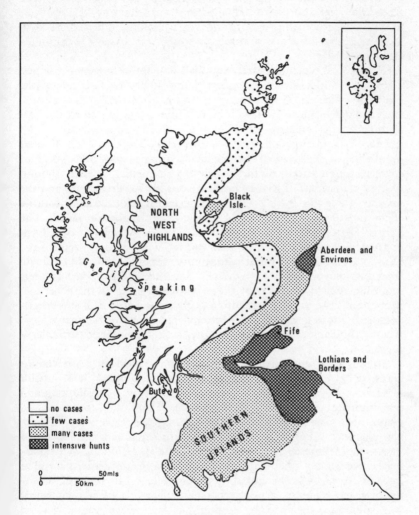

DISTRIBUTION AND INTENSITY OF PROSECUTIONS

Tranent and Prestonpans were places which featured both in the first witch-hunt and in all the major hunts. They were also among the last places to have limited local hunts. Inverkeithing in Fife, Dumfries, and Aberdeen were also places of long-term witch-hunting. There seems to be a self-perpetuating element in witch-hunting. Where there were local memories of actual burnings it was relatively easy to stimulate them again.

Other places which regularly supplied witches were fishing villages. The connection of witchcraft (first demonstrated in Scotland in the North Berwick trials) with disasters at sea made these places natural areas for witch-hunts. Bo'ness in East Lothian, and indeed all the East Lothian fishing villages, the Fife, Buchan, and Aberdeenshire coast and the Ayrshire ports of Ardrossan, Inverkip, Largs, and Ayr itself all regularly provided cases. The incidence of cases does not appear to correlate immediately in time with any particular disaster, though specific accusations of having been responsible for drownings and the sinking of ships are included in the indictments. More striking was the effect on a fishing community of a large-scale slaughter of sailors. The burgh of Pittenweem lost over 100 adult males at the battle of Kilsyth in 1649. The effect on the women was far worse than it would have been in a purely agricultural community, for women could cultivate land, but they could not go to sea. Seventeen ships rotted at their moorings and the families of those who had sailed in them became pauperized. The burgh went into a decline from that date and witch-craft accusations began to rise.[2] Pittenweem is one of the many areas where a minute study of the pattern of accusation might be particularly revealing.

Although more detailed investigation may reveal such connections between local disasters and outbreaks of witch-hunting, it is difficult to make any general correlation between surges of witch-hunting and demographic disasters (see Appendix 1). There were outbreaks of plague in 1600 and 1607 when witch-hunting was at a low level. There was plague in Edinburgh in 1624 and there was a general plague and widespread famine in 1635 when again there was a lull in witch-hunting. There was a further plague and famine in 1644 just after the rise in cases of 1643.[3] None of these bears much relation to peaks of witch-hunting. In a sense this is not particularly surprising. While witchcraft was sometimes held to be responsible for rather vague general conditions like an increase in sin, rebellion, or disturbance, and occasionally for storm raising, it was rarely held to be responsible for large-scale disasters in which the suffering might be random. There were orthodox views about what caused the spread of plague and smallpox; witchcraft tended to be used as an explanation for individual misfortunes and illnesses for which no standard explanation was at that time available.

Although it is not therefore surprising that there should be no direct connection between calamities and witch-hunting, an indirect one in the form of an increase in the number of persons suffering displacement and deprivation might have given rise to an increase in the number turning to healing and sorcery as a means of livelihood and therefore vulnerable to accusations of witchcraft. However, this does not seem to have been the case. The severe famine of the 1690s, known as the 'seven lean years' coincided with the Renfrewshire outbreak, but it did not provoke any general witch-hunt. It was perhaps too late for that in any case. There appears, therefore, to be no satisfactory correlation on a national level between witch-hunting and demographic events. Whether there may be at a local level is an issue yet to be explored.

There are further problems about the connection between local and national witch-hunting. In the chronology of witch-hunting central control was important in varying degrees. The hunt of 1590–91 was stirred up to express Scoto-Danish Protestant solidarity. Witch-hunts were generated at the same time in Edinburgh and Copenhagen to account for the naval misfortunes of the various royal voyages sent during the equinoctial gales to take Anne of Denmark to Leith. For James they were an opportunity to identify his enemies and stir up support. The 1597 hunt was the culmination of a policy of first advertising the danger of witchcraft and then handing out non-accountable general commissions to try witches. It was brought to an abrupt end by the withdrawal of these commissions. The 1629–30 hunt was preceded by a Privy Council pronouncement about the necessity of tightening up on villains including witches, and so were the hunts of the 1640s. The Restoration hunt was accompanied by a Privy Council assertion of the necessity of ridding the land of witchcraft and its decline was preceded by Privy Council attempts to suppress the use of torture in witchcraft cases and discredit witch finders.

There are other factors, however, which make the relationship between governmental intent and a national witch-hunt less simple than this outline suggests. Although the General Assembly in 1649 did press for action against witchcraft in particular, the pronouncements of the Church and Government in the late sixteenth century and the Privy Council statement of 1628 expressed concern about law and order in general. Witchcraft was only one item among many. The outbreaks of 1629–30, 1649, and 1661–62 were all preceded by a gradual build-up of cases accompanied by expressions of governmental anxiety. During the investigation of the Inverkeithing witches in 1623 the Privy Council had noted its own special responsibility in this matter.

> Quhairfoir necessair it is for the grace of God and for purging this land of such hynous offenouris and for avoyding the heavie judgement of God that attendes the impunitie of such nefarious crymes that order justice be ministrat upon them.[4]

They then set up a commission 'to the provost and bailies of Inver-keithing James Stewart of Rossythe, James Ogan of Cawstoun, and James Spittel of Blair or any three of them, two of the gentlemen being always present, to hold justice courts and try Margaret Kinnell and Marjorie Gibson'.[5] In urban commissions burghers frequently out-numbered lairds, and it was normal practice to ensure that the land-owning classes were properly represented (see Appendix 2).

The pressure behind the Restoration hunt seems to have been slightly different. In 1658 there were a number of cases, and in 1659 in addition to an outbreak at Tranent about twenty cases came before the military Circuit Court at Stirling. Most of them were acquitted and reappeared for trial again in 1661 when the Privy Council was restored.[6] This may suggest that the pressure here came from below rather than from the government. It all depends, however, what is meant by 'below'. In arguing that witch-hunting is in general a ruling class phenomenon it should be borne in mind that in seventeenth-century Scotland there was at least a threefold stratification among those who had powers over the peasantry. There was the embryonic central administration, the landowners with their courts and rights, and the ministers and their Kirk sessions who acted both as propagators of the new beliefs and values and as a primary police force both for misdemeanour and major crime.

In distributing responsibility among sections of the ruling class much attention has been given to the third tier, the ministers and Kirk sessions. The rationalist school concentrated almost exclusively on them.[7] While their role in primary social control and ideological in-doctrination was of great importance their power to operate the witch-processing machinery may have been over-emphasized while that of the nobility and gentry has been relatively under-examined. In the struggle for dominance between church and state, between reli-gious and secular forces (except possibly in 1649 when covenanting interests had a larger influence than at any other time) it was the secular powers who actually determined the level of judicial activity. In 1602 the General Assembly attempted to stimulate the search for witches in their initiation of 'visitations'. The 'visitor' was to ask all ministers if there were any witches in their parish.[8] This had no notice-able effect on the rate of prosecutions which remained minimal. In 1609 the Presbytery of Dalkeith argued before the Privy Council that they should be allowed to proceed against Geillis Johnston of Musselburgh but this was decided by the Privy Council against them.[9] During the next few years the Council issued a small number of commissions to bishops; to the Bishop of Aberdeen in 1613, to the Bishop of Galloway in 1614, to the Bishop of Dunblane in 1615, and occasionally to local ministers.[10] In 1624 the Council decided that all information and requests for commissions must go through a bishop, thus centralizing control further.[11] It was the Council who in 1628 eventually set in progress the first major hunt of the century by announcing that witches and others were to be tried at Circuit Courts throughout the kingdom. In 1649 and again in 1661–62 the central government kept control of witch-hunting for themselves against the demands of the presbyteries and ministers. Certainly these demands were considerable. The presbytery of Dunfermline in 1649 was begging Parliament to hand out commissions to them free: 'that we may have commissionis gratis, lest through the want of mone this worke which the Lord hes so miraculuslie begunne and so wiselie heirtofore caried on perish in hand.'[12] Central government, however, kept this form of revenue flowing. At six pounds, twelve shillings and fourpence (Scots)[13] a commission they were worth issuing in bulk, though it is not clear that this was a motive. The motives of both church and state seem to have been ideological.

At the end of the century, long after the secular powers had lost interest, the General Assembly was making provision for its own control. In 1699 it made a recommendation to the presbyteries concerning witchcraft, but got no response. In 1707 the Assembly codified the procedures to be taken in bringing to trial and trying witches, and the following year it defined the function of the Kirk session including in this its part in the trial of witches.[14] It is possible that this was in response to some cases which had recently occurred in Pittenweem and Dumfries, but the rules were in any case more or less redundant. The fact that the ecclesiastical authorities were continually making requests to central government for more judicial activity or for more authority to them has sometimes been taken to suggest that the basic responsibility for witch-hunting lies with the church councils: the General Assembly, the presbyteries, and the ministers. (The Bishops have oddly escaped this particular censure.) While it is undoubtedly the case that the church, as the front-line purveyors of the new ideology, was committed to the assault on witchcraft as a priority which transcended rival politico-religious problems, the principal difference between them and the central authorities was a difference in power.

What is more, in the interplay between local and central government it was the landowners rather than the ministers who requested most of the commissions, and they who conducted most of the trials from which the clergy were normally excluded except as witnesses. It was not only the ministers and presbyteries whose activities the state wished to control. It was also that of 'inferior judges': the barons, sheriffs, and baillies who had powers, very often including that of 'pit and gallows', over their local peasantry in a variety of crimes other than the four pleas of the crown. This meant that it was possible for a local baron to execute for murder, provided that he termed it slaughter and carried out the sentence summarily. 'Inferior judges' were therefore accustomed to considerable local powers which with regard to witchcraft were only given to them in individual cases through special Privy Council permission.

The great majority of witches were tried in this way and the commissions were normally given to named landowners and their grand tenants, local magistrates, and very occasionally ministers. More often ministers operated in the background obtaining confessions from the accused, and gave evidence at the trial. It would be possible to make a fairly comprehensive list of members of commissions for trying witches, and some representative examples are given in an appendix.

It has been suggested by Levack that the initial impetus for the 1661–62 hunt came from the Earl of Haddington who expressed anxiety about law and order in general during the period when the Cromwellian regime had withdrawn but the Restoration government had not yet been set up.[15] Haddington insisted that his tenants had threatened to leave his land if the witches who were harassing them were not rounded up and brought to justice. This may seem to support the theory that witch-hunting started with the peasantry, but it is not really very clear what this threat amounted to. It was a time when the population was rising and land, partly because of early capitalization in the Lothians, was in short supply. Even if we take the statement at its face value the peasantry needed someone of substance to pursue their witches for them, but it is also possible that there was an element of rhetoric in Haddington's assertion. In any case a demand from below that witches be pursued was in the first instance a demand from the local landowner, the second tier of the ruling class.

Another example of the role of landowners is the case of Sir George Maxwell of Nether Pollock. Maxwell had been appointed in January 1662 to a commission to try Beatrix Lyon, Jon Boig, and Jonet Morrison of Inverkip, so he was familiar at first hand with the process. When he fell ill in 1676: he 'was surprised at Glasgow, in the night-time, with a hot and fiery distemper', he attributed it to witchcraft and eventually identified culprits who confessed to bewitching him with waxen images. The Privy Council granted a commission and

> in regard of the singularity of the case, they ordered the process to be very solemn, commissioning for the trial some judicious gentlemen in the country, viz. Sir Patrick Ganston of Ganston, James Brisbane of Bishopton, Sir John Shaw Younger of Greenock and John Anderson younger of Dovehill. To whom they added Mr. John Preston, advocate (a gentleman well seen in criminals, and who exercised the office of justice-depute for several years), a *sine qua non* in the commission. And that the whole process might be the more exact, they appointed George Lord Ross assessor, with power to vote and decide.[16]

In fact this commission was not particularly exceptional in being composed largely of 'judicious gentlemen in the country'. The 166_ commission of which Sir George Maxwell himself was a member also contained a high proportion of gentry. In a routine case in 1649 for trying Janet Small, Margaret Blair, Jean Walker, Catherine Allan, and Janet Robertson of Carriden in the Presbytery of Linlithgow the commission to try was given to Sir Robert Drummond, the lairds of Dundas elder and younger, Mr. James Restow of Crictoun, James Campbell in Lithgow, Robert Cuthbertson, younger, John Dick in 'Queensferry, George Allan in Bo'ness, James Allan of Stales, Alexander Gib and Florence Gairdner in Graypannes. Five was to constitute a quorum. This assize consisted of about half lairds and half grand tenants.[17]

There are only a few individual pursuers of witches who have reached some fame in the annals of Scottish witch-hunting. Apart from James VI, there are the witch-prickers, especially John Kincaid, and some individual ministers. Most, however, are unknown and it would be interesting to put through a computer the names listed in commissions to find the landowners who appeared most repeatedly in the lists. It was very often those who put in the request for a commission who were first to be named as commissioners. We have detailed lists of names for those who tried witches on nearly all Privy Council commissions and many lists of assizers (jurymen) for the Court of Justiciary cases, and it should become clear if there were any names in particular which kept cropping up. The extent to which the local ruling class rather than the central ruling class controlled the supply of suspects is an indication of the extent to which social control was still local. The fact that a central demand for a tightening up on law and order tended to result in a national witch-hunt may be partly a reflection of the fact that, along with the much rarer treason this was the only crime which was centrally administered. The extent to which such demands also resulted in a more general crime (or control) wave is still unresearched.

In local witch-hunting the ministers and Kirk sessions worked with the gentry as a third tier in the chain of social control, though in some cases membership of the Kirk session overlapped with that of the gentry. The fourth tier was that of the peasantry themselves. Their level of interest in the pursuit of the witches in their midst is hard to measure because recorded complaints to the Kirk session while occasionally spontaneous seem frequently to have reached the point of record in response to encouragement by the session. Yet the neighbours' complaints were an essential part of the process, and their willingness to lay charges and their choice of individuals to lay charges against must have been affected by local conditions and pressures which only microscopic analysis of surviving local records could reveal.

Although the rise and fall of witch-hunting has to be related in the first place to the concerns of central government, and in the second place to the interest of the local landowners and church authorities in bringing forward charges, that does not mean that the analysis of witch-hunting should be, as it often has been in the past, conducted mainly at the level of ruling class activity. While the idea that peasant discontents can in themselves generate witch-hunting (as opposed to witch accusation) if unsupported or unstimulated by the authorities is discounted, that does not mean that peasant life was not strongly affected by witch-hunting. On the contrary, witch-hunting drew on endemic fears and hostilities in the peasant population. What we have learned from the English studies of Thomas and Macfarlane is that neither the accusers nor the accused are randomly selected, and that the accusations reflect and are a key to the conflicts of rural life. The next chapters consider the peasant experience of witchcraft and witch-hunting as a phenomenon essentially imposed on the powerless by the powerful rather than as a spontaneous peasant movement. Through witch-hunting popular peasant belief was actually altered, and the significance of endemic fears for an increasingly Christianized and increasingly literate Calvinist laity was redefined. The nature of this process and the part it played in the battle for the minds of the seventeenth-century peasantry by the local and central rulers of seventeenth-century Scotland is explored in the remainder of the book.

CHAPTER EIGHT

WHO WERE THE WITCHES?

The witches of Scotland were typical of the witches of rural Europe.
They were predominantly poor, middle-aged or elderly women. The
sources are not often directly helpful in establishing social detail. It is
unusual for the occupation or age of a suspect to be recorded. Marital
status is given in about a third of the cases. Quite often we have nothing
but a name and sometimes not even that. Of the 3,000 or so accused
collected in the *Source Book* only 192 have their occupation or status or
that of their husbands recorded. They can be classified as follows:

Nobility	16
Burgess	14
Craftsmen	46
Indweller	1
Sailors	10
Lairds	2
Ministers/teachers	14
Prosperous tenants	10
Midwife/healers	12
Wage labourers	16
Innkeepers	3
Musicians	3
Servants	23
Beggars and vagabonds	21[1]

These figures are in fact extremely misleading. Fortunately there is
internal evidence in a fairly substantial run of documents which shows
that it would be absurd if one were to project from the figures given
above to the mass of other witches.[2] Indeed the status of the accused
seems to have been mentioned in the documents only when it was
slightly unusual. The average witch was the wife or widow of a tenant
farmer, probably fairly near the bottom of the social structure. If she
was categorized in the records at all it was as spouse, for example, to
John Graham in Kirkton. It is evident from the accusations that the
quarrels which generated them were about the exchange of goods and
services in a tenant and sub-tenant economy.

It is hard to speak with great certainty in the absence of more detailed
local research on one of the major witchcraft areas such as Fife or East
Lothian, but the impression given is slightly different from the English
scene, where it is clear that the witches were ninety-three per cent

women, and that they were absolutely at the bottom of the social heap. They were the wives or widows of wage labourers; they were on the poor law; they were beggars.[3] The Scottish ones appear on average to be slightly further up the stratification scale. Those really at the bottom of the Scottish scale were the large but unknown number of people who were in a sense outside the system. They were the criminals, paupers, gypsies, entertainers, and wandering wage labourers, all generally summed up under the title of vagabond. Some of the witches whose status is specifically named do fall into this class. A few are identified in the records as being downwardly socially mobile. Jean Hadron, tried in Glasgow in May 1700, was mentioned as being poor and seeking alms and was a baker's widow;[4] Margaret Duncan, who was tried along with her, was a merchant's widow.[5] Catherin Mac-Taiged, who was tried in Dunbar in May 1688 was the wife of a weaver who became a beggar. John Shand of Moray tried in 1643 was described as a fugitive;[6] Marion Purdie, tried in Edinburgh in 1684, was once a midwife.[7] But these glimpses in the records are fleeting. What detailed research on one area might establish is to what extent accused witches belonged to a class which was being dispossessed from small-scale collective farming and was having to make a living from inadequate land supplemented by wage labouring. In the present state of knowledge it looks as though, while a few belonged to the class of outsiders: wage labourers, servants, and the dispossessed, many of the accused witches had a more or less stable domicile and might be related to people in the neighbourhood who had a formal stake in the feudal structure. The majority, however, appear to have been at the bottom of the formal feudal structure itself; they had at least a house with a kailyard, some were part wage-earner, part tenant-farmer; others were sub-tenants and tenants in a farm-toun. In other words they had a position in society, albeit a lowly and often semi-dependent one, and they did not mean to drop out. Unless someone had a fixed position in the community their reputation was not likely to have a chance to grow. Exceptions of course were those who were banished for witchcraft and who had to move for that reason, or whose reputation travelled with them. The case of Janet Anderson who moved to a different locality voluntarily and brought her discharge from the Kirk session of her former parish with her caution for witchcraft recorded on it has already been mentioned.

An indication of the importance of being within the system before being in danger of witch accusation is given in the Kirk session records of Rothesay. This was a burgh on the island of Bute in the Clyde which had a few cases of witchcraft although it never had an epidemic. A woman called Bessie Nicol, daughter to Duncan Nicol, a weaver, was called up by the Kirk session in 1706 for

imploying Elspeth NcTaylor, spouse to James Stewart, thatcher, by charmeing to find out and recover a gown that was lost and for that end to have given the said Elspeth a fourtie pennie piece with a litle salt in a clout (cloth) to performe the charme.

It might perhaps be thought that Elspeth NcTaylor, the charmer, and therefore potentially the witch, might have been the worse offender but in this distant outpost of the Kirk the local session lacked courage:

In regard the forsaid Elspeth NcTaylor alledged to be imployed to perform the charme is notourlie known to be most intractable, incapable and infamous and irreclaimable the Session waves troubling themselves with her.[8]

Suspects were then from the settled rather than the vagabond or out-cast poor, and they were predominantly women. Witchcraft was, as elsewhere in Europe, overwhelmingly a woman's crime. It was also in Scotland almost the only woman's crime in this period. If one looks impressionistically at those unanalysed central criminal records it appears that apart from a little adultery, a little incest, a surprisingly small amount of infanticide, and (as Covenanters) a bit of rebellion, women were not reaching the Court of Justiciary. At a lower level, however, they were being constantly subjected to the variety of degradation rituals which comprised the lesser punishments of the Kirk sessions, town councils, or baron courts.

The relative figures for men and women at least are firm apart from the 300 or so witches whose names (unless they are duplicates) we do not know. The number of male witches fluctuated, but overall amounted to about one fifth of the whole.

Percentage of male suspects by decade[9]

Decade	Female	Male	Male percentage
1560–9	10	2	16.7
1570–9	4	1	20.0
1580–9	10	3	23.1
1590–9	144	36	20.0
1600–9	24	9	27.3
1610–9	62	19	23.5
1620–9	347	49	12.4
1630–9	133	38	22.2
1640–9	396	57	12.6
1650–9	308	55	15.2
1660–9	577	77	11.8
1670–9	162	29	15.2
1680–9	32	3	8.6
1690–9	36	11	23.4
1700–9	63	13	17.1

If one leaves aside those decades in which the numbers are too low for percentages to have much significance it becomes clear that the proportion of men dropped fairly sharply during the major panics. In the quieter periods the proportion of male suspects was from twenty per cent to twenty-seven per cent; during the epidemics it dropped to eleven per cent to twelve per cent. When demand rose, the supply was more definitely female. The trend, which is the opposite of what Midelfort found for south-western Germany, is quite marked but it is not clear how it should be interpreted. It looks as though male witches needed time to build up a reputation, and that during a crisis, when an instant supply of witches was required, accusers were more likely to resort to classic stereotypes. It looks also as though convicted witches, under pressure to name accomplices, felt they were more likely to convince if they named other women.

Whatever one may make of this fluctuation, however, it is clear that overall the figure for men is higher than Macfarlane found for Essex. But Soman, working on appeals to the Parlement of Paris, has found that half the appellants were men.[10] Midelfort for south-western Germany[11] and Monter for Switzerland[12] found the overall proportions similar to those of Scotland. The very low proportion of male witch suspects found in England seems rather unusual. The substantial proportion of male witches in most parts of Europe means that a witch was not defined exclusively in female terms. If she were the problem would be simpler, but the two principal characteristics of the witch, malice and alleged supernatural power, are human rather than female characteristics, yet at least four out of five persons to whom they are ascribed are women. Witchcraft was not sex-specific but it was sex-related.

There are two distinct problems about this. The first is that of why witchcraft in Europe was so strongly sex-related. The second is what bearing this sex-relatedness had on outbreaks of witch-hunting. It is argued here that the relationship between women and the stereotype of witchcraft is quite direct: witches are women; all women are potential witches. The relationship between witch-hunting and woman hunting, however, is less direct. Witches were hunted in the first place as witches. The total evil which they represented was not actually sex-specific. Indeed the Devil himself was male. Witch-hunting was directed for ideological reasons against the enemies of God, and the fact that eighty per cent or more of these were women was, though not accidental, one degree removed from an attack on women as such.

So far as the woman stereotype is concerned witches were seen to be women long before there was a witch-hunt. The stereotype rests on the twin pillars of the Aristotelean view of women as imperfectly human—a failure of the process of conception—and the Judaeo-Christian view of women as the source of sin and the Fall of Man. Since witchcraft involved a rejection of what are regarded as the noblest

human attributes women were the first suspects. Women were intrinsically and innately more prone to malice, sensuality, and evil in
general, and were less capable of reasoning than men were, but were
nevertheless to be feared by men. There are a number of ingredients in
this fear: through their life-bearing and menstruating capacities they
are potential owners of strange and dangerous powers. Shuttle and
Redgrove quoted Pliny's description of the menstruating woman:

> If they touch any standing corn in the field, it will wither and
> come to no good . . . Look they upon a sword, knife, or any edged
> tools, be it never so bright, it waxeth duskish, so doth also the
> lively hue of ivorie. The very bees in the hive die. Iron and steel
> presently take rust, yea and brasse likewise, with a filthy, strong
> and poysoned stynke, if they but lay hand thereupon.[13]

They make the point that this presentation of the harmful attributes of
the menstruating woman tallies with descriptions of the characteristics
of the witch. These characteristics fit all mature women some of the
time. The theory is, however, more historically specific than Shuttle
and Redgrove suggest. Pliny himself refers throughout the passage not
to the effects of contact with the menstruating woman but of contact
with the menstrual blood itself (*mulierum effluvio*).[14] The translation
quoted is stylistically sixteenth- or seventeenth-century, though its
source is not given, and it is this free adaptation which shifts the evil
effects of the menstrual fluid to the woman herself. It is not too
fanciful to suggest that this shift reflects an intensified misogyny in
this period.

Women are feared as a source of disorder in patriarchal society. Not
only are menstruating women to be feared. So too are women as
child bearers. It is only by exhibiting total control over the lives and
bodies of their women that men can know that their children are their
own. They are feared too in the sexual act. The fact that they are
receptive, not potent, and can receive indefinitely, whether pleasurably
or not, has generated the myth of insatiability. Because it was thought
that women through these insatiable lusts might either lead men astray
or hold them to ridicule for their incapacity, witches were alleged to
cause impotence and to satisfy their own lusts at orgies with demons,
animals, and such human males as could also be seduced. James VI was
giving a version of the prevailing view when he argued as to why
women were more disposed to witchcraft than men:

> The reason is easie: for as that sexe is frailer then men is, so is it
> easier to be intrapped in these grosse snares of the Devill, as was
> well proved to be true, by the Serpents deceiving of Eve at the
> beginning, which makes him the homelier with that sex ever
> since.[15]

It is perhaps worth noting that the stereotype of the witch is the mirror-opposite of the stereotype of the saint. The witch, through a special relationship with the Devil, performs impious miracles; the saint, through a special relationship with God, performs pious miracles. In the peak period for saints (thirteenth to fourteenth centuries) sanctity was sex-related to males in much the same proportion as witchcraft was later to females.[16] The female stereotype is in fact so strong that in some periods the words woman and witch were almost interchangeable. In twelfth-century Russia when the authorities were looking for witches they simply rounded up the female population.[17] In Langedorf in 1492 they charged all but two of the adult female population.[18]

The presence of up to twenty per cent of males in the European witch-hunt has a variety of explanations. Monter found that male witches in his survey tended to predominate in areas which had a history of confusing witchcraft and heresy.[19] Midelfort found that male suspects tended to be accused of other crimes as well.[20] Urban male suspects could be a source of income to the authorities. This has some parallels with Scotland. The agnatic system of marriage prevailing in Scotland in which the wife retained her father's surname makes it difficult to tell when suspects are related by marriage. The Scottish male suspects whose identity has been pursued have so far all turned out to be either husband or brother of a female suspect, a notorious villain as on the continent, or, in a few cases, a solitary cunning man. The difference between Scotland and England in the proportion of males accused can be accounted for by the fact that the English had very few multiple trials in which male relatives might be embroiled, and the fact that in England cunning folk normally escaped being accused of witchcraft.

Although it can be argued that all women were potential witches, in practice certain types of women were selected or selected themselves. In Scotland those accused of witchcraft can be described, though not with precision, under four heads: those that accepted their own reputation and even found ego-enhancement in the description of a 'rank witch' and the power that this gave them in the community; those that had fantasies of the Devil; those who became convinced of their guilt during their inquisition or trial; and those who were quite clear that they were innocent, and who either maintained their innocence to the end or confessed only because of torture or threat of torture. They are all equally interesting in relation to the image of the witch in the community, but those who embraced the role of witch are also interesting in relation to the actual attraction of witchcraft for women.

This attraction of witchcraft is clear when we ask why the witches were drawn from the ranks of the poor. Apart from the obvious fact that it was socially easier to accuse those who were least able to defend themselves witchcraft had a particular attraction for the very poor. It has been pointed out by Thomas that the English witches, who were more clearly than the Scottish ones at the bottom of the stratification ladder, were people who felt themselves to be totally impotent.[21] The normal channels of expression were denied to them, and they could not better their condition. Witchcraft, Thomas suggests, was believed to be a means of bettering one's condition when all else had failed. The fear of witchcraft bestowed power on those believed to be witches. A reputation for witchcraft was one possible way of modifying the behaviour of those more advantageously positioned. More than that, it was a direct way of providing benefits for themselves. Although the Demonic Pact does not loom very large in English witchcraft it is made something of a centrepiece by Thomas in the psychology of the self-conscious witch. Those who committed what is well described as the 'mental crime' of the Demonic Pact (that is those who not only consciously believed that they were committing effective acts of malefice, the social crime, but also that they were able to do this because of their relationship with the Devil in the Demonic Pact) also revealed in their confessions the exact nature of the promises which the Devil had made to them.[22] We have moved a long way in rural pre-industrial England and Scotland from the classic aristocratic pacts of the Dr. Faustus type where great creative gifts are on offer in return for the individual immortal soul of the human concerned. The economic value to the Devil of the soul of a seventeenth-century peasant was not so great. With these people, in whom hope is expressed in the most circumspect of terms, we are in the world of relative deprivation. Seventeenth-century English women at the margins of society did not expect that their soul would qualify them for silk and riches. Instead they said that the Devil promised them mere freedom from the extremes of poverty and starvation. He told them, typically, 'that they should never want'.[23]

The witches of Scotland used exactly the same terminology as those of England, but since the Pact loomed much larger they used it more habitually and more extensively. The Devil's promises were much the same from the time when the pact is first mentioned in Scottish cases until it faded from the collective imagination. John Feane in 1591 related that the Devil had promised him 'that he should never want'.[24] In 1661 it was the same. The Devil promised Margaret Brysone 'That she should never want', Elspeth Blackie, 'that she should want nothing', and likewise Agnes Pegavie and Janet Gibson. Bessie Wilson was told by the Devil, 'thee art a poor puddled (overworked) body. Will thee be my servant and I will give thee abundance and thee sall never want', and Margaret Porteous was told even more enticingly, that 'she should have all the pleasure of the earth'.[25] Thomas also noted that English witches in their exchanges with the Devil were sometimes offered small sums of money which sometimes then turned out to be worthless.[26] One of the witches in this particular group from Dalkeith in 1661, Agnes Pegavie, also mentioned that the Devil, after making these rather limited promises, gave her 12d in silver which she found afterwards to be only a 'sklait stane'.[27]

Equally good indicators of their expectations and sense of the economically possible are the more elaborate confessions which include descriptions of witches' meetings. The food and drink said to have been available at these meetings varied a bit; very occasionally it was said to have been unpalatable, usually in circumstances in which the Devil was also perceived as being generally unkind to his servants and beating them up for failures in wickedness. More often it fell within the range of normal peasant fare: oatcakes and ale. Sometimes it was the fare of the landed class: red wine, wheaten cake, and meat.

There are other suggestions than hope of alleviating poverty as to why women might be attracted to witchcraft. The explanation of the Gonja woman in West Africa interviewed by Goody echoes that of the seventeenth-century European manuals. Although some women gave specific motives one answered 'because we are evil'. Goody suggests that while there are a number of contexts in which men may kill there are few in which women may legitimately use aggression even if they are able to.[28] In situations of domestic stress and tension in which men resort to violence, women use witchcraft. The female witches in the seventeenth-century Scottish courts may be the equivalent of the males accused of slaughter and murder. This is to assume what is sometimes forgotten in analyses which involve oppressor and oppressed, that women are not more virtuous than dominant males any more than the poor are more virtuous than dominant landlords. They are merely less powerful. Another angle on the theme of psychological motivation is suggested by Warner in her novel *Lolly Willowes*. Here witchcraft represents adventure and excitement which are normally excluded from the lives of women.[29] Women may turn to cursing to give vent to aggression or exercise power. They may fantasize about the Devil to bring colour to their lives.

The women who sought or involuntarily received the accolade of witch were poor but they were not in Scotland always solitary. The women who were the classic focus of witch accusations were frequently, it turns out, impoverished not because they were widows or single women with no supporters or independent means of livelihood, but were simply married to impoverished men. The figures which we have obtained for marital status are again not very good, but they are better than those for social status. About half of those whose status is recorded were in fact married at the time of their arrest.[30] Some were solitaries, but solitariness as such does not appear to have been an important element in the composition of a Scottish witch. Nor does ugliness appear to have been of very much importance. Macfarlane has drawn attention to the stereotype of the ill-favoured witch,[31] though Thomas discounts its significance.[32] The presence of a popular literature on witchcraft in England which was almost absent in Scotland may have made the factor of personal appearance a more significant one there. The stereotype of the ugly, old woman certainly existed in Scotland,[33] but there is little evidence connecting this stereotype with actual accused witches.

So far as personal as opposed to social characteristics go we are left with the variable of character. This is a notoriously difficult concept to deal with historically. One can sometimes identify character traits in particular individuals. But it is usually hard to say whether these are deviant in terms of standard behaviours of the period. It has been observed by Heine that 'character has lost its narrow psychological significance and has increasingly been endowed with social content and meaning'.[34] It has become associated in role theory with the acting out of socially prescribed roles. We may observe some of the personal characteristics of the witch; we do not know whether they are characteristic of all seventeenth-century Scottish women near the bottom of the socio-economic hierarchy. This problem was recognized at the time, and much exploited by defence lawyers. The successful defender of Elizabeth Bathgate of Eyemouth argued in respect of a witness who claimed to have been bewitched after being shouted at by the accused, that nothing has been 'libelled to procure his distress but a sort of Railing and Flyting (quarrelling) which is common to women when stirred up by their neighbours and especially by websters as common objects to women's spleen'.[35]

When all this is said, however, the essential individual personality trait does seem to have been that of a ready, sharp and angry tongue. The witch had the Scottish female quality of smeddum: spirit, a refusal to be put down, quarrelsomeness. No cursing: no malefice; no witch. The richness of language attributed to witches is considerable. Helen Thomas of Dumfries was accused by Agnes Forsyth in August 1657 of having said, 'Ane ill sight to you all, and ane ill sight to them that is foremost, that is Agnes Forsyth.'[36] In similar vein Elspeth Cursetter of Orkney in May 1629 hoped that 'ill might they all thryve and ill might they speid.'[37] More aggressively, Issobel Grierson was alleged in 1667 to have said 'The faggotis of hell lycht on the, and hellis caldrane may thow seith in.'[38] Agnes Finnie of the Potterrow in Edinburgh, who was accused in 1642, was alleged to have said that 'she should gar the Devil take a bite of the said Bessie Currie', and to John Buchanan at Lambarr, 'John, go away, for as you have begun with witches so you shall end with them.' And her daughter Margaret Robertson, not to be outdone when called by one Andrew Wilson 'ane witches get' (offspring), replied, 'if I be a witches get the Devil rive the Soul out of you before I come again.'[39] Less dramatically, but packed with economic menace, Elizabeth Bathgate told George Sprot, 'for work what you can your teeth shall overgang your hands and ye shall never get your Sundays meat to the fore.'[40]

The witch may have been socially and economically in a dependent position, but the factor which often precipitated accusations was the refusal to bring to this situation the deference and subservience which was deemed appropriate to the role. In her dealings with relative equals too she was likely to be just as aggressive.

It is one thing, however, to produce a static ideal-type of the commonest features of the witch. She is a married middle-aged woman of the lower peasant class and she has a sharp tongue and a filthy temper. The problem as with so many stereotypes is that its explanatory force is limited in that not only did a considerable number of Scottish witches not fit the stereotype; an even larger number of people who did, and who lived in the danger zones for witch accusation and prosecution, were never accused or identified in this way. It is at this point that the labelling theory of sociology may have something to contribute, for labelling theory stresses the dynamic elements in the process of identifying and thereby creating a socially deviant person. There is a continuous interaction between the individual and society. 'At the heart of the labelling approach is an emphasis on *process*; deviance is viewed not as a static entity but rather as a continuously shaped and reshaped *outcome* of dynamic processes of social interaction.' These, it is argued, occur on three levels of social action; collective rule making, interpersonal reactions, and organizational processes.[41]

Without the collective rule making by which witchcraft was reconstructed as an offence against society in 1563 and the nature of it redefined during the 1590-91 treason trials, there could have been no Scottish witch-hunt. It is possible to develop this argument further and say there would have been no demonic witches. There were, essentially, no demonic witches in the Highlands and Islands during the period of the hunt, and none in the rest of Scotland before the late sixteenth century. There were plenty of specialists. There were charmers, healers, sooth-sayers, poisoners, owners of the evil eye, and there were cursers. Many of these, particularly the successful cursers, would have been called witches. The difference between them and the seventeenth-century east-coast and lowland witch was two-fold: in the first place, the meaning of the label changed to something at once more precise and more universally anti-social: the new witch was not only the enemy of the individual or even of the locality; she was the enemy of the total society, of the state, and of God; in the second place the existence of the third level of social action, the new organizational processes, both created a demand for the production of witches and at the same time made the production more rewarding to the community. It was these factors that generated activity on the second level; that of interpersonal relations.

In the process of building up a reputation in a community there was one important element which provides a link between the static description of the social and personality types which were most likely to attract accusations of witchcraft, and the identification of those individuals who actually ended up in the courts. This was the accused's friends, relatives, and associates. There was nothing like a link with someone already suspected to set the labelling process going. We have already mentioned the daughter of Agnes Finnie. The label of 'witches get' was often the first stage. Evil powers were believed to be transmitted from parent to child (a belief which sits uneasily with the demonic pact). Those cases that have come to light tend to be the ones where mother and daughter were executed together (partly because it is otherwise difficult to identify the relationship when the mother retained her own name while passing her husband's on to the daughter). In 1673 in Scalloway in the Shetland Isles, Margaret Byland and her daughter, Suna Voe, were both commissioned for trial.[42] Two years later, also in Shetland, an unnamed old woman and her daughter, Helen Stewart, were executed together.[43] There must have been many more cases where the label was passed on, and the daughter either lived with the label for ever, or was accused formally at a later date. The term 'witch's get' was part of the normal currency of rural life.

Other relationships had their effect as well. In 1629, the sheriff of Haddington was given a commission to try John Carfra, Alison Borthwick, his wife, and Thomas Carfra, his brother.[44] They were also charged with having consulted with Margaret Hamilton and Bernie Carfra, who was, no doubt, another relative, and who had already been burnt for witchcraft.[45] Husband and wife teams were quite common. In West Lothian, in February, 1624, Elspet Paris was tried along with her husband, David Langlandis,[46] and the following month William Falconner, his sister Isobell Falconner, and his wife Marioun Symsoun were tried with a group of other witches.[47] In the same area, in Kirkliston, near Edinburgh, in 1655, William Barton and his wife were strangled and burnt.[48] Mere acquaintanceship however would do perfectly well. When Elspeth Maxwell was tried at Dumfries in 1650 it was alleged that she had been an associate of a woman who had been burnt three years before,[49] and this was a very common item in the depositions. Yet these links and associations are still only an occasional factor in the making of witches. The build up of reputation seems normally to have taken some time, and to have been a dynamic process of social interaction between witch and neighbours with steady mutual reinforcement. When Agnes Finnie, whose cursing powers have already been mentioned, said, 'if I be a witch, you or yours shall have better cause to call me so,'[50] she was giving a classical demonstration of the move from primary to secondary labelling (acceptance of the label and the accompanying role).

Unfortunately we can tell very little about the crucial initial stage in the process of becoming of ill repute, since the depositions usually bring together a set of accusations allegedly made over a period, but certainly gathered together at one point in time. Sometimes the dates of the malefices are identified, but even some of these may have been recalled, or seen in a new light after the reputation had been established. This is another of the areas where an intensive local study, matching early complaints against witches in the Kirk session with cases which later came to the courts, might be particularly illuminating.

The length of time over which a reputation could be built up varied greatly, a factor which lends support to the suggestion that many reputed witches could live with the reputation for a lifetime and die in their beds, even during the seventeenth century. Some witches who were eventually accused had lived with the label long enough to have acquired a title. In Inverkeithing, in 1631, Walker the Witch was active.[51] Janet Taylor, who was banished from Stirling in 1634 was known as the Witch of Monza.[52] Others had names which simply identified a peculiarity which could make them socially marginal. 'Deiff Meg', whose deafness clearly contributed to her reputation, was tried with four others in Berwick in 1629.[53] More mysterious was Archibald Watt in Lanarkshire, who was known as 'Sole the Paitlet, a warlock'.[54]

Others had a long term reputation without acquiring any special title, and with or without such a title many lived with the reputation for years before they were eventually brought to trial. Janet Wright of Niddry, near Edinburgh, was said in 1628 to have been by her own confession for the last eighteen or nineteen years 'a consulter with the devil has resaved his marks, renunced her baptism and givin herselfe over to the devill's service';[55] and William Crichtoun of Dunfermline in 1648 'being straitlie posed and dealt with by the ministers and watchers, he came to a confession of sundrie things, and that he hade made a paction with the Devill to be his servand 24 yeirs and more since'.[56]

Labelling theory takes us only so far in suggesting why particular individuals who shared the classic characteristics with many others were selected from them for accusation. It explains the build-up of social reinforcement, but, apart from the selection of daughters of witches, not the beginning of the process. In the last resort it can only be said that these individuals were in the wrong place at the wrong time.

When we turn from the selection of the individual back to the classic characteristics, however, there still remains a problem. What is the relationship between the type of person accused of witchcraft and the growth of witchcraft prosecutions? There is some evidence to suggest that the relationship is a direct one. Witch-hunting *is* woman-hunting or at least it is the hunting of women who do not fulfil the male view of how women ought to conduct themselves. An example from anthropology is that of the Nupe in the nineteen twenties. Nadel describes how the women were money lenders and traders and the men of the Nupe were very often in their debt. These women lived independent lives, took lovers, and rarely had children. They challenged the conventional ideal of women as servicing men and children, and it was they who were accused of witchcraft.[57]

We do not at present have enough evidence to say whether the status of women was radically changing in Europe in the fifteenth, sixteenth, and seventeenth centuries in a manner analagous to the more limited and specific case cited by Nadel. It has been argued that the witch-hunt was an attack by the emergent male medical profession on the female healer.[58] There is a certain amount of evidence for this. In Scotland in 1641 in the ratification of the privileges of the Edinburgh chirurgeons it was noted that unqualified females had been practising chirurgy illegitimately in the city,[59] and a number of witchcraft suspects were identified as midwives. The connection, however, is not direct enough. The main usurpation of midwifery by males took place in the eighteenth century after the witch-hunt was over. The objection to female healers was concentrated in the towns where the emergent male professionals had their strength. While witchcraft prosecutions may sometimes have married conveniently with the suppression of female healing, male professionalization of healing really cannot account for the mass of the prosecutions.

A different argument is that capitalizing agriculture reduced the role of women to that of a mere producer of children rather than a particip-ant in peasant production.[60] Anyone pursuing this argument however is likely to get into difficulties. Not enough is known to support or, what is worse, to make suspect, any large scale theory on the economic history of women. In particular the timing of that major change seems to have varied greatly in different parts of Europe, and in most areas took place after the end of the witch-hunt. The suggestion that this period saw an increase in the number of unsupported women is, again, difficult to substantiate, and the witch-hunt was not primarily directed against them.

If we turn to the sphere of ideology the case for witch-hunting being seen as a woman-hunt is more convincing. The stereotype of the witch was not that of the child-woman; it was that of the adult, independent woman. The religion of the Reformation and the Counter Reformation demanded that women for the first time became fully responsible for their own souls. Indeed preachers went out of their way to refer to 'men and women' in their sermons. The popularization of religion, however, took away from women with one hand what it gave to them with the other, for the particular form of religion was strongly patriarchal. The ritual and moral inferiority of women was preached along with their new personal responsibility. The status of women became ambiguous under the terms of the new ideology.

Witchcraft as a choice was only possible for women who had free will and personal responsibility attributed to them. This represented a considerable change in the status of women in Scotland at least. Up to the time of the secularization of the crime of witchcraft their misdemeanours had been the responsibility of husbands and fathers and their punishments the whippings thought appropriate to children.[61] As witches they became adult criminals acting in a manner for which their husbands could not be deemed responsible. The pursuit of witches could therefore be seen as a rearguard action against the emergence of women as independent adults. The women who were accused were those who challenged the patriarchal view of the ideal woman. They were accused not only by men but also by other women because women who conformed to the male image of them felt threatened by any identification with those who did not.

This explanation is the most plausible of those which identify witch-hunting as woman-hunting because unlike the other explanations the timing seems right. Nevertheless while witch-hunting and woman-hunting are closely connected they cannot be completely identified as one and the same phenomenon. The relationship is at one degree removed. The demand for ideological conformity was simply a much wider one than that aspect of it that concerned the status of women. The present discussion over the direct connection between the alleged uniqueness of English witchcraft and the allegedly unique status of women in England[62] is therefore misconceived. The pursuit of witches was an end in itself and was directly related to the necessity of enforcing moral and theological conformity. The fact that a high proportion of those selected in this context as deviants were women was indirectly related to this central purpose.

CHAPTER NINE

THE PROCESS
FROM ACCUSATION TO EXECUTION

There were two principal ways in which the process of prosecuting an individual for witchcraft might be initiated. The first was through the accusations of neighbours. The second was through accusations made by other accused witches. Either or both might occur, but although the initial impetus came frequently from another witch, the evidence of neighbours was regarded in law as more significant. The process by which a witch was made was the same as that by which she was convicted.

Indeed it is hard to overemphasize the importance of reputation in the production of a witch in Scotland. Alongside the individual charges of malefice, supporting them and finally summing them up we find frequently that the accused was 'of ill fame', 'a rank witch', 'by habit and repute a witch', 'of evil repute', 'had been long suspected of witchcraft', was 'brutit' with witchcraft, or, in legal terminology was of *mala fama* or *diffamatio*. While in modern jurisprudence it is thought improper to consider the character of the accused in the court proceedings, in seventeenth-century Scotland it was a legal virtue. Reputation was considered by lawyers and demonologists to be in itself a sign (though not a proof) of witchcraft. Sir George Mackenzie, while accepting that lawyers did take cognisance of *mala fama*, deplored this:

> consider how much fancy does influence ordinary judges in the trials of this crime, for none now labour under any extraordinary Disease, but it is instantly said to come by witchcraft, and then the next old deform'd or envyed woman is presentlie charged with it; from this ariseth confused noise of her guilt, called *diffamatio* by Lawyers who make it a ground for seizure . . .[1]

It was not only in witchcraft cases that societal labelling was an important element. It was a standard method of assessing guilt. Arnot was still lamenting this in the late eighteenth century:

> 'Habit and repute' is a very dangerous doctrine of the law of Scotland, at this minute in full force, by which a man may be hanged altho' hardly any charge be exhibited against him, but that he has a bad character. For instance, if a man is charged with

stealing a pair of old shoes, value threepence, and with being by habit
and repute a thief, if the jury find such indictment proved, or such
prisoner guilty, the Court would by law be bound to sentence the
prisoner to be hanged; if my temerity may be pardoned, for
supposing that any such thing exists as a precise established rule of
criminal law in Scotland.[2]

The lack of such 'habit and repute' could work in favour of the
accused when other things were against her. This is demonstrated in
the cases of Janet Thomson and Marean Yool who came to trial with a
group of witches from Tranent in 1659. The Justice General asked for
more information on them because he was not satisfied with their
confessions of meeting the Devil and other witches. The elders of the
parish quizzed the parishioners for evidence of their having practised
malefice or uttered spells, but none was forthcoming. Their neighbours
declared them to be of good reputation and the charge was dropped.[3]
Accusation by another suspected or convicted witch, though the
process often started this way, was regarded as the weakest form of
accusation. George Guidlet in 1671 declared in an appeal against his
imprisonment that there was no stain on his reputation: 'ther having
nevir been so much as a Dilation (formal accusation) of ane dyeing
witch against him'[4] and was set free. Blameless reputation, however,
could not always save them. In Carron, in Stirlingshire in 1670, it was
noted that the wife of one Goodaile, a cooper in the parish,[5] was accused
by several witches who had been burned, and was herself executed.
She in turn 'delated many Women, some of them of good repute,
who afterwards confessed, and died so'.[6]

The point at which reputation and accusation led to arrest is hard to
identify. Except for those cases in which the same witch is noted more
than once in the surviving records, we have only the evidence of a
particular case collected at one point in time, and it is not always clear
which of the accusations was the first one in time, nor which was the
one which set the inquisitorial process going. For proceedings to go
ahead it was necessary for an approach to be made by an individual or a
number of individuals to the Kirk session. In a number of cases the
matter was dealt with at this level. The accused could be admonished,
fined, possibly banished. A possible redress was for the accused to
counter-accuse of slander. In some instances slander cases came prior to
any formal accusation, simply on the basis of spreading false rumour.
In the vast majority of these slander cases the class relationship was
reversed. The person accused of slander would be in a dependent
position. It was possible for the dependent person in a disturbed
relationship to press an accusation of witchcraft, but hard to make the
accusation stick unless there was already some existing reputation. To
be accused of witchcraft at Kirk session level, however, did no-one's
reputation any good. Even if the charge was refuted or the accused

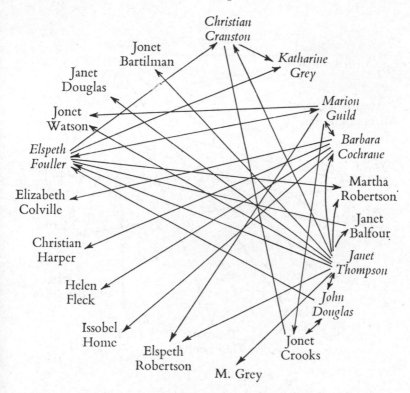

let off with a caution, the fact of having been previously accused encouraged the build-up of reputation.

While some witches appear from their dossiers to have been on an inevitable path towards arrest in an ever-deteriorating relationship with their neighbours, others seem to have been caught up in a mass hunt. The impetus may have come from laird, minister, or tortured suspect. Under those conditions any isolated quarrel may have been enough to bring them into the system. The diagrams above show the networks of two East Lothian hunts of 1659.

Whether the impulse came from above or below the Kirk session then had to decide whether or not to take the matter further. There was a limit to what they themselves could legally do if they wished to bring the witch to justice. Of course the Kirk session could in fact do a great deal of damage to an accused witch if they so wished. They could effectively take away her livelihood by banishment which would turn her into a vagabond or wage labourer. Sometimes the Kirk session imposed minor punishments for particular offences. They

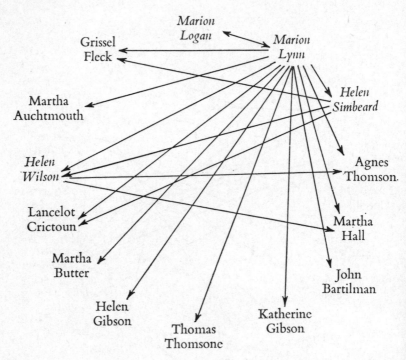

might admonish or fine. If, however, they wanted to rid the community of that particular witch, or if they were actively looking for witches, then it was necessary for the Kirk session to collect the type of evidence which would impress the Privy Council or Parliament.

The collection of evidence began with statements about malefice and ill fame given by other parishioners to the Kirk session. Sometimes the witnesses would be asked to repeat them under oath to magistrates or other officials. The witch would probably be imprisoned in the tolbooth if it was a burgh; but normally in the kirk steeple or in some barn or outhouse. Katherine Rowan was moved from the tolbooth of Culross to the steeple in 1643 'that room might be made for others delated as guilty of sorcery and witchcraft'.[9] There were no purpose-built gaols in seventeenth-century Scotland since imprisonment was not a standard punishment, it was normally a pre-trial convenience. These *ad hoc* prisons were not necessarily very secure and escapes seem to have been common. Imprisoned witches would be guarded by neighbours paid to watch them. Sometimes this was the local locksmith who might double as hangman. During this period the minister and elders would come in and interrogate them and attempt to secure a confession.

They were well aware of the type of evidence that would convict a witch in the High Court or obtain a commission from the Privy Council. Malefice alone would not normally be enough; it was an indication. *Mala fama* similarly was a sign rather than a proof, though *mala fama* was particularly useful in legal terms in that it could be made to imply a long-standing pact with the Devil. The main purpose of the preliminary informal inquisition was to extract a confession of the Demonic Pact, which was regarded by the courts as the essence of witchcraft. Confessions of particular acts of sorcery or witchcraft were all useful, but these were usually additional to the essential confession of witchcraft as the law understood it. The courts were properly satisfied only by a statement that the accused had renounced her baptism and become the Devil's servant.

Various methods were used to extract the confession. Officials used sleep deprivation, pricking for the witch's mark, threats of torture, and direct torture. The purpose of torture was either to inflict punishment or to extract confession of guilt or information about the guilt of others. Scottish practice in this as in other legal matters seems to stand somewhere between the English and the continental. The English officially condemned torture and though the English practice was somewhat different they were certainly inhibited by the illegality of torture.[10] Roman Law seems to have taken torture for granted, though in practice there may have been some of the ambiguity which certainly surrounded its use in Scotland.[11]

Scotland had a number of standard instruments of torture, but it did not have the rack, which was the regular instrument used by the inquisition, and there seems always to have been anxiety about the desirability or usefulness of torture. It is possible that the Scots actually invented sleep deprivation as a means of extracting information because of this ambiguity about direct torture. Known as 'waking' or 'watching' the witch, sleep deprivation was an almost routine method of extracting confession of the Demonic Pact. The Culross witches of 1643 for whom Katharine Rowan was moved were 'to be warded, watched by gentlemen, money to be contribute for their necessities'.[12] Two years later at nearby Dunfermline the Kirk session register records

Arrangement for watching landward witches. To begin at 6.00 p.m. for 24 hours. Any failure penalised 24s. To begin at Muirtown [near Auchterarder] and so to continue through so many of the touns of that quarter till the next session day. Masters of households to come or send enough honest men, magistrates and landward baillies to assure adequate numbers, remit 6s/day for four watches of Margaret Donald, the witch. Five days total.[13]

In 1649 the Presbytery recommended to the magistrates of Dunfermline that incarcerated witches be constantly waked and watched, 'and that they be dealt with as others in the lyke case are in other paroches.'[14] Margaret Thomsone appealed to the Privy Council in 1644 complaining against the tutor of Calder and the minister of the parish for 'waking her the space of twenty days naked, and having nothing on her but a sackcloath and that they had kept her in the stocks separate from all company and worldly comfort'.[15] Many references to expenses for the watchers demonstrate its routine nature. The authorities started to have doubts about it about the same time as they were campaigning against direct torture. From 1662 on, instructions to avoid torture were commonplace and a commission of 1677 to try witches in Dumbarton were directed that 'If found guilty without the use of torture hindering them to sleep or other indirect means, then justice may be administered upon them'.[16]

There is some individual variation in the amount of sleep deprivation required before hallucination begins but not very much. It is curious that the authorities thought this a reasonable method of getting at the truth because they were well aware of the hallucinogenic effects. The Jesuit, John Ogilvie, in 1616 was 'compellit and with holden perforce from sleep, to the great perturbation of his brayne and to compell him *ad delirium*'.[17] The magistrates of Dunfermline begged the Privy Council for another three days grace in which time they were sure that the witches would have cracked through sleep deprivation.

The application of direct torture which frequently accompanied or succeeded sleep deprivation was in a sense more logical. Persons threatened with pain or more pain might still be lucid. In the 1590s the government reinforced by James VI made a positive recommendation that torture should be used to extract a confession and the names of accomplices. He argued that the Devil had such a grip on his servants that only extreme pain could cause this grip to slip. Nor was torture reserved for witchcraft cases. It was used in many criminal cases where there were no witnesses; it was used against the Covenanters and it was used in other political cases in the reign of James II. As Duke of York he particularly enjoyed being present on such occasions.[18] It is also clear that, as in France, it was often merely threatened. Simon Graham was accused of arson in 1624, and the instructions of the Privy Council were to 'examine the said Symon and threattin him with tourtour. Bot yf threating will not serve to draw a cleir confession oute of him, we are weele pleased, yf so you shall think convenient that he salbe put in the bootis'.[19]

The details of the tortures used are fairly familiar. The 'boots' whereby legs were crushed, sometimes known as the cashielaws, the pinniewinks (thumbscrews), burning with hot irons, 'thrawing' with a rope, the 'turcas' for tearing out nails, were all mentioned in the complaints and appeals of imprisoned witches. Some complaints were less about specific torture to induce confession than about general brutality. John Trinche's complaint to the Privy Council about the treatment meted out to his mother, Marion Hardie, who had since died, is typical. He said that Duncan Kendla and others had gone to the pit (place of imprisonment) and without a warrant against her

> put violent hands in her persoun, band her armes with towes, and so threw the same about that they disjointed and mutilat both her armes and made the sinews to loupe asunder and thairafter with their haill force drew ane great tow about her waist, kuist her on her backe and with thair knees they birsed, bruised, and punced her so that she was not able to stirre, strake the heid of ane speir throw her left foote to the effusionn of her blood in great quantitie and perrell of her lyffe. Wherethrow she lay bedfast in great pane and dolour a long tyme thairafter.[20]

The case of direct torture which has always attracted most attention from commentators was that of Alison Balfour of Orkney whose aged husband, son and seven year old daughter were tortured in front of her in 1594 'to this effect that hir husband and bairnis beand swa tormentit besyde hir mycht move hir to mak ony Confessioun for their relief'.[21] Accounts of the torture of relatives of principal suspects are commonplace now in reports by Amnesty from Latin America. In late sixteenth-century Scotland it was regarded as exceptionally barbarous.

Serious disquiet about torture as a means of getting at the truth seems to have been first expressed in November 1649. The Committee of Estates (operating in the Parliamentary recess) gave a commission to Sir Alexander Murray of Blackbarron, Sir David Murray of Stane-hope, and several other lairds for the trial of several witches from villages south of Peebles, orders them 'to use all legal and accustomed wayes according to the Lawes of the kingdome And to do everie thing necessarie and lawfull quich may conduce to the tryall of the said persones Provyding they use no torturing to force them to confesse'.[22]

The English judges made a further attempt to put a stop to the use of torture in witchcraft cases in 1652,[23] but it was in general use again during the Restoration hunt and was proclaimed illegal by the Privy Council in 1662.[24] This did not effectively stop the practice, but the registration of governmental disapproval in place of the governmental approval of the earlier witch-hunts was a significant change. For some time before this, however, a confession extracted 'without torture' was regarded as being more valid than one with.

Both deprivation of sleep and the infliction of pain were directed to the extraction of a confession and the incrimination of others. The various ordeals were different. They were intended to provide additional circumstantial evidence of guilt. Swimming the witch was an ordeal

widely known on the continent and in England. The witch had her
wrists tied to her ankles and was thrown into the water. If she sank
she was innocent; if she floated she was a witch. The Devil would keep
her up. The purpose of this was not to drown the suspect. Ropes and
planks were kept handy lest she sank. However, despite the evidence
of place names, such as 'witches' pool' in Kirriemuir, and despite
David Livingstone having explained it to his followers on the Zambesi
as an ancient Scottish custom,[25] it seems to have been a very unusual
ordeal in Scotland. The witches' lake in St Andrews was a bay of the
sea so-called from the ashes of witches having been thrown there.[26]
This may have been the origin of other witches' pools. There is an
unreliable reference to the swimming ordeal in Atholl in 1597.[27]

The ordeal of bierricht in which the accused was ordered to lay
hands on the corpse of someone he or she was supposed to have
murdered was occasionally used in Scottish witchcraft cases. A similar
type of evidence was used in the case of Elspeth McEwen of Dalry.
'One of the most convincing parts of the evidence against the accused
was, that the minister's horse which was sent to bring her up for trial
trembled with fear when she mounted and sweated drops of blood'.[28]

A type of ordeal was also used in cases of possession when the
possessed person was taken into the presence of the accused and
immediately threw a fit, but by far the commonest of the ordeals in
Scotland was pricking for the witch's mark. In England the search
was for supernumerary nipples at which familiars might suck. These
again were rarely presented as evidence in the Scottish trials. It was the
mark they looked for nearly every time.

The witch pricker therefore was a key figure in the process of
gathering evidence. His role was to examine the suspect for unusual
bodily marks and then to test these marks by pricking them to find
out whether they were insensible. The theory was that the Devil
consummated the Pact by nipping the witch, and that the permanent
mark thus made was insensible to pain and would not bleed. The
finding of such a mark constituted evidence of the Pact.

In 1643 Janet Barker was investigated before her trial in Edinburgh:

James Scobie, indweller in Mussilburgh, being sent for and brocht
in before Jonet Baker as he that had knowledge in finding out and
trying the devillis mark he fand out the said mark betwix her
schoulderis in the quhilk he did thrust ane lang preane [pin] the
quhilk preane abaid stiking thrie quarteris of ane hour, and yet the
said preane was nawayis felt sensible be the said Jonet and at the
drawing thair of schoe confessit that nocht only sche hirself but
also umquhile [deceased] Jonet Cranstoun, had resavit the devillis
mark about the same part quhair sche was markit.[29]

There are many similar descriptions of pricking for the witches'
mark. The pricker George Cathie in Lanark 'by consent of the suspected

women . . . did prik pinnes in everie one of them and in diverse without
paine the pinne was put in as the witnesses can testify'.[30] Jonet Paiston
was pricked by John Kincaid, the most famous of all the prickers.

> She did nather find the preins when it was put into any of the said
> marks nor did they blood when they were taken out again: and
> when shoe was asked quhair shoe thocht the preins were put in,
> schoe pointed at a pairt of hir body distant from the place quhair
> the preins were put in, they being lang preins of thrie inches or
> theirabout in length.[31]

Alexander Bogs was reported to have tried one woman, 'and finds the
mark on the middle of her back, wherin he thrust a great brass pin
of which she was not sensible nor did any blood follow when the pin
was drawn out'.[32]

The absence of sensation may sometimes have been caused by the
shock of the experience to which they were being subjected, but the
prickers were undoubtedly a consciously fraudulent body of men with
knowledge of anatomy. They understood the principle of confused
sensation and which parts of the body could be most successfully
assaulted.[33] They may have had knowledge of the points used by
acupuncturists. The possibility of fraud was well recognized by the
time of the Restoration hunt. In 1662 not only Kincaid himself, but
also a Mr. Paterson, and John Dickson, were all exposed as having
used trickery some of the time.[34] Paterson and Dickson both turned out
to be women in disguise, which suggests that witch pricking was a
male preserve. Paterson was responsible for dealing with the suspects
(fourteen women and one man) brought to him (her) by the Chisholm.
It was said that

> after rubbing over the whole body with his palms he slipt in the
> pin and it seems with shame and feare being dasht they felt it not,
> but he left it in the flesh deep to the head, and desired them to
> find it and take it out. It is sure some witches were discovered but
> many honest men and women were blotted and broak by the
> trick.[35]

The accused themselves were also aware that the process might not
be entirely fair. Elsbeth Maxwell, mentioned earlier as a sufferer from
reputation through association who was tried in 1650 in Dumfries with
six others,

> being tryit be the man who professes to discover witches by satans
> mark, befoir shoe put off hir shoes and stockings said God help us
> we have meslet (blotched) skins we sit neir the fyer, and being
> blindfolded notwithstanding that shoe was sensible in the shyne
> and shrieked yet being questioned thairafter whare she fand pain,

shoe could not point the part nor did any blood appeir at all, the
pin being thrust in place full of vains and sinews in her leg . . .[36]

Showing evidence of feeling pain was not enough to prove innocence. Alison Patersone who was tried at the same time as Elsbeth
Maxwell, 'being prickit on the gaird of the richt arm she feanit to be
sensible bot no signe of blood followit'.[37] The methods used by that
particular pricker became clearer when their fellow suspect Bessie
Graham was pricked:

The said Bessie Graham being tryed on the Lefft shoulder thair wes
no signe of blood nether could she tell the place quhair she was
thrust and at the same tyme being twitched vpoun the shoulder
with the finger of ane that stood by she seamit to be more sensible
of that nor of the pin quhairwith she was pricket.[38]

Despite the exposure of many professional prickers the system
retained its credibility throughout the hunt. As early as the 1590–91
hunt Agnes Sampson was pricked for the witch's mark. As late as 1699
the Glasgow synod were discussing the expediency of having 'those
in readinesse at the Justiciar Court that has skill to try the insensible
mark'.[39] Pricking was so routine that many indictments simply noted
that the accused had confessed and the mark been found.

Witch pricking was a link between popular and official belief. It was
normally done in the witch's own locality and was a visual aid by
which the populace were tutored in the relationship with the Devil.
It was sometimes voluntarily resorted to by the accused as an ordeal
through which her innocence could be established.

Catie Wilson of Lauder was imprisoned in 1630, 'her husband', not
in this case herself, 'being content she should be tried by jobing'.[40] As
late as 1718 Margaret Olsone in Thurso was pricked and should have
the last word:

Upon a vulgar report of witches having the devil's marks in their
bodies, Margaret Olsone being tried in the shoulders, where there
were several small spots, some read, some bleuish, after a needle
was driven in with great force almost to the eye, she felt it not. Mr.
Innes, Mr. Oswald, ministers, and several honest women, and
Bailzie Forbes were witnesses to this. And further, that while the
needle was in her shoulder as foresaid, she said, 'Am not I ane
honest woman now?'[41]

Indeed she was not, but her fate is not known. For the most unfortunate the next stage was the application to the Privy Council,
Parliament, or in 1649 Parliament's Committee of Estates, for a
commission to try the witch. Another possibility was direct recourse
to the Court of Justiciary or its travelling Circuit Courts. The Privy

Council commission was preferred and the greatest number of witches were processed in this manner. The advantage of this to the local community was that the witch did not have to be taken to Edinburgh; she could be tried and executed locally. This was less expensive and was more likely to result in a conviction.

It was at this point in the proceedings that the central ruling class in the form of the Privy Councillors came into the process, though sometimes the cases were coming in in response to their own exhortations. They would consider the evidence, and either ask for more or grant a commission to a group of local landlords and grand tenants to hold a trial and carry out the sentence. Sometimes this group would be headed by the local sheriff, but this would not make it a normal sheriff court or baron court. Its powers were derived from the Privy Council Commission. This was true even in the regalities but did not affect the normal rights of regalities as they made clear in a case of 1643:

> The Lords of Secreit Counsell declares that the Commission this day past for tryell of some witches in the Queensferry sall be no wayes prejudiciall to the Earle of Dunfermline his right of regalities of the lordship of Dunfermline within quhilk the burgh of the Queensferie is comprehended.[42]

The arguments and evidence used at the trials are discussed in the chapters on the belief system. The court would fix a date for the execution, usually only a few days ahead. This allowed just enough time to engage a hangman, usually the local locksmith, and arrange for supplies of fuel.

From lists of expenses for the burning of witches and from a few eyewitness accounts we have some information about the procedure. It was a great public occasion. The whole community would be in attendance, and stakes were needed, in 1597 in Aberdeen for example, 'to withstand the press of the pepill.'[43] The execution was frequently preceded or accompanied by a day or days of fasting and a round of sermon preaching to which all the ministers within reasonable travelling distance would contribute. In 1628 in Peebles Alexander Dikisoun even extracted a pair of shoes price 20 shillings from the burgh for this purpose.[44]

The witch was normally first strangled (wirreit) and then her dead or unconscious body was burned, sometimes in a tar barrel. It took sixteen loads of peat, a relatively low heat fuel, sometimes supplemented by wood and coals, to burn a witch. Although prior strangulation by garotting was usual witches were sometimes burned alive. An account of witches being burned at Brechin in 1608 describes how

> they were brunt quick (alive) eftir sic ane crewell maner, that sum of thame deit in despair, renunceand and blasphemeand; and

PROCESSING A WITCH★

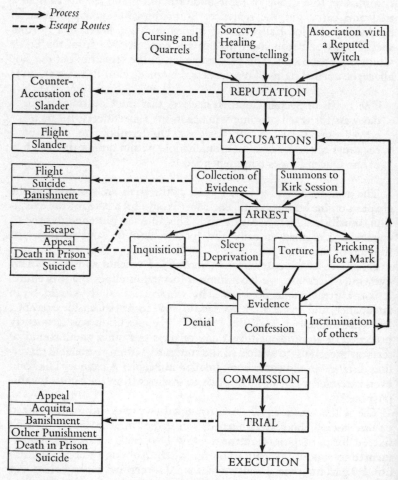

★ Adapted from a model in S. Box *Deviance, Reality and Society*, London 1971.

utheris, half brunt, brak out of the fyre, and wes cast quick in it
agane, quhill they wer brunt to the deid.[45]

Of the aftermath of a witch-hunt we have little knowledge. The
psychological cleansing effect on a community has been suggested but
this is speculation. One could speculate equally about the tainted
relatives, the orphaned children, the questioning, the sense of anti-
climax. All we have in the records is the counting of the financial cost.

Witch-hunting was only cost-effective if the witch, through her
attack on life and property, was herself regarded as an economic threat.
The people who gained from a witch-hunt were the minor officials:
the witch watchers and jailers, the organizers of an execution, the clerks
of the courts, and above all the witch prickers. In an arrangement with
John Dicksone (alias Christian Caddell) he was engaged to be present
for a year from March 1662 in the neighbourhood of Elgin. He was
to be paid six shillings expenses a day and a bonus of 'sex pundis
scottis fur the persone that sal be tryed be him and fund guyltie having
ye foresaid mark'.[46] This seems to have been the standard rate for the
job. John Kincaid was paid 'VI lib Scotts' in 1649 for 'brodding'
Margaret Dunham in Lauder and a further three for 'meat and drink
and wyne to him and his man'.[47]

The Lord Advocate, his Depute, and other prosecuting lawyers
were also offered a bonus for convictions in the Restoration hunt.[48]
Apart from these payments there were few to gain financially from a
witch-hunt. Partly because of them the total process of pursuing a
witch to execution could be expensive for the parish. The witch had
to be fed and guarded prior to execution. Messengers to Edinburgh
required a fee and expenses. The commission itself had to be paid for.
The hangman and his assistant required payment, and those who supplied
rope and fuel and refreshments for the hangman. A witch's estate was
automatically forfeited to the crown, but this was hardly a major
source of revenue. The locality would extract their expenses first. In
1649 the expenses for imprisoning and executing Margaret Dunham
were 92 pounds 14 shillings (Scots), and from this they deducted 27
pounds 'quilk the said umquile (former) Margrit Dinham had of her
ain',[49] leaving the parish of Lauder a deficit of some 65 pounds 14
shillings. In some cases the expenses were reclaimed from the witch's
surviving relatives. David Aikman of Nether Williamston in Midlothian paid the Kirk session for expenses for his wife's execution in
1644,[50] and a year earlier the burgh of Pittenweem had claimed the
liability of the relatives for expenses. John Dawson had to make payment of his grassmail (the grass that will keep a cow for a season) and
£40 Scots for the expense of executing his wife.[51] John Crombie was
ordered to pay £80 Scots for the expense of executing his,[52] and
Thomas Cook had to pay 'three score of pounds Scots' for the execution
of his mother, Margaret Horsburgh.[53]

In 1649 the Presbytery of Dunfermline petitioned Parliament for financial assistance in dealing with the 'great and daily discovery of witches within their bounds' in that 'commissions for putting them to an assize cannot be obtained without great charges'.[54] Disposing of a witch was nearly always an expense to the local authority rather than a source of revenue. If neither the estate of the witch nor the means of her family were adequate, the bill was met by laird, presbytery, or burgh. Those who profited were pricker, hangman, and central government.

Previous accounts of Scottish witch-hunting have stressed the cruelty and inexorability of the system. It was assumed that under the inquisitorial system derived from continental procedures a witch once named would be successfully pursued to the death. The system was undoubtedly intensely cruel. The only humanity that appears in the records comes from the appeals by children and husbands of the accused against their imprisonment. It was not, however, inexorable. It was savage, random, and inefficient.

There were various escape routes from the process. The principal ones were a counter charge of slander against the accusers, a good defence in the Kirk session, flight before arrest, escape after arrest, legal appeal, and suicide. Ways out provided by the system itself were admonition, minor penalties, banishment, acquittal, or death in prison. From the point of view of the accused escape through flight or banishent was a very serious matter, probably resulting in vagabondage. Suicide or death in prison (which are not always distinguishable in the records) may not seem like escape from the system at all. From the point of view of the pursuers, however, the system had been cheated, and debate followed as to the proper way of disposing of the body of an accused but not yet convicted witch.

A slander charge was the first line of defence and was most successfully pursued by the more powerful. William Clerk complained to the Kirk session at Culross in 1643 that his daughter was being abused by the people 'in calling her a witch bird'.[55] He may perhaps not have done her a favour in that such a complaint could give more substance to an evil reputation, but some found it worth doing.

In the Aberdeen Kirk session minuted for 7th October 1604 Helen Gib, the spouse of Charles Wilson, complained that Helen Cassie had 'maist schamfullie sclandert the said Helen Gib upon the hie streit in calling hir ane commoun witche be practizing the same in sic godles maner as the witness culd testifie'. Helen Cassie defended herself by saying that she had not actually spoken those words, but that she had seen Helen Gib practising sorcery with drops of water in a cauldron. It was Cassie's word against Gib, and it turned out that she had formerly been a servant to Gib. Cassie was condemned to make publick repentence for her slander.[56]

Also in Aberdeen, on the 8th October 1684, there was recorded in the Register of Convictions of Delinquents, a slander case between social equals.

> Elspet Ffrazor spouse to Andrew Perrie taillior in the said burgh being convict by the depositions of famous witnesses of injuring Andrew Brown taillior in the same by saying he was the devill's servant and in blooding and sticking of him in the head amerciat the said Elspet in [sum left blank] made to be payed to the dean of Gild for the use of the toune and ordained hir to be imprisoned while the same should be payed and to seeke pardon of the partie injured before the baillies.[57]

The relative likelihood in relation to rank of charges being made to stick, however, is shown in the account given by Fountainhall of the East Lothian cases of 1678.

> Eight or ten witches, all (except one or two) poor miserable like women were pannelled, some of them were brought out of Sir Robert Hepburn of Keith's lands, other out of Ormiston, Crighton, and Pentcaitland parishes. The first of them were delated by those two who were burnt in Saltpreston in May 1678 and they delated and named the rest, as also put forth seven in the Lonehead of Lasswade; and if they had been permitted were ready to file by their delation, sundry gentlewomen and others of fashion; but the Justices discharged them, thinking it either the product of malice, or melancholy, or the Devil's deception, in representing such persons as present at their field meetings who truly were not there. Yet this was cried out on as a prelimiting them from discovering these enemies of mankind.[58]

For those who were unable to press slander charges successfully, the best remedy was flight. The Porteous Roll of Ayr had a list of persons in 1658 who were to be arrested and examined for witchcraft. When they went to the homes of Margaret Cunningham, Agnes Mortoune, Jonet Holmes, Margaret Jameson, Violet Guillieland, Jonet Hamilton and John Walker, there were 'none such there when officers went to summon them for trial'. Jonet Wilsonne, Christian Meving, Annabell Gottray, Jennet Tait, Bessie Fullerton, Margarat Laurymer and Margrat Allan, were found to be dead.[59] It is not clear from the record whether they had been long dead, had committed suicide, or whether relatives were covering their flight.

In one case in 1626 Elizabeth Ross of Weymis fled as far as England and the Privy Council wrote to all justices of the peace and magistrates in England to aid in her recapture.[60] In 1628 the provost of Tain was given a commission to apprehend and try four witches 'long suspected of witchcraft and who have all fled from justice'.[61]

Some managed to make their escape from prison. The elders in the parish of Mid Calder were 'to mak tryell and search for ane woman callit Marioun Ramsay quha is fled out of Prissoun in Leith and is suspect of witchcraft'.[62] Not all managed to make their escape good. Marion Durie's husband Robert Brown had some influence in the Presbytery of Dunfermline. The Committee of Estates in 1649 considered a supplication from the presbytery to remove Marion 'out of the said steeple and put her in some other prison house'. They went on to point out that 'the work of God in discovering and punishing that abominable sin is greatly obstructed if ease and liberty be provyded for or any incuragence given to persones so tainted with that gross obbomination. And seeing the said Marion since she was incarcerated brybed the watch and escaped and since has been taken again at Burntilland and the devell mark fund in dyverse parts of her body . . . to permit carcerate for the said cryme to a confession Without prescrepvency a depute day bot leaving them to the best opportunity according to the nature of the business.' They also asked that her husband be charged expenses.[63]

If escape from prison was not possible then an insistence on innocence coupled with an appeal through lawyer or relative sometimes succeeded. Given the pressures upon the suspects during their imprisonment it is remarkable that so many of them asserted their innocence to the end. Not only were they subjected to ordeals and tortures, they were often cold, and hungry. One brother and sister were fined for trying to visit their imprisoned mother. Some were left lingering in prison because of the slowness of the legal process or because they had been forgotten. Grissel Rae, Margaret McGuffock and Janet Howat complained in 1672 that they had been transported from Dumfries to Kircudbright 'wher they have even since continued in a dark dungeon in a most miserable conditione being always at the point of starving having nothing of ther own nor nothing allowed them for ther sustenance. And one of ther number Issobel Pain who was in prisonis with them dyed the last winter through cold hunger and other inconveniencess of the prison And the petioners are in such . . . miserie that it ware better for them to be dead than alyve.'[64]

Problems seem to have arisen when there was not enough evidence to obtain a commission or to convict but setting the witch free would cause trouble. David Rotson petitioned on behalf of his wife Margaret Philip to the Kirk session of Dunfermline in 1649, that she 'so long being detained in ward and under suspicion of witchcraft and sterving for want ather that she be fund guilty or clean of that crime'. She was freed on caution and banished from the parish.[65]

Appeals b came increasingly successful after the end of the Restoration hunt, but even during the national panics successful appeals were recorded. Some processes were delayed or abandoned on grounds o pregnancy. Isobel Falconer of Eyemouth tried this on. She 'mos subtilie and falslie alledgest and confidentle and impudently affirme that sho wes with chyld, and upon the falce informatioun procured an warrant from our Councaill for continency of hir tryall till she wer delyverit of her birthe; quhilk as yitt now after mony yearies is not done and meanwhile sho continewis in hir divilishe practises'.[66]

Others were released without action on their part. Some accused witches were liberated during the pre-trial proceedings. The lawyers at the High Court or the Privy Councillors simply decided that there was not enough evidence to warrant proceeding. The likelihood of this happening depended on the type of external political factors described in Chapters 5 and 6. During the Cromwellian period such abandonment of proceedings against witches was common. In October 1652 the English Commissioners for Administration of Justice investigated a number of witches. Two of them described the tortures they had been put to before they had confessed, and claimed that four other had died under the torture. The judges appointed the sheriff, ministers, and tormentors to be found out, and to have an account of the grounds for this cruelty.[67] But even at other times when the English were not around to protect them, witches sometimes were liberated before the trial on the grounds that the evidence was not sufficient. Both this and the possibility of acquittal increased as the century wore on. The overall acquittal rate in the High Court trials was nearly 50 per cent.[68] Others were cautioned, banished, or branded.

The only way of ensuring that reputation would not return you to the trial process was death. Many witches died in prison. Elizabeth Fouller, one of those accused in Tranent in 1659, died there of 'ane fluu'.[69] Many committed suicide. It is not always clear which deaths were through neglect, which through torture or ill treatment, and which were suicide. Either way the system was cheated of a victim and the community of the psychodrama of an execution.

Janet Hill hanged herself in prison before her trial in 1629. Her body was dragged at a horse's tail to the Gallowlee and buried under the gallows.[70] When Janet Smellie died in the tolbooth in Ayr in 1650 the town council of Ayr on the advice of the minister Mr. Robert Adair ordained 'that her corpes sall be drawn upon ane slaid to the gallows foot, and burnt in ashes'.[71] The friends of Lady Pittathrow, one of the gentry who got caught up in a feud between the Inverkeithing minister Walter Bruce and the secular authorities and committed suicide in prison, were reprimanded for giving her a normal burial.[72] Margaret Kirkwood of Haddington hanged herself in 1673. 'Some say shee was so strangled by the devill and witches', observed Fountainhall.[73] In such an escape from the processes of God the Devil was thought to look after his own.

CHAPTER TEN

TWO CLASSIC CASES

From their Circuit Court trial on Monday 15th May, 1671, until their execution on the afternoon of Thursday, 18th May, two women of uncertain age, Janet Macmurdoch and Elspeth Thomson, were imprisoned together in the tolbooth of Dumfries. They came from neighbouring parishes, but there is no particular reason to suppose that they had met before or known of each other's existence, although the areas over which their reputation had spread overlapped.

The introduction of a small-scale study is a reminder, amid discussions of trends, figures, explanations, national purposes, and general functions, that every successful accusation of witchcraft represented at best social misery, at worst tragedy and death for the individual so accused. These particular cases were chosen because they are relatively well documented, though not well known, and because they illustrate the kind of case which can be regarded as most typically Scottish. The women were accused by neighbours of specific acts of malefice and at the same time of being of evil reputation. The dossier was collected by local officials. At the Circuit Court the central accusation of the indictment was that of having made the Demonic Pact. We have no account of how the focus of the accusation was so transformed, but the gulf between local and official concerns is clearly shown. The documents for the cases fall into two groups: the original depositions made by neighbours, and the final indictments which contain these original depositions with the additional legal requirements for a conviction. The substance, though not the *ipsissima verba* of their confessions are contained in these.[1]

Janet Macmurdoch was married to James Hendrie, a tenant farmer in Airds, by Loch Ken in Kircudbrightshire. The accusations against her were collected under oath, listed and signed in April 1671 to prepare the case for the Circuit Court judges. Her first accuser was the intermediary for her feudal superior, John Moor of Barlay, aged about forty. He was baron-baillie for her landlord the laird of Broughtone, and the initial trouble between them was over payment of rent. John Moor had in May 1665 impounded her livestock for the unpaid rent; she 'promised him an evil turn', and shortly after a cow and a calf of his had died. When he challenged her with this she told him 'he should get ane worse turn', and soon after his child died 'of an extraordinary sickness, sweating to death'. John Moor added that she had been reputed a witch and been 'under evil report' for many years. Her second accuser was John Murray of Laik, aged sixty. (The form 'of Laik' as opposed to 'in', means that like John Moor he was of owner-occupier (bonnet laird) status). He claimed that about a year before he had caused Janet to fall 'by ane accidentall twitch of the foot'. One might think that given Janet's reputation that was excessively careless of him, but whatever the nature of the encounter she went away cursing. Within the space of five or six weeks two of his calves 'ran wod (mad) and ramished to death', and later one of his horses met the same fate. He further added that she had been under evil report for a long time.

Robert Brown in Castleton, aged about forty-six, added his testimony. About three years before he had turned Janet's animals off his grass where she had carelessly or deliberately let them wander. She angrily told him that he should not have so many nolt (black cattle) to eat the next year's grass. Within a month his wife died of 'ane strange and sudden dissease', and the curse was fulfilled more precisely when within the year he lost fifteen nolt and three horses. He also noted that she was under evil report. John Morries in Clean quarrelled with her for a similar reason. He had 'poinded her goods', that is, appropriated some of her livestock, in retaliation for Janet's horse eating his corn. She had gone off 'discontent and murmuring' though the witnesses did not know what she had said. Since this was supposed to have happened nine years before this is not surprising, but the very next day before midday John Morries' child was drowned in a peat bog. He too added that she was of evil reputation.

The accusation of William Gordon of Minibouie, another fairly substantial farmer, echoes even more closely than John Morries that of Robert Brown. Like Robert Brown he had chased Janet's livestock off his grass and she had followed scolding. She told him that she hoped he should not have so many geir (cattle) as he had then to eat the next grass. This happened at harvest time, and before the following Beltane (May Day) twelve of his oxen and seven or eight of his horses died. Since this was the same year that Robert Brown lost a lot of horses and cattle (1668) there may have been some local disease of livestock that year.

Not all her accusers were men. Margaret Maclellan, a fifty-one year old married woman in Boghall, employed Janet's daughter, Isobell Tagit, as a servant. Isobell had been sent to muck out the byre, and Margaret Maclellan, thinking that she had been overlong, went out to see what she was doing and found her sitting in the middle of it playing with dung. She reproved her and suggested that she was using some of her mother's devilish tricks. Isobell reported this to Janet who came round to Boghall and said to Margaret 'Why called you me and my daughter witches, for you shall get some other thing to think upon?' Within a month of this threat Margaret Maclellan's husband took 'ane extraordinary sickness and disease and continued therein by the space of seventeen days and thereafter grew stupid and senseless'. This apparently continued until Janet 'came to his house undesired'. After Margaret had given her meat and drink Janet said that this, 'had comforted her heart, and god send you comfort of your husband'. After this reconciliation Margaret's husband

> suddenlie grew better in so much as he turned himself in the bed whereas formerlie he was insensible and could not do the same unless he was lifted by four men. At the very same instant his best mare died and he cried out during the time of his sickness, before he began to recover, 'what had you done with his horse for his best mare was blown away'. And this was before the mare died.

Janet does not appear to have had a general reputation as a healer, but she was credited with the ability to remove an illness which she was responsible for and transfer it to an animal. It was her refusal to do this which was the last straw in her relationship with Jean Sprot and Robert Cairnes: a couple who, unlike her other accusers, lived in the same farm-toun as Janet, and who would have been closely involved with her in the distribution of strips of land and the sharing of equipment.

About seven years before the collection of the accusations she came to Jean Sprot to borrow meal and was refused because Robert advised his wife to have nothing to do with one of her reputation. She told Jean that she should rue it more than the worth of the meal, and that night the milk of Jean's cow was mixed with blood and flesh. The next trouble came a year later when Janet came to see her after one of her lambs which was being herded by Robert Cairns had been worried. She told Jean that 'it should be as dear a lamb as was tupit of any ewe', and soon after nine of Jean's lambs 'took ane trimbling and sweating and some died'. Neither fowl nor beast, it was observed, would eat their flesh. When she challenged Janet with being responsible for this Janet sneered at her for thinking so much of 'worldly geir', and told her to thank God she kept her own health. The same day she 'contracted ane strange disease and was sore tormented with vehement sweat and pain for the space of three days'. At that point Janet turned up again, accepted a drink from her, and after drinking a little 'she bade God send her her health and said she should warrand her free from sickness at that time'. Within an hour Jean was on the way to recovery and the relationship seems to have been restored.

Two years later in 1667 there was another recorded contretemp. between the women. Janet went round to Jean Sprot alleging tha Jean's cow had stolen her grass and went and plucked it out of the cow's mouth. The cow then refused to chew the cud, sickened, and died. Jean Sprot 'having salted the said cow when she put the leas piece thereof in the pot it did swell so big that it filled the pot, and the broth was like beastings and the flesh like lights, and her husband and her self and sundrie others having eat thereof did swell likewise'. Jean was forced to throw the lot into the peat bog but neither dog nor fowl would touch it. In 1668, the year which many of the accusations against her related to, Jean's husband, Robert Cairns found Janet in his barnyard on the sabbath day with a sheaf of corn, and reproved her. Whereupon Janet in anger 'bade the divill pyk out his eyn (eyes)'. The Friday after at midnight he contracted a sudden disease and died the following Sunday morning. During this short fatal illness he sent for Janet to restore his health, but on this occasion she refused to come. The dying Robert, according to his brother John Cairns who signed this accusation, 'left his death upon her, and ordained his friends to pursue her as a witch and necromancer'.

It is not clear whether the death of Robert Cairns was the key episode which stimulated the process of formal accusation since it took place three years before the final gathering of accusations taken under oath, but certainly Robert's family and friends took his injunction seriously. Christian Gordon, who was a close neighbour, but was not otherwise identified in the accusations, supported the testimony of John Cairns and Jean Sprot. She said that Robert had desired Janet to come to him 'to forgive and be forgiven before he departed this life', and that when she refused 'he left his death upon her'. She also supported Jean's story about the state of her cow's milk after Janet had promised her an ill turn, and she claimed to be the messenger who had persuaded Janet to come to see Jean when she lay ill, and described the healing ritual with the drink which Janet had successfully performed 'to the great admiration of the said Jean Sprot'.

Jean Sprot added to her testimony that her husband had charged his brother to pursue Janet 'to the death'. She also noted that when Janet first came to the town (farm-toun) 'she went thryse widdershines (anti-clockwise) round about all the yards barefooted and after that she went thryse widdershines round about the stockyard'. This revealing accusation suggests that Janet may have been a newcomer to the area, perhaps brought in through marriage. The ritual of beating the bounds was a widely practised fertility rite, but it would have been performed with the sun. To go against the sun, widdershins, was associated with a deliberate intention to evil.[2]

There is no indication that Janet was tortured before her trial, but she was examined by the local minister, Mr. Ross. The only response to her accusers prior to her confession recorded in the coded form of the final indictment is in the brief account of this encounter. She argued that Jean Sprot ought not to be accepted as a witness since 'she was a witch as well as hirself': she was able to tell fortunes from the way a person walked. It is easy to see from this last desperate effort to incriminate her accuser in the very same breath as she identified and accepted her own status as a witch, that under the right conditions such counter accusations could stimulate further prosecutions. It was clearly a very thin and rather hopeless attempt on this occasion because these were circumstances in which the community was anxious to nail a particular individual rather than to uncover a general conspiracy in which anyone could be a participant. Janet was a classic, individual scapegoat witch.

The accusations and indictment leave us with a puzzle. Janet is said to have been spouse to James Hendrie in Airds, but he remains a completely shadowy figure throughout. He is mentioned only as identifying Janet. He was not apparently involved in any of her quarrels with the neighbours, nor does he appear to have been active in working the tenancy; the references in the documents are all to Janet's goods, Janet's rent, Janet's horse. It is clear that married women could own property, and Jean Sprot also has ownership of livestock attributed to her, but the most likely explanation is that Janet was in fact a widow, and the scribe had not adopted the normal style of 'relict'. He also described Jean Sprot as 'spouse' of Robert Cairns although we know Robert to have been three years in his grave at the time of the preparation of these documents for the circuit judges.

If Janet was in fact a widow this does a lot to explain her predicament. She was by no means at the bottom of the social scale. She had a tenancy; she had enough land and livestock for a subsistence; she was not in that peripheral state of being a kept wage-earner, though her daughter was. Servant status was usually a temporary phase most women went through when young.[3] Yet it looks as though she was something of a problem in the local economy. She had failed to pay rent on more than one occasion. She was short of grazing for her animals; no less than four of her quarrels with neighbours were about her animals and someone else's grass. She stole corn. She ran out of meal and tried to borrow some. She was not managing to cope, and was in some sense dependent on the good will and helpfulness of neighbours.

Most of her accusers were more substantial than she. Robert Brown had fifteen cattle and three horses die through her alleged malefice, and presumably had some livestock remaining. Jean Sprot had more than nine lambs. The rest had cows, calves, horses, and land to graze them on. Three of them were lairds. In this aspect of her relationship to her accusers her case is classic. It is one of the standard features noted by Macfarlane in his Essex study: richer accuses poorer.[4] He was not prepared to commit himself on the question of tension between age-groups,[5] and it is equally difficult here. Unusually for Scottish cases we are given the age of the accusers which range from twenty six to sixty, but most were over forty. This suggests that there was no significant age disparity between Janet and her accusers. Neither age in itself nor a particular type of age-relationship seems very important in building up a reputation nor provoking an accusation. Reputations took time to build up, and so, except during epidemics of multiple accusation, it was rare to find a young woman and even rarer to find a young man accused of witchcraft.

Position in the social structure seems to have been much more important, but her dependent and marginal economic position in the locality was not in itself enough to turn her into a reputed witch. She was not only dependent; she was ill-tempered in the way in which she managed her dependency. The classic witch not only had particular social and economic traits; she had particular character traits too. There was for the community a dissonance between her semi-dependent status and her independent and undeferential demeanour reflecting her ambiguous role as lone female. Supporting the feckless and inefficient is acceptable so long as they are grateful. Janet's best chance of a reasonably equable existence would have been to display the deference which the neighbours would have felt to be appropriate. But Janet had the fatal ingredient of an aggressive, forceful, and quarrelsome personality. She was deferential to no-one, and if anyone crossed her she swore at them. Along with most alleged practitioners of malefice she had 'smeddum'. She answered back, right to the end. On the occasion when the minister went to see her he chided her for not putting on 'well-favoured clothes', Janet's reply was that they were good enough for the hangman, and that her own children should wear her plaid and not the hangman. Undoubtedly this unquenchable capacity to answer back and demonstrate her control of the situation in which she found herself, helped to propel her into a state of secondary deviation[6] in which she herself accepted, identified with, and made an ego-prop out of the label of witch. Not all accused witches so accepted it. Some denied it continuously; others accepted it bemusedly, prefacing their curses with 'if I be a witch'.

It is not clear that Janet's co-prisoner, Elspeth Thomson, accepted herself as a witch at all. It was her misfortune to be accused by the family of her husband William McGhie. The McGhies consisted of five brothers: William, Donald, John, James, Thomas, and their sisters Rosina and Janet; and more than half the accusations against Elspeth came from them and their spouses. William did not actually appear as a witness against his wife, but was cited by other witnesses as having made complaints or told stories about her.

As in the case of Janet the focal point of the accusations was the death of a man who had had bad relations with her and who had previously attributed his misfortunes to her; in this case her brother-in-law, Donald McGhie. The accusation was made by Donald's widow, Elspeth Coupland, who claimed that Elspeth Thomson and her husband had quarrelled on several occasions, and though she herself did not blame Elspeth for his death Donald had been constantly 'on his guard for her'. After these quarrels there had always followed 'some

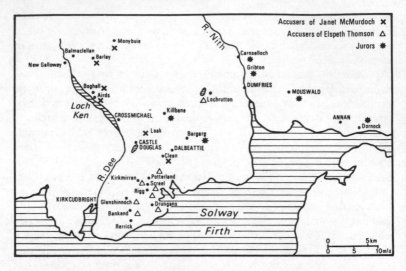

DISTRIBUTION OF JURORS AND ACCUSERS IN KIRKCUDBRIGHT 1671

mischief on his goods, his children and sickness on himself'. A child of hers had actually died and finally her husband; and he had said before he died that 'he hoped he had as many friends behind him as would pursue her for it'.

The occasion of their final dispute was when Donald refused to cut peats for Elspeth. Another brother, James McGhie, declared that Donald had said to him five days after he fell sick that Elspeth Thomson 'had then gotten the sight she desired of him and that as ever before he was still feared for her and that they still discorded and he blamed her for all evil that befell him'. The matter of Donald's death was confirmed by an ordeal commonly used in Scotland.[7] Elspeth was made to touch the corpse and 'immediatle upon the touching thereof the blood rushed forth at his nose, navel and ears and his corpse bled all the way to the burial place'. James also said on his own account that because he 'refused a day's work to her she said she hoped not to be cumbered with his work for a year after, whereupon he fell sick, and since that he declaired he was never so able as formerly'.

Elspeth's sister-in-law, Rosina McGhie, accused her of causing the death of her child. There had been a quarrel between them because Elspeth had not been summoned to the birth and baptism of Rosina's child, and after that Rosina fell sick. Her husband, John Crosbie, explained that the sickness 'was occasioned by a fear she got thinking that Elspeth Thomson came to her and was like to murder her and her chyld'. John Crosbie procured her recovery by going to Elspeth Thomson's house and taking three 'rugs of thatch' from the roof of her house and burning them in front of his wife. Two other witnesses also claimed on different occasions that they achieved the restoration to health of relatives who had quarrelled with Elspeth by the same means. It is not clear whether a rug of thatch was a symbolic amount or a substantial part of the roof of Elspeth and William, but the procedure seems to have been a standard response to trouble with Elspeth, and Macfarlane, in his discussion of informal counteraction against witchcraft, noted that the Puritan writer William Perkins referred to burning the thatch of the suspected party's house.[8] Despite the fact that Rosina recovered, their child died. Rosina gave her own version of the episode, claiming that they had first quarrelled about Elspeth's hindering of Rosina's milk. When she had gone to Elspeth's house to ask her to 'pray God to send her good of her milk', Elspeth had replied 'the Devil take both the good and the ill of it', but was eventually prevailed upon and reluctantly uttered 'God send all folks good of their milk', whereupon her milk was restored. Then Elspeth came round to her house to borrow a heckle (a small loom), and seeing it lying by the bed

> she observed her to fathom and grope the bed with her hands, and on her going forth a terror did strike her mind least her servant should have put the child in the bed, fearing some hurt from her. Whereupon she instantly returned and did cast in a whelp into the bed three times and immediately the dog lost the power of his hinder quarters and became so odious and loathsome to look on that her husband was forced to hang him and put him out of pain, but after that she took an extraordinary swelling and sickness herself, which she thought was occasioned by another fear that she visibly saw Elspeth Thomson come to her bed endeavouring to destroy her and her child but she using all means and loudly calling to her husband it was not possible for her to waken him.

After this episode which it is clear from the way both she and her husband described it referred to a dream, she sent for Elspeth to come and heal her. Elspeth refused although many others tried to persuade her. Other witnesses, including Rosina's sister Janet McGhie, corroborated this.

While over half the accusations against her came from the McGhies and their spouses, there were other neighbours to bear similar stories. These accounts are less specific in their renderings of actual curses and their immediate consequences than those against Janet McMurdoch, and they do not have the reiterated refrain that she is of evil reputation. This may well reflect the views of the local scribe, minister, or magistrate about the most effective way of presenting the evidence, or it may reflect very local belief structures and fashions of speech. Since the attribution of evil repute was common parlance throughout the witch-prosecuting areas the former seems more likely.

One feature of the accusations against Elspeth which is missing in those against Janet is the imputation of her direct relationship with the

Devil. This came largely from her husband, but was reported by others. James Corkney in Barrhead reported that William McGhie had described to him that one morning in his bed he saw the Devil looking in his face. 'Being terribly affrighted his wife gripped him fast and said what needed him be so feared for she was not feared for all that.' This or another visitation was mentioned by Elspeth Coupland, the widow of Donald, who said that William had told her that 'there came one tyme a great heaviness over him, and that the Devil came like a rat, and bit his left arm'. Further reinforcing the suggestion of alien powers, though not directly identified with the Devil, William's brother James McGhie, the one who had been permanently affected after refusing to work for Elspeth, made the accusation that there were two mysterious holes beside the hearthstone in Elspeth's house. He said that she had asked him to put his fingers there but that he had refused, and that his brother William had told him that out of these holes the ashes would often fly up to the crook (the chain for hanging kettles) and that under the hearth a great din could be heard 'like the rusking of a dog', and that Elspeth had confessed to him that these holes had been there since Janet Callan, who had been burned as a witch, had lived with them. Even in communities where witches were identified singly, and where the belief in conspiratorial companies of witches was not strongly held, witches were still reckoned to learn their trade and inherit their powers through association with other witches whether mother or friend. Janet Callan had been burnt in 1659 in Dumfries after a multiple trial with nine others.[9] Elspeth's husband William was not exempt from this guilt by association although he appears to have played some part in building up Elspeth's reputation. His brother James, a leading witness in the case, said that on an occasion when Donald had called Elspeth a witch it was William who loyally responded by promising him an ill turn, though it was Elspeth whose power was credited with actually achieving Donald's death.

Unlike Janet, Elspeth does not seem to have been an economic problem in the community. Her reputation was established in her own immediate family all of whom appeared to be of reasonably secure small tenant status. Her sister-in-law, Rosina, mentions a servant, which suggests that there were households supporting more than the immediate nuclear family, but servants seem sometimes to have been the older children of other small farmers, so it is difficult to make very much of this. It is possible that Elspeth, like Janet, was brought into the neighbourhood as an incomer, but unlike Janet's case there is no direct evidence of this. Elspeth was also a woman of middle age or at least mature years, though she may well have been younger than Janet. She had a sister-in-law young enough for child-bearing; she herself had a daughter old enough to have been sent out to work. One of the accusations against her came from another brother, Thomas McGhie, to whom she had offered her daughter's services. These were refused and as a result of the quarrel and subsequent threatening Thomas too fell ill.

The similarities between the two sets of accusations are, of course, as interesting as the differences. In both communities a woman was a focus of discord and quarrels, and although Elspeth was labelled primarily by her own extended family there was plenty of support from other neighbours for her evil reputation. In both communities the woman was accused of causing a variety of misfortunes, but in particular of causing obscure and sudden diseases to afflict those who had annoyed her. Both, in more than one instance, were alleged to have caused death. Yet no one accused of causing death by witchcraft was ever prosecuted for murder; such people were prosecuted for the more serious and more all-embracing crime of witchcraft. Both were credited with the power to remove illnesses, though less with the power of healing in general than with that of shifting those illnesses which they were supposed to have inflicted in the first place. This frequently involved transferring the disease, which was regarded as having a life of its own and which must therefore be transferred to some animal rather than eliminated.[10] What the accusations sought to establish above all was the quarrel, the threat, and the resulting misfortune or affliction. These accusations were all collected together at one time and couched in a form which the scribes assumed would have maximum effectiveness in the court for which they were intended: the Circuit Court of Justiciary due to arrive at Dumfries in May 1671. Nevertheless these accusations of malefice on their own would not have procured a conviction. The relationship of the witch with the Devil could be imputed from evidence of malefice, but it was better if it was substantiated by further testimony of the witch's general reputation, of her using mysterious powers, or of the practice of sorcery through the manipulation of objects, and finally, through the witch's own confession of the Demonic Pact.

The evidence collected for both these cases did not in itself offer enough to the legal authorities to confirm them as authentic cases of witchcraft. In Janet's case the scribe had collected additional affirmations of her evil reputation, but the case was incomplete without the confession. As in so many cases there is a gap in the evidence. We have nothing other than the accusations and the final indictments. These final indictments contain only the legally significant points of their confessions. We have no evidence about how they were actually obtained, but it is clear that it was only necessary to fill in the details of a document which had become common form. The indictment went as follows in the case of Elspeth (variations for Janet are given in brackets):

You ar Indyted and accused that wheir notwithstanding of the divyne law of the (omnipotent) almightie god set doune in his sacred word especiallie in the 20 chapter of Leviticus and 18 chapter of Deutronomie All witches sorcerers and users and practisers of sorcerie and witchcraft are to be punished by death As also by the acts of Parliament and Municipall lawes of this natione (realme) And namelie be the 73 act (9 parl.) of parl: of Queen Marie of worthie memorie It is expreslie provydit statute and ordained that no maner of persone nor persones of what-somevir estate degrie or conditione they be off take upon hand in any tyme heirafter to use any maner of witchcraft sorcerie or necromancie nor give themselves forth to any such craft or know-ledge theirof theirthrough abusing the people under the paine of death As in the saide laws and act of parliament at mair length is contenit Nevertheles It is of veritie that you (ye) the said Elspeth (Janet McMurdoch) haveing shaken of all feare of god and reverence and regaird of the divyne ordinance Lawes and acts of parliament of this kingdome has these fyften or sextein (number left blank for Janet) yeires bygane betaken yorself to the service of sathan (Sathan) the enemie of your salvatioune Ingaged to be his servant And taken his marks upon yor bodie practised used and excercised divers and sundrie devilische charmes witchcraft and sorcerie And hes thereby hurt and damnified his majesties subjects in their goods and persones And hes bein the cause of sundrie other deaths by your sorcerie and witchcraft And also ye have had severall tymes carnall dealling or copulationne with the devill And so defylled that bodie of yours which should have been a temple of the holie ghost by giveing the use theirof to the devill as said is And so testifie and manifest your guiltieness of the saids Crymes.

This indictment was by 1671 pure common form. The only problem was to fill in the names. Sections of the 1563 Act were cited, the Biblical references given, general malefices including causing death were asserted, and the whole was summed up in the Demonic Pact complete with the Devil's mark and carnal copulation. Unlike some other recorded cases there are no details about either of their con-fessions. It may well have been that the Pact by this time had become a legal fiction, not deemed to have an interesting physical reality in the courts, and that the witches were simply required to assent to the general formula; but it is possible that the Pact may still have been thought to have had a specific rather than a spiritual reality. However the legal authorities viewed the pact, the wide gap between the concerns of the neighbours and the concerns of the court is clearly demonstrated. The pollution of the body implicit in the carnal relationship with the Devil is intrinsic to the legal formulation, yet it is quite clear that neither of these two women had been in any sexual trouble. Among all the recorded quarrels there is no suggestion of sexual rivalry. Neither of them had a reputation as a whore: conceptually quite distinct from a witch though not incompatible; nor were they, as menopausal women, accused of jealously thwarting the sexual activities of others, though this was certainly something of which witches were from time to time accused. The witch's mark, too, which appears in the indictment, is something which was not mentioned in either of the sets of pre-trial accusations. There was no official witch pricker mentioned as being in the neighbourhood. Those who examined them in prison must have found an appropriate mark, or the women must have offered suitable moles to their examiners in order to pre-empt an inevitable search.

The original accusations are appended to the main indictment as relevant material. They are more or less in the same wording, but in the case of Elspeth Thomson one of the witnesses, James Thomson (married to the sister of Elspeth Coupland and therefore another affine) was prevailed upon to elaborate his former testimony. He was alleged to have 'discorded' with Elspeth over 'ane turfe of heather'. Elspeth threatened to do him an ill turn, and he fell into a 'languishing disease' which had continued ever since for the past three years. Elspeth was prevailed upon to come to him after first refusing, and was asked by James to say 'God send him good health'. This she not only refused to do but said 'she wold not speak of god but of her lord'. Such an accusation was intended to convey directly that Elspeth had transferred her allegiance from God to the Devil who had become her lord. It is inconsistent with the earlier accusations in which Elspeth was reported as having uttered various requests to God to restore her victims to health, and it was no doubt added to strengthen the case.

The jury brought together to consider the evidence were small lairds and grand tenants from within approximately a ten-mile radius of Dumfries. It is interesting, but not surprising, that the extent of the reputation of the accused women was somewhat broader than Macfarlane found was typical of Essex. The reputation of an Essex witch rarely extended beyond five miles; Janet's accusers came from as far afield as ten miles in different directions, a span of twenty miles altogether, and over difficult terrain. Elspeth's accusers came mostly from a restricted area and a restricted kin group, but her accuser from Lochrutton lived over twelve miles from the centre of accusation. This distant accuser of Elspeth and the more generally diffused distribution of Janet's accusers reflects the more diffused settlements of population compared with that of Essex. Instead of the nucleated village there were scattered farm-touns with the estate and the parish as separate though overlapping foci of communication. Peasants would expect to travel long distances on foot or on horse or, if young or infirm, by sledge, to attend the kirk or to work for the laird. The communications network was wide and so thus widespread the rumour of a person's character.

Janet and Elspeth and their accusers lived to the west of Dumfries; most of the jury held land to the east, but two of them, John Grierson of Bargarg and John Maxwell of Killbane, lived within the orbit of both the women's influence and reputation (see map on p. 126), and it may be significant that they both found against the women. It is clear that the points were all debated in detail because two of the accusations against Janet—those of John Moor of Barclay, her landlord's baillie, and of John Murray of Laik, the old man who had knocked her over 'accidentally'—were found 'not proven'; so was that of William Gordon; while that of Robert Brown whose spouse was said to have died of a strange and sudden disease was found proven by one witness only.

The cases against them were found proven only by a majority of the jury of fifteen, and in the case of Janet McMurdoch only by one vote. The cases against five others tried at the same court were dismissed. The trend towards acquittal seems to have been well under way by this time although it was to be greatly accelerated in the years that followed. No reasons are given for the acceptance of some of these accusations as proven and others as not; no reasons are given why some jurors voted for the defendants and some against, but one can see here an indication of the way in which the witch-belief was gradually eroded. There was no overturning of the paradigm; no reasoned arguments against it. There was merely a reduction of the prominence of the character of the Devil in the script, an increasing reluctance to find particular instances of malefice as proven, and an increasing tendency to acquit.

The tide was not strong enough for Janet and Elspeth however. They were sentenced to be taken

on Thursday nixt the eightein of May instant betwixt two and foure houre in the afternoone to the ordinar place of executionne for the toune of dumfreis And their to be wirried att ane Stake Gibbett till they be dead And theirafter their bodies to be brunt to ashes And all their moveable goods and geir to be escheat and inbrought to his majesties use.

And much good, one might think, might Charles II have had of Janet McMurdoch's plaid. There were rarely many pickings to be had from the conviction and execution of a witch; more often the process was an expense to the local authority, though, as Janet herself implied, the petty officials involved would take what they could as perks of the trade.

The question remains to what extent these two cases can be regarded as typical. In one very obvious sense they were not typical of the majority of those who were executed, because most witches were convicted in the multiple trials of 1629–30, the 1640s and 1661–62. In these holocausts it seems likely that many perished whose local reputations were not clearly established but who were incriminated by other convicted witches either out of spite or in order to undermine their testimony (as Janet tried to do with Jean Sprot) or under torture. Micro-studies of such mass trials as the East Lothian ones of 1649 would be illuminating on this. But while Janet and Elspeth may not have been typical of the majority of those who were executed they may well have been typical of the much larger number of identified witches who died in their beds with their reputations acknowledged locally but who were never pursued to the courts. The relatively late date of these cases, too, has meant that although the Demonic Pact was still vestigially present, there appears to have been no attempt to link either of these women to a conspiracy of witches or to corporate Devil-worship. This very factor, however, lays bare the essence of peasant witch-belief: the woman with the deadly and threatening combination of malice in her heart and special power to inflict damage. Too frequent a demonstration of the first was always likely to produce a reputation for the second. It is to the interaction between these peasant beliefs and those of the representatives of the church, the law, and the government that we now turn.

CHAPTER ELEVEN

THE BELIEF SYSTEM
I THE PEASANT IN THE COURTS

We know more about the way in which a seventeenth-century Scottish peasant saw the Devil than we do about the way in which he saw God. It is much easier to conceptualize absolute evil than to analyse the components of an absolute good. Absolute good is defined in extra-terrestrial terms; it is that which we cannot understand. Absolute evil is not the inverse of this absolute good and therefore equally incomprehensible; it is simply the inverse of modest social goods. It is disease as opposed to health; madness as opposed to sanity; hatred and malice as opposed to love and friendship; cursing as opposed to blessing. The norms, practices, and values of a given society can never be perfectly fulfilled nor represent perfection. They cannot easily be defined by reference to some absolute good, because juxtaposition to such a good would show up the imperfections of existing human practices rather than justify them; instead these norms are defended by contrasting them with an absolute evil.

The anthropological truism that witch-beliefs represent a direct inversion of the values of the society in which they are held implies that we can learn more directly about the concerns and interests of the ordinary farmers and fishermen of seventeenth-century lowland Scotland through the complaints which they raised about witchcraft than we can by reading examples of sermons which were preached to them. The rhetoric of the general good is much less specific than complaints of particular evils. Nevertheless the two inter-relate. The inversions of witchcraft are simply the more explicit side of the belief system.

There are two disadvantages in treating seventeenth-century culture as an alien belief system which, provided they are borne in mind, do not seem to be overwhelming. One disadvantage is that it may seem to minimize both the extent of the bitter debates and disagreements about belief with which followers of Scottish religious history will be familiar, and the scepticism and distance exhibited by some members of the legal profession and others over aspects of witch-hunting. Much of the conflict described as religious, however, was at the political exterior rather than the theoretical core of a basic Calvinist consensus, and the scepticism over witchcraft was, even among the most sophisticated, a minority attitude. The second disadvantage is that since the term belief system derives from functionalism it may suggest a static approach to patterns of belief which is expressly eschewed here. The intention is to look at the way in which the witch-beliefs of both the educated and the peasant inter-related with formal and popular theology during the hundred years of prosecutions for witchcraft. Some degree of stability is assumed, but it is also taken for granted that in a changing society belief is not static.

The evidence for witch-beliefs in Scotland comes partly from the relatively scarce contemporary references in journals, sermons, histories, and tracts, but mainly from the records of the courts, local and central. The material from the courts offers three types of evidence: the accusations of neighbours, signed (or marked by the illiterate) and witnessed; the confessions of the accused; and the indictments and summing up of the court.

The accusations represent in their most uncontaminated form the ideas of peasants about what witches could do. They also indicate these peasants' most central concerns. Although some of them contain a good deal of allegedly verbatim reporting the accusations cannot, however, be regarded as 'pure', since they were collected and arranged by scribes, ministers, and magistrates who had a good idea of what kind of accusation stood some chance of standing up in court. Further, although collected together at one point in time the accusations often related to events in the past sometimes many years back.

The confessions are the most difficult of the three types to evaluate. Some were extracted under torture, but even those which were not were extracted under varying degrees of pressure. Voluntary un-provoked confessions such as that alleged to have been made by Major Weir in 1670[1] seem to have been very rare. Witch-hunting always began with the pointing finger extending away from the self. Some of the accused may have confessed with semi-suicidal intent, to avoid a sentence of death by burning alive or a future made intolerable by their reputation in the community; some may have confessed in order to attract attention; but it is reasonable to assume that most confessed under direct duress. In their content the confessions are much closer to the final indictments than they are to the original accusations which are principally concerned with details of individual malefices. The confessions sometimes reinforce these accusations by containing claims to powers of malefice: the formulation of Magdalen Blair to the effect that 'shee never gave a malison but what shee saw light',[2] and Isobal Ramsey that 'when she gave her malison it always lighted' are sufficiently representative to suggest that the phraseology was widely used and understood, but the main focus of the confessions was on diabolism. They normally featured the Demonic Pact and witches' meetings, and they range from those which mention only the Pact (the legal minimum for a conviction) to those which give considerable detail about activities at witches' meetings.

These confessions may well have been extracted by questioning, but one cannot go on to argue that because they were extracted and because they differed in content and in their concerns from the accusations, they were therefore alien to popular belief; for unlike the final indictments, which are common form, the accounts of the happenings at witches' meetings given in these confessions contain varied and diverse details. That many of these details were manifestly impossible makes them, as Cohn has persuasively argued,[3] unreliable throughout as evidence for what actually occurred, and, since there are no really satisfactory criteria for distinguishing what people said from what they believed, the confessions of individual witches are not even evidence of what they as individuals thought had occurred. None of this, however, affects their value as evidence for collective beliefs. Witch confessions represent an agreed story between witch and inquisitor in which the witch drew, through hallucination or imagination, on a common store of myth, fantasy, and nightmare, to respond to the inquisitor's questions. As a source for this common store the confessions are invaluable. The final indictment and sentences of the courts simply contain the purest legal formulae about what the educated thought witches did and what they thought they were.

Together these three types of source cover the beliefs and preoccupations of peasant, minister, magistrate and lawyer. The main gap in the evidence is the questions which were asked by the inquisitors of the accused. These questions survive in some criminal archives, those of France and Massachusetts for example, but in the Scottish cases the details of how the confession was extracted have to be inferred. There is nevertheless quite enough evidence to suggest a difficulty about the clear separation of witch-beliefs into a static popular culture on the one hand and a dynamic educated culture on the other.

Until the work of Thomas and Macfarlane on English witchcraft was published students of European beliefs concentrated on the problem (which is still with us) of the apparent shift of educated opinion from scepticism to credulity. 'Folklore' was a separate field of study. Thomas discerned at least two overlapping systems of belief in pre-industrial England: the magical and the religious, and demonstrated the complexity of modes of thought in that society. The similarity of English magical beliefs to those discerned by ethnographers in primitive societies was established, but this identification created a problem. It was reasonable to assume that English beliefs which were demonstrably common to many pre-industrial societies had been endemic for centuries, and that therefore the causes of the rise in prosecutions for witchcraft were to be found elsewhere than in popular belief, which must be regarded as essentially static. The fact that the content of the English trials closely reflected village beliefs and showed little of the adulterations of the preacher reinforced this assumption: popular beliefs were concerned with malefice, cursing, and misfortune; not with diabolism. Furthermore the similarities between the beliefs of English villages and those of African tribesmen led to the search for parallel explanations for the rise and fall of accusations and to the emphasis on stress among the populace caused by social change rather than on the direct influence of the ruling classes.

The difficulties inherent in applying this explanation to Europe have been discussed, but the insights from the English material concerning the endemic nature of popular witch-beliefs have encouraged scholars of European witchcraft to look for similar concerns among European peasants. This has produced a variety of responses, but the central problem for all European researchers has been that whatever the extent to which the interests and beliefs of European peasants are similar to those of English peasants, a very high proportion of European suspects were initially brought to trial through the confessions of those already examined and tortured rather than through the accusations of neighbours. The extent to which these suspects were previously of ill fame is therefore often bypassed. The charges in these cases were principally of diabolism; the pace and intensity of the witch-hunt controlled from above. While some, such as Monter,[4] have simply denied the relevance of English interpretations to European material, others, principally Cohn and Kieckhefer,[5] have developed a model based on a distinction between learned or educated and popular belief. Both identify diabolic witchcraft as learned; simple sorcery and *maleficium* as popular, but Cohn presents a highly sophisticated account of the popular origins of this educated demonology, especially the elements which stressed night-flying witches, orgies, and cannibalism.[6] These popular fantasies were rationalized by the developing figure of Satan in Christian theology. Thus the educated witch-belief always had a strong popular component. This educated belief, however, can be contrasted with popular beliefs in *maleficium* and sorcery which reflect everyday interests and fears as compared to collective social fantasies. As Cohn has observed, 'behind the accusations from below and the interrogations from above lie divergent preoccupations and aims'.[7]

The logic of this position, however, is that the simple distinction between learned and popular is, even at a high level of generality, somewhat strained. It is nevertheless possible to follow initially the methodological pattern suggested by Kieckhefer and consider the belief patterns shown in the accusations as representing the most primitive levels of belief. It is from these accusations that we learn the popular assumptions about sorcery as used in white magic: healing, fortune telling, finding of lost property, and other forms of divination; and in black magic: cursing and malefice, and counter black magic. Even at the popular level, however, analysis of the Scottish material is not entirely simple. In the first place, as we have noted, collections of signed accusations by neighbours, while relating to many incidents over a period of time, were all gathered together for the purpose of getting a conviction or a commission. While there are instances of a witch entering the documents more than once, most of the evidence for long term reputation comes from one set of documents which it is reasonable to assume are full of retrospective reinterpretation. The Kirk Sessions, which were largely responsible for collecting this evidence, were well aware of what would convince in the Privy Council or the High Court and were intelligent in their selection of items and the way in which they were presented. There may well be a whole layer of popular beliefs which are not represented because no scribe thought them worth sending up to Edinburgh. The accusations which were signed and sent were extremely circumstantial. In the second place the accusations reveal other elements than pure sorcery, whether black, white, or counter magic; they frequently emphasize the long term reputation of the witch, and her known association with the Devil. The importance of reputation relates to the demands of Scots law. It also stems from a view of witchcraft as an attribute of particular individuals rather than an activity which a wide range of people might practise; a view more characteristic of Europe than of witch-doctor cultures. In Scotland the references to the witch's association with the Devil, frequently appearing as an addendum to an accusation of malefice, suggests that the peasantry had either absorbed or generated at least some of the diabolism developed by ecclesiastical lawyers. In fact, while the distinction between the concerns of the learned and the concerns of the peasantry is clear from the documents, so too is the mutual influence. Cohn has suggested that it was this interaction between the learned and the popular which was instrumental in promoting the witch-hunt.[8]

The beliefs which relate to magic, religion, and witchcraft are beliefs about power. The sources of power and the extent to which the individual is a prey to them or can manipulate them are the focus of any belief system. Adam Smith's observation that man is an anxious animal was intended to apply to anxieties about status, but it has wider applicability. He is anxious about his health and its relationship to his inevitable death, and about the health of his kin. He is anxious about property, status, and the stability of the society in which his property and his status are held. Beliefs supply reassurance, mechanisms for control, and scapegoats for misfortune. In so far as religious beliefs are about the sources of power it may be expected that changes in technology or in social structure will be reflected in changes in the belief system. The systematic teaching of new ideologies stemming from changes in the elite will also affect the cosmology of the peasant.

The healer is a source of hope in the community. But his power is two-edged. If he should fail, demand extortionate and uneconomic returns for his services, or become hostile, then he becomes a source of menace and a focus for anxiety. The refusal of Canon Law to distinguish between black and white magic, while based on the idea that all power not sanctioned by the church is either ineffectual or demonic, regardless of whether it is intended to heal or harm, in fact reflects a peasant reality: that the healer can be dangerous. The healer represents power at the most basic local level and is therefore the natural starting point of a scale which ends with power at the most abstract and political level: that ascribed to God and the Devil.

Healing in seventeenth-century Scotland can be divided into official and unofficial. Official healing was that sanctioned by the emergent professional associations and taught in the universities. Official healing was 'scientific'. This is not to say that official healers had got their facts right in terms of twentieth-century positivist science; it is merely to say that scientific healing in this period was based upon current physical knowledge and was susceptible to intellectual discussion and experiment within the current paradigm. There are difficulties about overlap, however. It would seem reasonable to classify the wearing of an amulet as a cure for colic as unofficial medicine, but for the seventeenth-century wearer it was based on contemporary scientific assumptions about the physical properties of certain substances and their effects on the functioning of human bodies. Perhaps the clearest common element in official and unofficial medicine, however, was the necessary acknowledgment of a particular healer's power.

Unofficial healing, which in the early days of the medical and surgical professions meant nearly all healing, consisted of both practical or commonsense remedies and ritual healing, though these were sometimes combined. Practical healing concerned the use of particular herbs and minerals of established utility. No-one was in the least interested in reasons. These could be used without the intervention of any specialized healer, but very often recourse would be had to one known to have special knowledge of how to mix herbs and apply them. Practical healing is therefore difficult to separate from ritual healing of which the essence is the spell, the charm, and the power of the wise man or woman.

Thomas has detected in England three basic assumptions behind the folk medicine of this period. The first is that disease is a foreign presence, and this assumption was shared by official healers as well. The second is that religious language possessed a mystical power which could be deployed for practical purposes. The third was that the working of certain charms and potions owed their efficacy to the healer himself. It was this last belief which proved so deadly to the healer when inverted. Thomas also observed that 'these practices did not reflect a single coherent cosmology or scheme of classification, but were made out of the debris of many different systems of thought'.[9]

All this is applicable to Scotland, though in Scotland the belief in the power of language was not restricted to traditional religious forms, but was ascribed to all language used with intent. The form of an instruction, a blessing, or a curse on the lips of a person of power was immaterial. The belief in the power of the individual acted as an umbrella for the diversity of detailed beliefs about healing.

The principal source of charms were the prayers of the pre-Reformation church. Paternosters, aves, and creeds, either straight or adulterated, were frequently uttered, and the suggestion that the persecution of witchcraft was a disguised persecution of Catholics may stem from an anachronistic interpretation of the residual use of old charms and familiar names as representing a conscious allegiance to Rome.

William Kerrow in Elgin in 1623 offered a charm for all fevers as follows:

> The quaquand fever and the trembling fever
> And the sea fever and the land fever,
> Bot and the head fever and the hart fever,
> And all the fevers that God creatit.
> In Sanct Johnes name, Sanct Peteris name,
> And all the sancts of heavin's name
> Our Lord Jesus Chrystis name.[10]

Janet Brown in 1643 healed injuries with a widely used charm:

> Our Lord forth raide;
> His foal's foot slade;
> Our Lord down lighted;
> His foal's foot righted;
> Saying Flesh to Flesh, blood to blood,
>   and bane to bane
> In our Lord his name.[11]

Another version of this one was known in Shetland:

> The Lord rade
> And the foal slade
> He lighted
> And he righted
> Set joint to joint
> Bone to bone
> and sinew to sinew
> Heal in the Holy Ghost's name.[12]

It has been suggested that the central part of this charm was known in Germany and Norway and was older than the rest. The words had an inherent efficacy of their own, and the appeal to an external god was an addition. A charm was in this sense a different type of utterance from a prayer or invocation.

The examples mentioned above are typical of many, and are similar to English ones cited by Thomas. They could be used on their own or in conjunction with other performances. Threads were sometimes wound round the afflicted person and then buried. Wool was regarded as having special potency. Mould, earth from graveyards, water which was south running, had been charmed, or used to wash a dead person, were also used.[13] The purpose was always to extract or remove the alien substance which was causing the disease. The idea that the disease thus removed must be transferred to someone else was quite common, and that was another factor which put the healer in a dangerous social position. The person who had power to remove also had power to place a disease, and it was quite common for witches to be accused of both putting on and taking off a disease. Sir George Mackenzie argued that 'it is against the confest principles of all Criminalists, that *una venefica non potest esse ligans et solvens in eodem morbo* cannot both put on and take off a disease; for it seems that the Devil thinks, that it were too much to bestow such favours upon one of his favourites'.[14] But this argument clearly went counter to popular belief. The complaints against Janet and Elspeth in Dumfries in 1671 were all about the cavalier distribution and redistribution of disease and misfortune, though not entirely at whim. The fundamental belief behind the idea that the witch could control the cure as well as the infliction of a disease did not relate to the amount of power which the Devil might be supposed to hand out to his servants. That was an issue which was very much a concern of the educated. The popular understanding was that the disease was the result of a broken relationship with the witch and that the removal of the disease could only be effected in the context of at least some formal acknowledgement of a restored relationship. An example of this is taken from the trial of Magdalen Blair of Stirling, who was noted for claiming powers of malison, in January 1659. William Luckisone accused her, in effect, of acting as a witch finder in the case of his illness:

William Luckisone maltman declares that about six yeirs since or thereby he contracted a sore sickness, and in the meantime having occasion to visit Katharine Luckisone, his sister, now spouse to James Andersone, and finding her and Magdalen Blair sitting together in the foot of Andrew Curran's yard the said Katharine asked at Magdalen what she thought ailed the deponer [witness, William]. And Magdalen thereupon asked at the deponer if there was any enmitie or discord between Issobel Bennet and him, And he answered that there was none that he knew of, except that at sometimes when her fowles would be in his father's victuall, he would throw stones at them to call them furth of it. Whereupon Magdalen desired that he would go to Issobel Bennet and take a grip of her coat tail and drink a pint of ale with her And crave his health from her thrie tymes for the Lords sake and he would be well. But he did it not.[15]

Issobel Bennet was a far from random choice by Magdalen in that not only was a discordant relationship known to exist between her and William Luckisone, but she was also of ill fame in the neighbourhood. She was tried two months later and sentenced to banishment.[16]

Amidst the diversity of beliefs about healing, the factor which stands out most clearly is the figure of the healer herself. It was she who had the power, and this power was strengthened, as it is in modern medicine, by secrecy, impressive procedures, mystery, and arduous performances by the patient. The sufferer was not expected to understand exactly how he was being healed or the purpose of the consultation and the relationship between him and the healer would dissolve. The same held true when the healer was being brought in for veterinary purposes. When Robert Hutton's mother-in-law sent for Bessie Paine to cure a sick cow 'the said Bessie paine . . . caused the Cow to be put throw ane hanck of green yairne speaking some words which the personnes present did not understand and yreftir the Cow was cured'.[17] Agnes Johnstoun's accusation against Bessie Graham in 1650 included her response to a request to heal her child. Bessie 'Tuik the bellt and wettit it' (a common form of divination) 'mutering some speiches with greit gauting eftir which she told the said Agnes that the chyld was seik and wald not leive and it provit so and the chyld died presentlie'.[18]

In fact the charm, the failed charm, the favourable prophecy, the unfavourable prophecy, and the curse are closely connected, and essentially fall from the lips of the same person, the person of power. In seventeenth-century Scotland blessing and cursing, black and white magic, went hand in hand, and this assumption was shared by peasant and lawyer alike—and by victim and practitioner. Popular belief and practice reinforced Canon Law rather than Civil Law.

Accusations of healing, such as that cited, were listed alongside accusations of malefice, and Bessie Paine was not only said to have cured. It was alleged that she came to a house in which she had formerly lived (from which we may assume she had been evicted) after the new tenant had moved in, 'and sitting down upon her knees upon the hearth staene she said "all the witchcraft which I have I leave it here"'. The new tenant, Robert Sturgeon, as a result of this curse upon his house, was reckoned to have lost within a year and a quarter above thirty cattle dead, 'and nothing he took in hand did prosper during his possession of that rowme (place).'[19]

The belief in the efficacy of the spoken word, whether as charm, blessing, or curse, was not simply a popular one. It had been demonstrated in the past by the pre-Reformation church which had regular services of general commination in which formal sentences of excommunication were uttered against lists of specific types of malefactor. Despite the objections by John Knox to that particular practice it was reinforced in the post-Reformation church by the rituals of prayer, fasting, preaching, and public discipline. It was demonstrated by those who regarded themselves as victims of witchcraft when they formally left their death upon the head of the accused before dying, and equally by Covenanters who regarded themselves on the scaffold as victims of villainous agents of the state. One after another they left their blood formally on individual named persons.[20] Social control in seventeenth-century Scotland was demonstrated continuously by competitive performative utterances. Indeed, it could be argued that the performative utterances of fully literate societies, identified by Austin almost exclusively in terms of their grammatical construction, are merely a system of control and communication in which utterances may be intentionally rather than effectively performative. Even in Austin's account grammatical form is not quite enough to identify a fully performative utterance; there must be a social agreement that the words, at a marriage ceremony for example, do constitute an action.[21] Performative utterances dependent on supernatural power were also partially supported by social recognition. The performative element might be diluted by an exhortatory element, but a person who was formally cursed was deemed socially to be a cursed person.

Like a charm, a curse could sometimes be obscure, incomprehensible, or unheard. Some of Janet Macmurdoch's accusers, for example, noted that she had gone away muttering or murmuring. More frequently, however, they were audible but highly general. The malediction on the house: 'all my witchcraft I leave here', uttered by Bessie Paine, was typical of this type. Accused witches were said to have told their accuser simply that they would have cause to regret this or that act or speech.

Alexander Maclay in Killearnan in Ross-shire testified in 1699 that he challenged Murrock Nickinairich for allowing her beasts to eat his father's corn. The woman 'threatened him at a high rate and told him that Challenge should be repented of by him'. The next day he fell ill and remained so until Nickinairich brought him a drink of milk, whereupon he recovered.[22]

The general rhetoric of cursing in which the witch very often acknowledged or reinforced her status as a witch has already been illustrated. Sometimes the mere raising of the question of witchcraft was enough to assume a cursing had occurred. Janet Anderson and Janet Dicksone quarrelled after which Janet Anderson 'desired the Lord to bless her'. Janet Dicksone immediately asked Anderson if she thought her to be a witch and Anderson promptly denied it. This did not avail her however and she fell sick and remained so "til the said Janet Dicksone was apprehendit be the Magistrate as ane witch and thereafter the said Janet recoverit'.[23]

Margaret Wallace of Glasgow in 1622 was accused of bearing a deadly hatred and malice against Cuthbert Greg because of certain things he said against her and she threatened him more precisely that he would not be able to work. Shortly after he had a strange and unnatural disease.[24] What was most acceptable to the authorities, however, was when the alleged curse was specific, and related closely to the alleged misfortune. The forementioned Magdalen Blair had a quarrel with a neighbour about a horse which he had left standing outside her door, whereupon 'shee strake the said Richards horse saying God send he shoot to death And the horse died suddenlie the same day after he was taken hame'.[25] Katherin Davidson, an accuser of Margaret Bezok at Fortrose in 1699, said that she was 'threatened by the said Margaret that she should have neither sock nor coulter going upon that ground, and that thereafter she lost ane ox that dyed suddenly and another ox that fell and brake his bones'.[26]

Equally precise was the threatening of Christian Wilson of Dalkeith, tried in 1661. When James Clarke came to visit Christian's sick son Christian asked why his wife Helen had not come also. When James said his wife would not come into the same house as Christian

she thereupon with threatening words said that James Clarke's wife should be childless before her and also did sorely threaten himself. Immediately James Clarke his child procreat betwix him and that wyfe took present sickness and raged to death before twelve o'clock that same night although there was no one in more perfyt health than that chyld was at the time the said Christian made hir expressions. Some dayes thereafter fell ane heavy sickness upon James himself . . . Lykeas he died a littell thereftir.[27]

Curing, cursing, and general harming, all feature in the neighbourly accusations. So too do anti-witchcraft procedures. Those wishing to undo the effects of witchcraft sometimes appealed to other reputed witches for advice. Others tried directly to mend their relationship with the witch. A more aggressive defence was the burning of thatch taken from the witch's roof or some other piece of her property. This amounted, in effect, to counter sorcery. All these represent basic primitive beliefs to be found in all simple rural societies, and they were echoed in detail in other parts of Europe. The Scottish accusations, however, do tend to contain elements which are rare in the reported English accusations and which Kieckhefer found to have been excluded from the *ipsissima verba* of European peasant accusers in an earlier period. These elements can best be described as the new popular demonic. They would probably not have been found in Scotland a century before; they cannot be paralleled exactly in other pre-industrial cultures; yet by the middle of the seventeenth century they were part of popular culture in Scotland.

The first of these appear in the accusations of 'ill fame' or reputation, which accompany the more specific charges. The accusation of ill fame was given a more diabolic slant by saying that the witch had trafficked with the Devil for a long time, or had long been in the company of the Devil. Sometimes the accuser also said that they had actually seen the accused with the Devil. Janet Miller, herself an accused witch, claimed to have seen 'Isobell Keir and Margaret Harvie and ane blak man with thame, all siting at one tabill covered with ane Whyt cloth and sum boylet beif and bread thairon'.[28] Two witnesses at the trial of Elizabeth Bathgate saw her conversing 'with the Devil in the likeness of a man having grey cloathes'.[29]

Others were said to have been seen not with the Devil as such but clearly on demonic occupations. William Gledstains saw Elsbeth Maxwell of Dumfries in 1650 'as he thocht ryding upoun a cat and leiding two in hir hand'.[30] Although these references in the accusations to specific or implied diabolism are quite frequent, the main concern of the accusations is always malefice. The strongest evidence for a well rooted and well understood popular demonology lies neither in the accusations nor the confessions, but in the ordeal of pricking for the mark described in Chapter 9.

It is to the confessions, however, that we have to turn to get a full picture of collective belief about the Devil and his relations with mankind, and this source has been affected by interaction with officials more than have the accusations. To turn from those parts of the trial papers which list neighbourly accusations to those, for the same cases, which record the confessions of the accused, is to leave the arena of local concern and enter a twilight world in which fantasy was given a legal formulation; in which peasant and lawyer combined to produce an agreed statement which had meaning for both. In these confessions the capacity to perform malefice played little part (although some of the accused did boast of their powers in this respect) since this aspect of witchcraft could be adequately proved by witnesses and was not absolutely essential to a conviction. The principal emphasis was on the Demonic Pact. Nocturnal meetings with other witches were a frequent but optional extra.

In the first phase of witch-hunting the elements of witchcraft which were taken as evidence were a random juxtaposition of ill fame, malefice, private demonic encounters, and communal meetings. The Pact, however, came to be regarded by the Scottish judiciary, despite the number who continued to be convicted on other evidence or while maintaining their innocence, as the single most essential element in an indictment. The legal significance of the physical, formal pact came from Canon Law. Despite the dominance of the idea of the Sabbath on the European continent, the legal manuals made the Pact central to the prosecution's case and certainly in France the Pact was the essential element in a conviction. The crime was ultimately that of being a

witch rather than that of performing any particular acts of witchcraft.
By the 1620s the account of the Pact in the Scottish confessions and
indictments had developed into a common form which did not vary
much for the rest of the century.

A condensed example of the Pact is given in the commission to try
Jonnet Dempstar in Fife in 1626 who confessed 'the renunceing of her
baptisme, ressaveing of the devellis mark, and geving of hir soule and
bodie over to the devillis service'.[31] An example of a developed version
from the Restoration witch-hunt comes from the indictment of Janet
Daill, wife of George Bell, who was tried along with four others from
Musselburgh near Edinburgh on the 29th July 1661:

> Notwithstanding that both be the law of Almightie God and be
> the lawes and actes of parliament of this kingdome the cryme of
> sorcerie and witchcraft is expressly forbidden and discharged, and
> the pain and punishment of death ordained to be inflicted upon all
> that are guilty and convict thereof. Nevertheless it is of verity
> that the said Janet Dale having shaken off all fear of God reverence
> and regard to the lawes of this kingdome Hes about fourteen yrs
> ago or thereby betaken herself to the service of Satan the enemie
> of her Salvation entered in a covenant and paction with him
> whereby she has renounced her baptisme and interest in Jesis
> Christ, and engaged herselfe to be the Devill servant and took ane
> other name upon her . . .

The indictment then described her meetings with other witches and
then returns to the Pact:

> She comeing from Dalkeith the Devill met her at Newtonhall
> burne in the likeness of ane man with grey clothes who promised
> to give her money and the marks upon her body ane upon her
> shoulder and between her thys and her body. wherefore she
> consented to be his servant and give herself over to him albeit she
> knew he was the devill. Next she had ane meeting with the Devill
> at the same place where the Devill had carnal dealling with her
> and caused her renounce her baptism.[32]

The following month five women and a man were tried in Edinburgh and their indictments were first summed up together in these
terms:

> ilk and ane of you haveing shaken off all fear of God Reverence
> and regard to the Lawes of this kingdome, hes betaken yourselves
> to the service of Satan the enemie of your salvations entered in a
> Covenant and paction with him whairby you renounced your
> baptismes and interest in jesus Christ engadged yourselves to be

the devills servants, and suffered your bodies quilke aught to have
been temples to the Holie ghost to be polluted defiled by suffering
him to have carnall copulation with you.[33]

The formula was the normal usage for the second half of the seventeenth century. It was given fuller detail in individual cases but
remained essentially the same.

How then did the Scottish peasantry see the Devil? In the earliest
case for which a detailed indictment has been found, that of Janet
Boyman of the Canongate in Edinburgh in 1572,[34] the demonic force
which she conjured up to perform her cures and malefices was
described as being like a whirlwind, 'and thairafter came the shape of
ane man and stood on the other side of the wall'. It is not clear from
the context that this human figure was Satan himself. It was not until
the trials of 1590 that his identity was made quite unambiguous. And
even in these trials, despite the fully formed figure of the Devil in some
witnesses' accounts, others did not appear to be so certain. To Catherine
Wallace the Devil 'appeared lyke a quale of hay at this convention',
and to Janet Straton too 'the divell appeared first lyk a tusk of hay'.
For Donald Robeison, however, 'the divell had ane blak goune and
ane skull bonnett evill favoured on his head'.[35] And for others accused
in these trials and their aftermath the Devil appeared in adult male
human guise though variously dressed.

By the early years of the seventeenth century the popular images of
the Devil were as stereotyped as they were ever to become. Occasionally he appeared in animal form, usually that of a dog, but sooner or
later he appeared like a man, often tall (meikle), often dark, but
dressed in a variety of ways. He appeared to Elene Case 'in the likeness
of a tall man in green cloaths';[36] to Janet Paxton, tried in 1661, he also
appeared 'clad in grein as was his Comon habit as ever she saw him
in',[37] Donald Mair of Killearnan in Ross-shire saw him at the end of the
century 'in the likeness of a Black Man with cloven feet and bigg
hands'.[38] To Beatrix Leslie he appeared first 'in the likeness of ane
uncouth beast', later 'in the lykness of a halfling lad' (an adolescent) in
which form he had intercourse with her. In a later confession she
changed her description to a 'meikle brown dog' later turning into the
shape of a man.[39] Agnes Pegavie earlier mentioned as the receiver of a
'sklait stane' saw him first 'in the lykness of a dog which foamed on
her' and later 'in the form of a meikle man'.[40] To another he appeared
'in the likeness of a man at the kirkland in dynsyre' and Bessie Flinkar
and many others 'in the likeness of her own husband'.[41] It may not be
too fanciful to suggest that when the accused identified the Devil as
appearing in the form of a known individual that she was responding
to questions about sexual intercourse with the Devil. Under pressure
the women would work out that if they had indeed had carnal dealing
with the Devil it must be most likely to have been any extra marital

intercourse in which they had indulged; the halfling lad in the barn, or the man in the kirkland in Dynsyre. In the absence of any such encounter it must indeed have been in the shape of their husbands.

It is also interesting to note that when we have the accounts of a group of accused who were alleged to have met together with the Devil there is little agreement between them as to his appearance. This is not, of course, conclusive proof that there was no meeting: witnesses rarely agree. But the collection of suspects at the Crook of Devon in Angus in 1661 had strikingly different coloured spectacles. Isobel Rutherford first saw 'three women with black heads and Satan with 'ane blue bonnet and grey clothes'. Bessie Henderson saw him as 'a halflong fellow with an dusti-coloured coat'; Janet Brough as 'an uncoath man with black cloathes and ane hood on his head'; another as 'a long old man with ane white beard'; Christian Grieve as 'ane little man with a blue bonnet on his head and rough grey clothes on him'. Robert Wilson, one of the two males accused at this trial, saw him more grandiosely 'riding on ane horse with fulycuit clothes and an Spanish cape'.[42]

Typically, he appeared as a thoroughly human, often rather scruffy, male (though Janet Man of Stenton saw him with his hat on his head like a gentleman),[43] of any age from puberty to pre-senility. He was identified as the Devil not by his appearance but by his behaviour, which followed a much more stereotyped pattern. He approached the intended witch: she rarely conjured him up. He then invited her to become his servant promising her in return certain economic benefits. The Demonic Pact initiated, in fact, a standard feudal relationship, reflecting standard assumptions about all significant human bonds in this period. We noted in discussing the social status of the accused that the benefits promised were rarely very extensive. There was little scope in seventeenth-century Scotland for hope of sudden wealth for the ordinary peasant. Hope lay in absence of dire misfortune; in avoidance of famine, disease, disgrace or displacement. The feudal inferiors of the Devil in Scotland were promised over and over again simply that they 'should never want'.

The formula for the renunciation of baptism also occurred repetitiously in the confessions and indictments. A ritual was performed in which the new witch put one hand on her head and another on the sole of her foot and promised to the Devil all that lay between. A variant was laying a hand on the head and giving all under it to the Devil. The sealing of the Pact often at a subsequent meeting involved sexual intercourse, the conferring of a mark or marks, and in some instances the conferring of a new name. Although sexual intercourse, usually called 'carnal dealing' to emphasize that there was nothing imaginary about it, was an almost essential ingredient in female accounts of the Pact, it cannot be said that details of sexual relationships were an important part of Scottish demonic beliefs. In so far as it was a sexually repressive culture, control over behaviour was exercised directly on fornicators and adulterers, as such. The evidence that we have suggests that the Scottish peasantry in the seventeenth century took it for granted that sex was uncomplicated and enjoyable for both sexes. They were in process of learning slowly, through endless reprimand, and payment of fines which were the main support of the system of poor relief, that God disapproved of it outside marriage. Accusations against witches that they caused impotence, common in Europe, did crop up, but were surprisingly rare. It was sexual repression rather than sexual performance which caused difficulties.

The accounts of demonic intercourse are therefore not very varied or detailed. Although one accused witch said that 'she fell in Satanis service through the lust of her flesh by seik a man who had promised her marriage', many had a specific complaint: that 'his nature was cold'. The idea that the flesh of the Devil was icy was common throughout Europe. It is not clear whether this idea is directly related to the educated scientific theory that the Devil took on a body of 'condensed air', [44] but it is an almost routine observation. From Margaret Watson, tried in 1644, we do get some indication of Satanic fore play. According to her indictment he came to her 'lyke ane blak man and gripped thee about the left pape and then had carnall deale with thee and thow discerned his nature to be cold'.[45] From this we may deduce that the Devil, in common with other left handers, caresses with his right hand.

The Devil's sexual relations with male witches are ambiguous. Sodomy with the Devil never appears in the indictments of male witches, but Thomas Black did find him 'lying heavy upon him in the shape of a man'.[46] And to John Scott in 1661 'the divell appeared . . . after twylight at the back of his oune house and took him in his armes and speired at him if he would be his servant'.[47] Some accused males provided the Devil with a female accomplice in their confessions. James Welsh had 'gone out to ease himself in the evening, and at the end of the barne there apperat to him Ane bonnie lass quha desyret him to ly wt hir and he refussit'. She was followed by the Devil himself who asked him to become his servant.[48] Patrick Lowrie in 1605, however, went to the logical extreme. To him 'the devil came as a woman named Helen McBrune. She gave him a belt with four claws like the devil's.'[49] With most male witches, however, the relationship does not appear to have been sexual. The Devil gave Robert Wilson 'ane sair stroke on the right shoulder'.[50] The principal seal of the Pact was the Devil's mark which was bestowed on all witches male and female.

The bestowal of a new name was another possible addition to the proceedings. Elspeth Blackie in 1661 was to call herself Janet Dalry; Janet Paiston was to be called General Jonet; Janet Man in 1659 who had seen the Devil as a gentleman was to call herself Bessie, but her co-accused, Bessie Lacost, claimed she herself had resisted being given a new name. 'The devil wold have called hir Jeanie but she said she wold not have two names shee was already called Bessie and he said Bessie be it then and thereafter did ly with her but she thought his bodie was harder and colder than a man'.[51] It has been suggested that certain names, usually Janet or Margaret, were specially associated with witches, but this suggestion is often related to the belief in a witch cult. In fact there was such a small number of female first names in common currency in seventeenth-century Scotland that it is impossible to deduce anything from their use among accused witches. Nearly all women were called Elizabeth, Margaret, Jane/t, Catherine, Christian, Mary/Marion, Ann, Agnes, Alison, Helen, Isobel, or derivatives of these. More idiosyncratic were Barbara, Euphemia, Beatrice, Annabel, Grissell, Marjorie, or Gilleis; but there the choice more or less ended.

Sometimes the Devil insisted on being given a particular name. He told Isobel Rutherford, who had seen him with a blue bonnet at Crook of Devon, to call him 'Viceroy': Bessie Henderson to call him 'Charles': Thomas Roy to call him Lucifer.[52] The Devil of the Stenton witches called himself 'Simon'. Most of the accused however seem to have called him 'my lord' if they addressed him directly.

The confessions of the Pact were reported in the final indictment either much as they had appeared in the pre-trial papers or somewhat pared down to the essential details of meeting the Devil 'knowing him to be the Devil', renunciation of baptism, and sealing with sexual intercourse and the bestowal of the mark. It was important to establish the witch's consciousness and responsibility for what she did, and many of the prefaces to the confessions emphasize that it was given 'freely and of hir awine accord'. Lawyers greatly preferred to have a confession of an explicit Pact rather than have to make an assumption of a tacit Pact through witnesses' accounts of her behaviour and performances. This preference reflected the changing focus of criminal law in which the rational punishment of individual acts of wrong doing was gradually replacing the restorative system of justice in which the satisfaction of the victim was of prime importance. At the same time it gave women for the first time personal responsibility for their own actions. It was a common feature of the confessions that the witch declared herself to be wicked, guilty, and deserving of the death penalty. Alison Fermer of Stenton after describing her activities summed up that 'for the which causes forsaid she deserves nott nor desyres to leive'. Bessie Lacost, the principal figure in the Stenton trial, described by Marion Angus as 'the officer' 'being seriously exhorted to declare the trewth whither ever schee had entered into and expresse Covenant with the deivell did most freelie and of hir awine accord confes that schee was a meiserable creature and one no worthie to leive for leiving so long in a direct league with the devill'.[5]

It is impossible to tell in these oft repeated declarations to what extent the accused had absorbed internally the truth of her statements

It no doubt varied greatly from person to person, but in so far as the accused fully accepted that they deserved to die, this represented a second revolution in their sense of personal identity and their relationship to the community and its God. Identification of the self as a deviant and witch, represented warfare on the dominant values; identification of the self as deserving to die meant reacceptance of these values and personal defeat. Not all of them made this second internal revolution. The range of possible postures were from innocent, confused, guilty but repentant, to guilty and unrepentant. 'And when I gave my malison it always lighted'.

The central points of the Pact and the personal responsibility of the individual accused formed the final indictment. The confessions, however, supplied a wider variety of detail than were needed for the indictment. Many indictments do not mention witches' meetings at all, but nearly all the multiple trials refer to them at least in passing. Some accounts of meetings are in fact simply an extension of descriptions of the Pact which is said to have taken place in the company of other witches. Some said that they went in the first place to a meeting to seek vengeance against some individual, and had then been pressed to make a pact with the Devil. The prime purpose of the demand for information about meetings was essentially to extract more names. Bessie Lacost said that 'Marion Wilson and Isobel Kemp who ar burnt and Alison Fermer who is yett alive did first take hir to the devill's companie' and that Alison Fermer, Jean Sydserffe, Helen Herriott, Marion Angus, and Jonett Wood, were 'also as great witches as shee'.[54] The last bit of power given to the confessing and about to be convicted witch as she was forced into her trap was the power to settle old scores. Not everyone on trial availed themselves of this. Helen Cumine, one of the Stenton group, said that she saw a great number of women, 'shee thought above fortie but ther was so great a mist betwixt her and them that she could not know them; lykways shee saw a great number of men in another place but ther was a great mist betwixt her and them too'. Bessie Henderson of Crook of Devon in 1661 compromised and identified her colleagues by their voices. 'She did not see them in regard of the weakness of her sight saying that she saw not well in the nicht this many a year.'[55]

Apart from the naming of names the actual details of what took place at the meetings were not legally significant and therefore reflect a wider range of collective belief than do accounts of the Pact. The most immediately obvious feature of Scottish beliefs is that they represent a less extreme collective nightmare than those of the European continent. Infant sacrifice is unknown; cannibalism, formal worship of the Devil, and communal sex are rather rare. The confessions which most nearly parallel those of the continent are those of Isobel Gowdie of Auldearn and those of the Forfar group of suspects. Not even in these there actual infant sacrifice, but unbaptized infants were said to have been exhumed and eaten. In the indictments of the Forfar group it was alleged that they 'went up to the church wall about the south eist doore, and raisit a young bairn unbaptised, and took his feet, his hands, a pairt of the head and butock, and maid a py thereof, that they might eat of it, and by that means might never mack a confessione (as they thought) of their witchcraft.'[56]

The descriptions given by the accused at these trials, which took place in 1661 and 1662, are quite exceptional in the richness of the detail which has been recorded, but at neither of them are accounts of formal devil worship given. The part played by the Devil was in eating, drinking, dancing, kissing, and copulating with them. Superficially they provide the best case for those who wish to maintain the reality of witches' meetings and they conform more closely than other Scottish confessions to a continental stereotype in that they refer to the number of their gathering being thirteen, and they refer to regular meetings: 'at Candlmas, Rood Day, Lammas and Hallowmass'. They are particularly detailed in descriptions of revelry: 'they daunced togither, and the ground under them was all fyre flauchter, and Andrew Watson hade his usuale staff in his hand, althou he be a blind man yet he daunced also nimblie as any of the companye, and made also great moviement by singing his old ballards, and Isobell Shyrrie did sing her song called Tinkletum Tankletum'.[57] They also, however, are particularly rich, as Cohn has pointed out, in example of incidents which can only relate to dreams, nightmares, and collective fantasies. Agnes Spark said that she

> heard people ther present did speake of Isobell Shirie, and say that the divell did always ryde upon hir, and that she was shoad lyke ane mare, or ane horse.[58]

Isobel Gowdie

> haid a little horse and wold say Horse and Hattock in the Divellis name! and we wold flie upon an hie-wey. We will flie lyk strawes quhan we pleas; wild strawes and corne strawes wil be horses to us and we put them betwixt our foot and say Horse and Hattock in the Divellis name! Quhan we wold ryde we tak windle-strawes of bean stakes and put them betwixt our foot and say thryse
>> Horse and Hattock, horse and gre,
>> Horse and pellake; ho! ho![59]

The Forfar group were also said to have gone out to sea as part of their group performance of a particular malefice: the sinking of ship: Elspet Bruice said that after drinking three pints of ail she and two other women went foorth to the sandis, and that ther thrie other women met them, and that the divell was there present with them all, in the shape of ane great horse; and that they concludit the sinking of ane shipp, lying not farr off from Barrie, and that presentlie the said company appoynted her selfe to tak hold of the cable tow, and to hold it fast untill they did returne, and she herselfe did presentlie take hold of the cable tow, and that the rest with the divell went in to the sea upone the said cable as shee thought, and that about the spaice of an hour thereafter they returned all in the same likeness as befor, except that the divell was in the shape of a man upone his return and that the rest were sore traiked (fatigued) and that the divell did kiss them all except her selfe, and that he kist her hand only, and that then they concludit another meeting to be at the nixt hallowes.[60]

The confessions of the accused at Forfar and Auldearn do not appear to represent the tip of an iceberg in the sense that many more as rich and detailed lie in the archives unpublished. The examination of numbers of unpublished confessions suggests that the most colourful confessions were published in the nineteenth century. The typical unpublished confession is scrappy. Those of Forfar and Auldearn, however, are typical in the sense that all the features which they mention in such detail are echoed in the often more fragmented confessions still in the archives. What they all have in common is not worship and ritual, other than those formal pacts which took place at meetings: the standard account of a witches' meeting is not of forbidden worship or an inversion of the services they knew. The Scottish Devil did not deliver long sermons which were patiently listened to. The standard account is an account of disorder. It is about eating and drinking and music and dancing. It is about gorrovage (uproar). It was common practice for Kirk sessions and burgh councils to forbid assemblies of more than a certain number under one roof. Enactments were made against 'penny bridals' (wedding parties to which the guests brought their own refreshment), and other forms of revelry and conviviality. The details of witches' meetings appear to reflect most frequently a particular kind of seventeenth-century deprivation.
Bessie Lacost, who had named all her neighbours, said,

that once at the Gallowhop the devill made them a feast of aill and wheat bread where they sat all about a great stone and the devill said three words like a grace but shee did not remember them that he dranke to them all and bad them be true to him and see that they were not fals and then bad them adieu. That in all there meitingis the devil whisles and they sung one to another and dawnced and mad gorrovage and ther last meitting was about half ane yeire since.[61]

Her neighbour and fellow accused, Marion Angus, describing the same set of meetings said that they

> had a meitting in the Gallowhope in the night tym and yair had a peace of flesche lyke beiffe. And eftir they had all eattene of the samen The devill haveing ane bonnitt on his head Tooke Bessir Lacost by the hand and the rest having one another by the hand daunced in ane ring rownd about the broad stoun in the Gallowhope and sung ane to another and stayed ther ane houre. Then the devill bad them be honest to him and ane to another and then bade them guidnight. And about three quarters of ane yeare yairefter They all mett at Sandies hill qua they sung and daunced a Whyl and returned hom.[62]

Bessie Flinker of Liberton said that 'she was taken upon the hills by a whirle of wind and masked herselfe, and there daunced with the rest'.[63] John Douglas of Tranent was the piper at meetings in 1659.[64] At Aberdeen in 1597 the accused were said to have danced at the 'mercat and fish cross', where it was particularly remarkable that no external witnesses saw them.

> You came [went the indictment] under the conduct and gyding of the devill, present with you all in company, playing before you on his kynd of instruments. Ye all dansit about baythe the said cross and the meill mercat ane lang space of tym; in the quhilk devyll's dans thow, the said Thomas was foremost and led the ring, and dang the said Kathren Mitchell because she spoilt your dans, and ran nocht so fast as the rest.[65]

Other details, such as times, places, numbers present, and method o: transport are diverse. The number thirteen, so beloved of twentieth-century demonologists, occurs fairly rarely and seems to have little o no significance. A large round number is the most frequent. On account to the 1649 Parliament alleged that there were 500 present.[6] At a convention upon a hill in Athole in 1597 there were exactl twenty-three hundred.[67] Elspeth Blackie in Liberton in 1661 though there were about 40 at the meeting: 'she kend non of them bot Elspet Mowat, the rest wer all masked'.[68]

Times varied, but were always at night. Midnight was commonl mentioned, but one suggested 'two hours before day'. The place were nearly always local and specific: the Bents of Balruddie, Gibson Craig, 'where the gallows stand before midnight', the gallowhop 'ane place in Stentoune paroche called the hom', Sandies Hill, or ver frequently the churchyard, or the Kirk itself: the hie Kirk of Lanar the Kirk of Carnwath were both mentioned. One defendant argue against a charge that she was running widdershins in the mill, that s

was in the mill simply wasting time when she should have been
attending to her 'stuff then grinding in the miln', but the prosecutor
argued that she was up to no good because 'it is the custom of witches
to have their meetings and dancings within milns'.[69] This could well
have been produced *ad hoc* by the lawyer since there is not a great deal
of support from the confessions for any particular preference for mills.

Apart from feasting, dancing, and disorder, the recurrent theme in
accounts of meetings was communal sorcery such as the Forfar ship
sinking, designed to effect more complex malefice than could be
achieved solo. Indeed the accounts of the use of corpses by witches were
usually for the purposes of sorcery rather than worship. A 1644 indictment said that the accused 'did lift corpses of deceissit persones fra
quhoum ye tuik membres to accompleische thy devillische designes
upone men and women'.[70] Sometimes there was no obvious sorcery
involved in the evil doing. Bessie Henderson's indictment said that
'Janet Paton in cruik of Devon was with you at ane meeting when they
trampit down Thos. White's rie in the beginning of harvest, 1661, and
that she had broad soals and trampit down more nor any of the rest'.[71]
All that was needed for that particular malefice was sufficient labour-
power. Elizabeth Bathgate's companions' malefice was performed to
avoid discovery. It was alleged that they

> met upon the shore of Eymouth under night and cruelly murdered
> David Hynd amongst them, who was watching the boats under
> night during the herring drove, for fear he should have dis-
> covered their unlawful actions and meeting.[72]

The same group also sank a ship. This was a common malefice among
witches in fishing towns and villages. The indictment alleged that

> the pannel and her associat witches being conveyed by the Devil
> from a meeting they had upon the shoar of Eymouth into a ship
> wherein George Holdie in Eymouth was with his company the
> pannel and her accomplices cruelly sank and destroyed the ship
> wherein they all perished with the ship and goods.[73]

Sometimes the accused said they had asked particular personal
favours of the Devil at the meetings with regard to a specific malefice.
Alison Fermer said that

> shee took the devell by the hand and desyre amends of Alexr
> Crumbie for his sonnes malt that daft Anna Crumbie took away
> and Bessie Calder brought back again and the devill said shee
> should gett a sufficient mendis of him. That shee desyred the malt
> barne to hir sonne for he had mor to plenische it with then
> Alex'r.[74]

Marion Angus explained to the court in 1659 that she went to a meeting of witches in order 'to seek amends of the devill of ane Englishman ane soldier that quartered in hir house', and the Devil on her promise to be his servant said 'he would switche the said Englishe man out of the town'.[75] Janet Wood in 1659 also had a specific request. Like Marion Angus she had a grudge against an English soldier.

Shee desyred amends of the Englische men that tooke hir self and the devill said they were out of Scotland he could not get amends of them. This schee denyed Only schee confessed that was ill tyme that the malt was taken awa & that the Englische took hir away to the Grange and left hir thair.[76]

The powers of the Devil ended at the Scottish border.

The confessions have a tendency to drift back from dream and fantasy to real life, to remembered injuries and injustice. The round of inquisition and questioning leading to the Demonic Pact and the private and communal fantasies surrounding it often ended up where it all began: with the simple and immediate quarrel, grudge, and malefice.

CHAPTER TWELVE

THE BELIEF SYSTEM
II THE CHRISTIANIZATION
OF THE PEOPLE

The evidence for how the peasantry saw God is less direct than the evidence for how they saw the Devil; we have largely to infer it from accounts of their religious instruction by the educated ministry of the Reformed Church. We turn here to the question of how the witch-beliefs which surfaced and were preserved as a by product of inter-changes between lawyer and peasant related to the central beliefs of official Christianity.

One of the current themes at present in the writings of European, and particularly French historians, is that Europe was effectively Christianized for the first time by the twin movements of the Reformation and the Counter Reformation.[1] This primary Chris-tianization had several facets, but it was characterized mainly by the systematic exposure of the laity to Christian instruction and moral exhortation through vernacular preaching, by an entirely novel shift from the idea that the religious life was to be lived only by religious specialists to the assumption that each individual was personally responsible for his own salvation, and by a move of first the urban and then the peasant laity from animist beliefs to a more spiritual form of religion.

It is a theme whose applicability to Scotland is very clear. What-ever may be said about the effectiveness of the pre-Reformation church there, it is not really disputed that in the fifty years following the Reformation, in those areas where Kirk sessions were set up and trained ministers sent, much of the populace was introduced through a most strenuous indoctrination of literacy, preaching, and the 'godly discipline', to a basic Christianity and to concepts of moral behaviour which would have been quite unfamiliar to their grandparents.[2]

Although this is not disputed, the emphasis in Scottish religious history has been on the differences in theology between varieties of Calvinism and between Calvinism and Arminianism; and on the differences in Church government between Presbyterianism and Episcopalianism. Following this, the analysis of witchcraft in Scotland in the past has been discussed in terms of the peculiarities of Calvinism rather than the peculiarities of Christianity.[3]

This is not to say that distinctively Calvinist beliefs did not affect the form of witch-beliefs, but simply that these may be peripheral to the main issues. It has already been clearly established by Teall[4] and reinforced by Monter[5] that there is no particularly Calvinist form of witch-belief. Calvin himself had little to say directly on the matter, though in his commentary on Exodus he appears to regard the sin of witchcraft as that of apostasy and superstition.[6] The major themes of Calvinism—the omnipotence of God and predestination to election and reprobation—however, clearly have direct bearing on the nature and identity of Satan and on the freedom of the witch. The three principal positions with regard to predestination adopted in seventeenth-century Scotland were supralapsarianism, infralapsarianism, and Arminianism. The supralapsarians expounded the most logical of Calvinist positions: that God preordained the Fall of Man, but had to struggle against the corollary that he was the author of sin. The infralapsarians held equally strongly the doctrine of the sovereignty of God but considered that the Fall was simply permitted rather than willed by God and that election and reprobation started with the Fall as an accomplished fact. Arminianism, stemming from the Dutch theologian Arminius, was radically distinct. Its exponents held that God had determined to elect all those who believed in Christ and to damn all those who did not, but like Calvinists they rejected the idea that man could acquire faith through his own free will; faith could only be obtained by God's grace.[7]

None of these positions in fact marry particularly well with the classic demonological view of the Devil. Most demonological treatises following the *Malleus Maleficarum* assert that the Devil, who is part of the creation, uses his powers 'by permission'. In this they guard against a Manichean position in which the powers of good and evil, God and the Devil, are seen to be evenly balanced. Even the less extreme Calvinist infralapsarian position regarded only the Fall of Man as being 'by permission'. All that followed, including the current activities of the Devil, was by God's will, rather than by permission. Calvinism, which stressed the omnipotence and sovereignty of God above all else, was as far removed from Manicheism as possible. Demonological theorists, however, had consciously to guard against the accusation that they were Manicheans, and although they made ritual protestations to protect themselves most of their treatises are open to this interpretation. It is perhaps noteworthy that demonological works tended to be published on their own rather than as part of an integrated scheme of theology. In theological as opposed to demonological treatises, whether Catholic, Calvinist, Lutheran, Arminian, or other, the role of the Devil tended to be highly spiritualized. He was a kind of unholy Ghost, not an incarnate or physically powerful form. Calvin's own position in regarding witchcraft as superstition and apostasy was entirely logical in this respect and bore very little relation to the demonological beliefs manifested in the continental and Scottish courts by those professing his doctrines. So far as the apostasy of the witch herself is concerned, however, as opposed to the alleged power of the Devil to incarnate himself, perform marvels, and seduce humans, there is no particular incompatibility with predestinarian doctrines. The fact that a consummation of the Demonic Pact appears in psychological terms to be the ultimate in human free will, does not preclude it having been predestined either from Eternity or from the Fall.

So far as witch-beliefs and witch-hunting are concerned, however, the different types of theological position prevalent in seventeenth-century Scotland are less important than the introduction of Christianity itself. The Calvinist supralapsarian and infralapsarian positions were characteristic of those who favoured a Presbyterian form of church government and the Arminian was characteristic of those who favoured Episcopalianism. It is not possible to discern any difference between these parties so far as witch-hunting or witch-beliefs are concerned. The main hunts were 1628–30 (Episcopalian); 1649 (covenanting Presbyterian), and the late 50s to 1662 (English occupation and Restoration Episcopalian). What is more, the party arguments about the sovereignty of God were conducted at a level of sophistication which was unlikely to be absorbed by the peasant parishioner. The factors which were common to all religious parties in Scotland (and to Reforming movements both Protestant and Catholic on the Continent) were the evangelical appeal to the individual to be responsible for his own salvation, the reiteration of trinitarian Christian doctrine, and the exhortation to the moral life. It has been suggested that the Presbyterian and Covenanting clergy were more fervently evangelical[8] but the evidence of surviving Episcopalian sermons does not really bear this out.[9] The striking characteristic of all preaching and instruction in the parishes of seventeenth-century Scotland is that it combined an established church concern with the church observances, morals, and demeanour of all the permanent residents, with a sect-like endeavour to turn them into highly-committed believing Christians. This of course was consistent with the twin Calvinist beliefs in election and the sovereignty of God. Only the elect will respond to evangelical appeals, but the reprobate must also be compelled to give honour to God in their outward behaviour. Preachers in practice divided their flock into three categories: those who had 'embraced Christ', who were often publicly indistinguishable from the second category: 'formal professors' or 'Christians within the law', and thirdly, 'sinners' or 'the reprobate' or 'the ungodly'. The term 'sinner' could technically be applied to anyone and had to be understood in context. A fourth category of 'witch', which was logically the inverse of those who had embraced Christ, was rarely included or discussed by preachers other than in the context of a witch panic or local execution.

Routine Christian indoctrination took most of the energies of the preachers without dealing with the most extreme form of hostility to the faith. Neglect of witchcraft as a regular issue went along with a highly spiritualized view of the Devil which bore only the most vestigial resemblance to the meikle black man who waylaid his female followers in barns, hill tops, and cross-road gallows. Andrew Gray who was a minister in Glasgow until his death in 1656 at the age of twenty-two, preached a sermon entitled 'Precious Remedies Against Satan's Devices', based on the text 'Lest Satan should get an advantage of us for we are not ignorant of his devices (2. Cor.ii 11)'.[10] Like many sermons this was addressed to grade two Christians: those 'under the exercise of the law and under the terrors of God'. The basic remedy which he offered was to 'embrace Christ', but the devices of Satan which he listed, some of which seem obscurely differentiated from each other, were fivefold. Satan's first device was to make Christians under the law misinterpret sermons, scripture, and providence; his second was to generate a spirit of discouragement; his third was to kill their convictions; his fourth was darkening the freedom of the gospel; and his fifth was to make them fall asleep.[11]

There was nothing unusual about this highly spiritualized view of the Devil. It was common in pre-Reformation theology; it was featured throughout the witch-hunting period, and still appears today in sects and denominations which retain the concept of a demonic force. In November 1589, Bothwell, who was later accused of being at the centre of the North Berwick group of witches, was in the High Kirk of St Giles on the stool of repentance where he was obliged to listen to a sermon preached at him by the Rev. Robert Bruce. His text, taken from 2nd Timothy 2, ended 'and that they may come to amendment out of the snare of the Devil which are taken of him at his will', and his highly evangelical advice to the congregation went as follows:

ye have only this to be aware of: for the Devill is ever readie at thine hand, and this provision is not necessair rather for ane hard heart, but gif men and women, through the wightinesse of their sinnes conceive over-deep a sorrow in their hearts, in this caice they would be helped. For, I say, at that time the Devill is present, and so soon as he perceiveth thee dung down with the consideration of thine own sinnes, that thou art, as it wer, presentlie in the pit of hell; then he is busie to make thee to doubt, to make thee to dispair, and to make thee to think that thy sinnes ar so manie, so uglie, and so great that the Lord will never forgive them, and casteth in this or that stay before thee, to terrifie thee, that thou come not to seeke grace at the throne of grace.[12]

The Devil, on the principle that earthly and bodily things were vile was deemed to represent the pleasures and temptations of this earth, but he was also regarded as being the author of more spiritual and sophisticated temptations. Robert Leighton, who was minister at New-battle in the 1640s and became Archbishop of Glasgow at the Restoration, reflected this when he wrote 'Consider whether it is better to be the slaves of Satan or the sons of God. Measure delight in God with the low base pleasure of sense.'[13] But he also on another occasion expressly denied the Devil's capacity and in this case his minions too, to incarnate themselves when tempting men and emphasized the most spiritual aspects of Satan's power.

fleshly pollution are things of which the devils are not capable in themselves, though they excite men to them and so they are called unclean spirits. But the highest rank of sins are those that are properly spiritual wickedness. These in men are the chief strengths of Satan, the inner works of his forts and strongholds (2 Corr.x 4).[14]

Though no doubt the most elegant sermons of the most famous clergy were those which were recorded by shorthand writers or other-wise found their way into print, there is every reason to suppose that their content was typical of the regular preaching that was taking place all over administered Scotland. The presbyteries kept a close rein on all their ministers. There was a considerable amount of reciprocal preaching at each other's great fasts and communions. Ministers were frequently told which texts they were to preach on.[15] The pressures to imitate and conform were much stronger than those to demonstrate idiosyncracies. This leaves a problem as to the connection between the new Christianity and the new demonology.

The seventeenth century, post-Reformation God is a totally spiritualized concept. He and the human souls who embrace him and are elected, stand in actual opposition to all earthly matters, although he does, in the form of Providence, sometimes concern himself with them. The inversion of the spiritualized God is therefore an equally spiritualized Devil. Descriptions of him are actually hard to distinguish from the promptings of the human ego. The spiritualized Devil is a great deal less precisely described than God, for it is relatively easy to describe perfection in spiritual terms. In mundane terms the reverse is true. There is no way in which the perfect trinitarian God can be related to the good society. Spiritual goodness is in opposition to society and it is significant that the attempt to describe the incarnate deity, the second person of the Trinity, is in terms of an individual opposed to society. Indeed the good society in a world where the dominant ideology is religious rather than secular can only be adequately described by its opposites. Society was in fact incapable of good since it was not spiritual. The Devil was used, therefore, to

describe two separate inversions: the inverse of a spiritual God and the
inverse of stable social life.

Belief Structure

GOOD

SOCIAL LIFE	GOD
THE DEVIL	THE DEVIL

THIS WORLD   OTHER WORLD

EVIL

The Devil was a transferable explanatory principle. It could be
used to explain misfortune and other violations of social life; it could
also be used to explain sin and unbelief. By one transference
ministers were able to turn to a physical devil when they operated as
policemen rather than pastors, and by another the convicted witch,
an enemy of her neighbours, became an enemy of God.

In practice the physical Devil who seduced witches seems not to
have been conjured up by preachers except when preaching directly
to convicted witches or at a fast before an execution. For the same
reason that witches were not part of the normal hierarchy of human
believers, formal believers, and sinners: they were monsters, not
humans, so the physical Devil, with the awkward questions he raised,
was rarely referred to in pulpit oratory. Unfortunately we do not
have the necessary evidence of witchcraft sermons preached by those
who were most prolific in classic evangelical preaching, to discover
exactly how they related the two Devils. The evidence runs only the
other way. Witchcraft sermons were obliged to confront all the
spiritual issues of damnation, salvation, predestination, free will, in
relation to the peasant encounter with the meikle black man whose
powers did not extend to England. We know too that the clergy were
centrally involved in collecting and processing the evidence that was
presented in court. They heard the first confessions and asked the
leading questions. There is no case for suggesting that their spiritual
right hand did not know what their physical left hand was doing.
Delumeau's suggestion that witch-hunting died down when the
peasantry had been finally wooed from their animist beliefs by the
preaching and education of a spiritual clergy,[16] rather underestimates
the extent to which the clergy shared and encouraged a very flexible
and ambiguous view of the relationship between the physical and the
spiritual.

The problem of the sources of physical and spiritual evil was there before Calvinism and is endemic to Christianity. The vernacular catechism published by the Archbishop of St Andrews as part of a pre-Reformation drive to evangelize the laity,[17] is ambiguously balanced between emphasis on the damage to the soul and the physical powers of witchcraft. After referring to 'superstitious' usages against 'fyre, water, sword, and noysum beistis', it continues:

> O thou wretchit and blind man or woman, that thinkes or says
> siclike wordis, knaw thou weil and understand, that quhen saevir
> thow speris or seikis for ony help, cousel, remede, consolation or
> defence at ony wytche, sorcerar, cownqerar, or siclike disseveris,
> thow dois greit injure to thi Lord God, because that thow takis
> the honour and service quhilk aucht to be gevin to God allanerly,
> and giffis it to the devil quihilk is deidly enemie to thy soul. For
> without dout, all Wytches, Nigromanceris and siclikes, workis
> be operation of the devil under a paction, condition, band or
> obligatioun of service and honour to be made to him.[18]

It is explicit that the Devil does have physical powers, but that these are minor:

> The devil sumtyme in smal matters schawis to the verite, bot to
> that effeck, that finally he may cause thee gif credit to his
> lesiningis and black falset in matters of greit wecht concerning
> thi saul. Sumtyme he will help the to get againe the guddis of
> thos world, bot his intent is, that finally he may cause the tyne
> the guddis of the world to come. Sumtyme he will help the to
> recover the helth of thi body, bot to that effeck, that finally he
> may bring the to the eternal dede of thi saul.[19]

The only difference between this and later, Calvinist writings is that the author does not seem particularly concerned about the source of the Devil's power in this matter and its relationship to divine power and divine volition. The pastoral concern and the spiritual signifi-cance of physical demonic powers are similar to that expressed in sermons a hundred and fifty years later. Indeed if we turn to two sermons which have been preserved from the very end of the witch-hunt we find that none of the problems had been resolved. A con-siderable amount of documentation has been preserved from the trial of the Paisley witches of 1697 and this includes one sermon which was preached to the Commissioners of Justiciary before they reached their verdict on the 13th April, and another which was preached to the seven convicted witches on the 9th June, the day before their execution.

James Hutchison, who preached to the Commissioners, was born in 1626. He was deprived of his living in 1662, reinstated in 1688, and retired in 1690, but seems to have been brought out for the purpose of this sermon at the age of 71.[20] His text was from Exodus, 11.18: 'Thou shalt not suffer a witch to live', and his purpose was to exhort the Commissioners, whom he likened to the judges of Israel, to do their duty and convict. He insisted that the particular kind of evil-doer referred to in the text was well translated 'witch' and added a great show of erudition, with reference to Hebrew, Greek, and Latin words, to demonstrate that this was indeed so. He then defined what was meant by a witch:

> By a witch is understood a person that hath immediate converse with the Devil. That one way or another is under a compact with him acted and influenced by him in reference to the producing such effects as cannot be produced by others without this compact.[21]

He compared the Demonic Pact with Christian baptism and suggested that while the external sign of baptism was a seal whereby a Christian child was to be counted as a visible professor of Christ,

> No less doth Satan require of them that will follow in his way than either personal covenanting with him and receiving his mark upon their flesh, or that the parent give their children to him and they receive his mark, and where this is I doubt not such a person is really a witch or a warlock, and even suppose it be a child it will be found afterwards (if the Lord's powerfully con-verting of the soul to himself prevent it not) that such persons will be as really in covenant with Satan, as the children of professing parents receiving baptism will be found to be in covenant with God.

Two of the accused, the Lindsay brothers, were pre-pubertal boys, and since the alleged victim, Christian Shaw, a laird's daughter, was a girl of about the same age, the status of children with regard to election, redemption, reprobation, and witchcraft was an issue at this trial.

Hutchison also attempted to distinguish between the sinner who did wicked things because the Devil had blinded him to goodness, and those who sinned directly because of the compact and were therefore guilty of witchcraft. The problem about whether it is worth distinguishing between categories of sinners and reprobates is solved by relating it to the kind of treatment which they should be accorded on earth. It was never suggested that the reprobate be physically punished or executed unless they had fallen foul of the law of the land. Certain sinners, too, may have been included in God's plans for a late redemption. But witches, who had personally committed themselves to reprobation were worthy of death along with others who had committed crimes so terrible that it was an offence to God to permit them to live.

Hutchison also discussed how it was possible for members of the visible church to become witches. He attributed this to the Fall and added:

> If God had not more to do with Adam's posterity it had been easy for Satan to have made Adam and Eve both witches. But that God had his Elect to bring out of their Loins and had a covenant of grace to transact with Adam and Eve.

Hutchison went on to draw certain inferences: (1) that children of witches might be justly regarded as being under a real compact with Satan; (2) that those who joined witches in murder by wax image were not only murderers but partakers in devilry; (3) that those who confessed to having been with witches were to be counted witches; (4) that the compact was to the effect that they were guided and influenced by Satan; (5) that 'carnal dealing' with Satan was witchcraft; (6) that when a person was thrown into a fit by another person touching them and only by that other then it was owing to witchcraft; and (7) that those that could 'tell secrets' or 'prophesie' were either guilty of witchcraft or else 'privie to the enchanters deals and "*socii criminis*" '. The reference to fits was a late addition to the structure of witch-beliefs. Only in the closing stages of witch-hunts did demonic possession feature at all frequently. In the Paisley witch-hunt it had been a central feature.

Hutchison concluded by emphasizing that it was the express command of God that such people as he described should be put to death. He reminded the judges that they were gods themselves in this act of judgement, and exhorted them to convict. He ended:

> Let this humble us all and let us bewaill it as a great evil that such a place as the west of Scotland where the gospell of Christ has been purely preacht should have so many in it under suspicion of the crime of Witchcraft. Ye that are free, Bless God that hath kept you from the wicked one, and pray that out of zeall to God and his Glory that he would bring their works of darkness to light that marrs your solemnities and are fearfull spotts in your feasts. I go no furder. Amen.

Hutchison emerges from this sermon as a cold and vindictive old man for whom the convicted witches have been completely stripped of human characteristics. He laid particular stress on the possibility of children being servants of the Devil, and added a socio-economic explanation for the easy entrance of witchcraft at this time. It was caused by the 'prevelancy of unmortified lust and corruption' and by the 'love of gain' in the west of Scotland. Further, witchcraft was the means whereby 'others of the poorer sort could get their malice and envy satisfied'. The theme that the poor and the greedy were particularly prone to the temptations of witchcraft goes back to James VI's *Daemonologie*[22] and reflects the fact that both those who were accused and those who appear to have been attracted to witchcraft practices came from oppressed groups and classes.

In contrast is the other Paisley sermon, that preached by the Reverend David Brown, a local minister in his early thirties,[23] to the victims themselves on the day before they were executed. The contrast may indeed be due partly to the fact that Hutchison was trying to galvanize a group of Edinburgh lawyers to convict; Brown was faced with human aspects of the servants of the Devil.

Instead of the standard witchcraft verse he took his text from 1st Timothy, 1.16: 'Howbeit, for this cause I obtained mercy, that in me first Jesus Christ might show forth all long suffering for a pattern to them that should hereafter believe in him to life everlasting.' The sermon opens with a discussion of the doctrine of salvation. Brown declared, with the aid of numerous citations from scripture, that Christ came not primarily to judge but to save sinners, and he directly criticizes Luther's view that Christ came as a judgement on sinful humanity. He demonstrated by elaborate arguments, carefully subdivided in the idiom of the period, the truth of his position, which appears to have been essentially Arminian. He then moved on to explain that even the most wicked of all sinners could avail themselves of salvation and suggested reasons why God is pleased to act in this merciful spirit. He concluded that one need never question 'God's good will to pardon', and continued his general evangelical argument in highly conventional terms: the sinner must know Christ, but knowledge is not enough; 'the devils believe and tremble'. As well as knowledge of the gospels there must be assent to their truths; there must be consent to Christ. Finally, the sinner must lean on Christ; there must be a 'recumbency and resting on him'. Full belief ensures divine mercy, but this does not mean that one is at liberty to sin in expectation of a late repentence. It is rather a stimulus, being assured of God's goodness in his mercy to lead in gratitude a good life. How terrible on the other hand will be the fate of those who, when offered this mercy, yet refuse it.

Brown then turned to the particular cases of those in front of him, and described their sin as 'the highest act of rebellion against the God of heaven and earth'. These preachers never failed unconsciously to glamorize witchcraft. In contracting with the Devil the witches have shown that they care not for Christ: 'there is your sin'. In waging war against Christ and against 'children, ministers, and others' they have

been guilty of 'war upon the whole of creation except the Devil'. He
went on to point out their danger:

> Will it not be sad that your heart should be hardened now, when
> ye are come to your extremity, and when it might be expected
> that messengers of grace should be acceptable to you. We are come
> to you, when ye are within a few hours of eternity, to intreat
> you, before ye perish for ever, to embrace the offers of Christ.
> For, first, ye go aback from the remedy, if ye close not with Christ.
> Again, you lay a foundation for a great many challenges through
> eternity, if ye close not with Christ; for though now conscience
> be secure, yet it will rise like a roaring lion at the last, and
> though ministers would weep over you, as if we were seeking
> from you some great thing for ourselves, yet ye will stand it out.
> What will conscience say, when the devil will be at the gallows
> foot, ready to harle you down to hell? and no sooner in hell, but
> conscience will say, when God sent his ministers to you, ye
> believed the devil, and would not yield to Jesus Christ, and what
> will ye say to conscience then? when conscience will say, now
> this is your lodging for ever; now eternity! eternity! what will
> ye do through eternity? ye are laying a foundation of challenges
> through eternity. Another thing that makes your case dangerous,
> ye declare you will not be in Christ's reverence for mercy. I will
> tell how so, if you will be in his reverence, why will ye not
> confess your sin, and renounce the deed of gift to the devil? ye
> declared your denial (of Christ) in the face of the courts, and
> frequently since ye have done. O how dreadful will your condition
> be if ye die in such a case! . . . Ye have murdered your own
> souls; your time is nigh a close, your glass is nigh run. Ye should
> confess therefore that God's people may pray for you. If ye would
> be out of the claws of the devil it will take all the prayers you can
> get.[24]

He ended: 'and now we take God to record that we have offered to
you Jesus Christ and if ye will not take him we are free of your blood.'

Brown's sermon demonstrates the way in which the normal idiom
of evangelical appeal, offered weekly or even oftener to their
partially literate peasant congregations, needed only the slightest
modification to be applicable to the abnormal case of convicted
witches about to be hanged. Hutchison's sermon was concerned with
the special crime of witchcraft and with the importance of law and
order. He wished to convince the justices (and some of the accused in
the case had already been acquitted) of the social, legal, and divine
necessity of conviction and demonstrate the power of the church. His
purpose was overtly political. Brown on the other hand was concerned with the particular individuals in the case, and was engaged in

the principal activity of seventeenth-century Scottish preachers: the struggle for peasant minds. The party differences were fought out at the elite end of the social and educational structure (though by the covenanting period these ideological distinctions within the basic framework had clearly penetrated very deeply). At the parish level the work of the preacher was still evangelical. Christianity itself was still felt to be insecure, and the central theme, at least of surviving sermons, was always the importance of personal commitment ('embracing' was the jargon word) to Christ. Brown's sermon, like so many others, was centred on the doctrines of atonement and salvation. Substantially the same address could have been given at any normal service. There was no mention of election, no particular stress on the omnipotence of God, no suggestion that the convicts were predestinately reprobate or that their deaths would be to the greater glory of God. Brown said nothing about the details of the behaviour of the witches. He was interested in witchcraft less as a social menace than as a sin against God, as the most defiant act, not of unbelief, but of enmity. Brown put witchcraft firmly at the centre of Christian dogma, where indeed it belongs. It was not a strange aberration superstitiously added on the orthodox Christian faith. Witchcraft had a natural, dominant place in the hierarchy of sin, second only to the always mysterious 'sin against the Holy Ghost' to which Brown makes a reference. A Christianity which does not actively oppose witchcraft has either no popular base as in the middle ages, or has lost its political ideological significance or had to trim its content to fit uneasily with a new scientific paradigm, as in the period beginning about 1700.

Although the preaching of sermons was routine at witch-trials and executions very few have survived. Our knowledge of the mental map of the preachers is based on these, on other routine sermons, journals, letters, and on a few pamphlets. As suggested the majority of pamphlets on Scottish witchcraft were printed in England for an English reading public. The kind of reading matter which had been available to the English for over a century was, in the late seventeenth century, still a luxury for the Scots whose literary diet was restricted to biblical studies, theological tracts, and other learned works. The English had a market for astrological, diversionary, and popular literature which exotic tales from Scotland helped to fill. By the end of the century, however, Scottish publishing houses had begun to explore this market.

Two of the most revealing of these bits of clerical journalism were the anonymous *Witchcraft Proven* published in Glasgow in 1697 and the *Tryal of Witchcraft*[25] published in 1705, also in Glasgow. These are particularly valuable sources because they deal with witchcraft in general rather than with individual cases. Both of them cover aspects of witchcraft which are dealt with by the lawyers such as standard methods of proof, but like the sermons, which consider questions o:

salvation, they concentrate on aspects which rarely appeared in the court material. In particular the witches' meetings, which in the confessions appear to have been jollifications, in the hands of the theologians emerge as inversions of Christian worship.

> nor is any place so piacular or sacred, but that the Devil and his Creatures (by permission) may meet therein, nay even the verie Churches themselves, where he makes bold to mount the Pulpit, black candles with a blew Low, burning all the while, both about the Pulpit and Binch, and in several parts and quarters through-out, and in all places wherever they meet.[26]

An even more detailed account of inversion is given by Robert Law in his journal entry for 1678. The reference is to the trial of Gideon Penman and the story is used to illustrate the evangelical devotion of those covenanting ministers who came back into the post-Restoration episcopal church under the Indulgence of 1669.

> The devill had a great meeting of witches in Loudian (Lothian) where, among others, was a warlock who formerly had been admitted to the ministrie in the presbyterian tymes, and when the bishops came in conformed with them. But being found flagitious and wicked was deposed by them, and now he turnes a preacher under the devill of hellish doctrine; for the devill at this tyme preaches to his witches really (if I may so term it) the doctrine of the infernall pitt, Viz. blasphemies against God and his son Christ. Among other things, he told them that they were more happy in him than they could be in God; him they saw, but God they could not see; and in mockerie of Christ and his holy ordinance of the sacrament of his supper he gives the sacrament to them, bidding them eat it and to drink it in remembrance of himself. This villan was assisting to Sathan in this action, and in preaching. The way how this was detected was thus: some of these witches being present at a sermon of an indulged minister, was struck with conviction and horrour of conscience, and made confession of it, and particularly delated this warlock minister, whereupon he was apprehended, and cast up in the tolbooth of Edinburgh; a sufficient evidence of the successfulness of the indulged ministrie in the work of the Gospell against all their open mouth'd slanderers. It seems the Lord is giving more length of reignes to Sathan in these days which should call us to be more in watching and prayer.[27]

This was elaborated on by Sharpe in his introduction. According to him the witches confessed that the Devil 'kissed them, but was cold and his breath was like damp air; that he cruelly beat them when they had done the evil he had enjoined them, for that he was, said they, a most wicked and barbarous master. That he adventured to give them the communion or holy sacrament; the bread was like wafers, the drink was sometimes blood, and other times black moss-water. That sometimes he transformed them into bees, ravens, and crows, and they flew to such and such remote places.'[28] This account of Penman's trial, for which the source is not given, unlike the majority of confessions, sees the inversion of reformed worship as the centre of the meeting, though it does also feature the orgy.

There were other ways, too, in which clerical writers laid different emphasis from those of lawyers. They were interested in the question of demonic and divine power and in this the theme was very obviously Calvinistic. According to the author of the 1703 *Tryal of Witchcraft*, probably the Reverend John Bell of Gladsmuir in East Lothian,

> Three things concur to the bewitching of a Person; viz. a Divine permission, a Devilish operation or the evil spirits working: and lastly, the Witches consent; so that the Devil does all, and they consent to all, which to wit, is done in their behalf, for no doubt Satan can go of, and for himself, where he hath no League with the witch.[29]

This eighteenth-century formulation has a very clear echo of the fifteenth century *Malleus Maleficarum* in which 'the three necessary concomitants of witchcraft are the Devil, a witch, and the permission of Almighty God'.[30] The Church, however, was offering an ambiguous message to its congregations on this matter. While some preachers dealt with the question of the Devil's alleged earthly prowess by avoiding it altogether and concentrating on the spiritual temptations presented by him, others admitted his powers though emphasizing that God's powers were superior and the Devil part of God's creation. Yet others had a concept of 'superstition', a word which they used freely to indicate false or impossible popular beliefs. Particularly in later demonological writings such as the anonymous tracts there is doubt cast on the physical possibility of witchcraft: 'They be often feasted (tho' but in show) with meat, drink, and musick of the best, or with whatever else may ravish and captivat the senses' said the author of *Witchcraft Proven*. 'They are carried in spirit through the air.'[31]

There are also problems for the Church about how Christians should counter witchcraft. The standard anti-witchcraft devices of the peasantry would not do: they were superstitious usages and near witchcraft themselves. Indeed the very concept of white witchcraft was argued against more overtly by the clergy than by lawyers. White witches according to the *Tryal of Witchcraft* are known as healers or blessers, but are themselves witches and in league with the Devil. The Church had no simple means for dealing with bewitchment other than initiating proceedings against the alleged offender which might lead to her death. Individuals believing themselves to be bewitched had only one properly godly recourse:

> the best means is fasting and prayer, for God only can best force us from Divels, and in the use of his means alone it is, that we are to expect a blessing: so that if we would prevent Witches and whatever else the Devil can do, let us always rely on God, who hath promised to such, that he will cover them under his wings.[32]

The only legitimate action apart from these ecclesiastical rituals which the bewitched or the anxious could take to protect himself from witchcraft, therefore, was accusation which might in turn bring the whole machinery of state into play. Reducing legitimate means of self-help against witchcraft may have been a factor in promoting large scale prosecutions.

We have to consider, however, what the relationship was in general between the Christian indoctrination which the peasant was receiving at least once a week, and his belief in witchcraft, and (despite the qualifications which have been made about the possible role of Calvinism as such) whether there were features in Calvinism which affected the particular forms or strength of witch-beliefs in Scotland.

Mair has made the point that in any society in which misfortune is seen to be the result of the just revenge of angry gods, witch-beliefs provide a particular psychological ballast.[33] Christianity in its Calvinist form exemplified though not consistently this view of earthly misfortune. Despite the emphasis of all preachers on the evil nature of the physical world, and the human body, all agreed that God operated in the physical world on behalf of his creation. God was expected to reward his faithful followers on this earth and likewise to punish sinners. Misfortune, in popular Calvinism at least, was held to be the just result of sin. According to Robert Leighton, Archbishop of Glasgow in the 1660s

> Though it were an error to think that all temporal evils are intended of God as punishments of some particular guiltiness and so to be taken as infallibly concluding against either persons or causes as evil, yet certainly the hand of God either upon ourselves or others is wisely to be considered and it will often be found a punishment pointing to the sin.[34]

The popular interpretation, reinforced rather than otherwise by the subtleties and modifications of the Archbishop, was that misfortune was not totally fortuitous; it was likely to be the just punishment of a just God for particular sins. Afflicted persons could therefore expect neighbours to weigh up why they deserved their illness, accident, loss of crops, death of child, rather than to sympathize with them on the cards which had been dealt to them. Witchcraft as an alternative explanation for misfortune therefore had a peculiar attraction over and above that normally required for such happenings in non-Christian societies. For the Calvinist believer abnormally afflicted it was a most welcome resource.

Another feature of the witch-beliefs which was especially strong in Calvinism was the idea of Covenant. Scottish theology which was strongly rooted in the Old Testament made the idea of a covenanted people peculiarly its own. It was reflected elsewhere in Europe in the rising secular concept of the social compact, but in Scottish hands it was firmly theocratic. The covenanted people were God's people, firmly bound to him in a special relationship by a special promise. The term has lingered long in Scottish vocabulary as in the phrase an 'uncovenanted mercy', meaning some advantage which was unmerited and unlooked for. The Demonic Pact was therefore, for the Scots, a particularly horrific inversion. The term 'covenant' was frequently used in the final indictments and the confessions as a synonym for the Pact.

So far as basic Christianity was concerned, however, even in Calvinistic forms which most consciously resisted it, there was in all its popular forms in this period a strong pull towards Manicheism. This attraction is evident both for those who used witchcraft as an explanation for their misfortunes and predicaments and for those who consciously or semi-consciously took on the name of witches. If the Devil is once admitted to have power (whether of himself or by permission makes very little psychological difference) then he may in any given set of circumstances be a better proposition than God. In the first place he made himself visible. As the renegade minister Gideon Penman observed 'they were more happy in him than they could be in God; him they saw, but God they could not see'. He promised them benefits in this life which God never did. There was a chance of faring better with him, either at the modest level of escape from penury which he normally promised or occasionally at a more ambitious level. Robert, known as Hob, Grieve of Lauder, whose wife, incidentally, had been burnt more than twenty years before, said that the Devil 'fitting his discourse to the man's tentation (temptation) made many promises to him that if he would become his servant, he would teach him many ways, how to be rich, and how to be made much of in the Country'.[35]

The breaking of a witch under interrogation was often aided by evangelical appeal by the local minister. Janet Man, one of the Stenton witches of 1659, whose view of the Devil was noted in the last chapter, said in her confession

> that she could not get a heart to repent for the devill was locked in her heart till once efter prayer made by the minister she got freedome to confess her other sinnes and then she thowght hir heart was something lifted up and now shee thankes god she hath gotten a heart to confesse the sinne of witchcraft too. She confesseth that she was guiltie of manie other sinnes such as neglect of the ordinances for the spaice of Tuentie yeires she had not receaved anie beniffeitt of the kirk, and that she leived nyne yeires in uncleannes with one Alex'r cathill and brought furth three children for him for which she never yett repented.[36]

Janet Man had in fact been a natural target for witch-labelling, though her list of sins contains nothing that would have otherwise got her into trouble with the criminal law. She was a social deviant. She had rejected patriarchal religion and had lived for nine years with one man to whom she had borne children. But conformity did not necessarily save women from trial and execution, and established Christian commitment could make it difficult for the clergy to extract a confession. When Janet Saers of Ayr, in 1658, the year before Janet Man, was urged by her local minister to confess, she answered 'Sir, I am shortly to appear before the Judge of all the earth, and a lye may damme my soule to hell. I am clear of witchcraft for which I am presently to suffer.'[37]

This dignified speech is one of the few in which an accused witch is recorded as making a direct reference to the Christian God. Janet Saers saw him primarily as judge, as ultimately more potent than the Devil, and as controlling a real future for her soul. At this level of belief the preachers had succeeded in making spiritual eternity more real to the peasant mind than the physical present. Janet Saers was one of their successes and the accusation of witchcraft was, from the point of view of the authorities though she may well have been in trouble with her neighbours, misdirected. Both these women differ again from Janet Macmurdoch who was not broken. The account of her confession in the indictment was entirely formal. Though she must in fact have offered this confession her own words recorded in the trial papers make her appear independent, neither confirming nor denying her witchcraft. 'If they say so, so I am.'

At the end of the day the accused witch had to make some kind of statement with regard to the most fundamental aspects of the beliefs of her society. Where does power lie? With God or the Devil? Who represents it on earth? Janet Man and Janet Macmurdoch accepted neither the values of the Church nor the social values of patriarchal society: they were followers of Satan on either count, and Janet Man freely admitted it and begged to be readmitted. She did in fact go free. Janet Saers can only have fallen foul of the Church by falling foul of her neighbours. She declared her long term allegiance to the Christian faith as preached in her parish, to no avail. The two inversions were conflated and an enemy of the people became an enemy of God.

CHAPTER THIRTEEN

THE BELIEF SYSTEM
III HOW TO DEFEND A WITCH

The last two chapters considered the basic features of the belief system as demonstrated by peasant, lawyer, and minister in court, pulpit, and pamphlet. It was suggested that there was a sufficient agreement about these basic features to justify calling the different strands of belief a 'system', and that despite strife on theological details and political implications, despite an amount of peasant abstention and detachment sufficient to cause continuous anxiety and distress to the clergy, there was a homogeneity about the conceptual map of the universe unthinkable in a pluralist industrial society.

This homogeneity becomes even clearer when we consider the arguments used by members of the legal profession in the defence of those accused of witchcraft. Those who have apportioned 'blame' among the witch-hunters have attached it primarily to the clergy, and attributed to the lawyers the virtue of quelling and reducing the witch-hunt. The fact that the belief in witchcraft was closely integrated with religion in this period lends credibility to this theory, but it underestimates the extent to which two other elites—the lawyers and the lairds—were involved. In all cases which went through the Privy Council local landowners sat on the commission and were the ultimate judges. They also sat on juries in the High Court of Justiciary. No-one was executed for witchcraft without their case being processed by members of the laity, and there are several cases in which lairds rather than ministers appear to have initiated proceedings either on their own behalf as victims of the witch or on behalf of others.

The case for suggesting that the lawyers had a moderating influence on the rate of prosecutions rests on the fact that cases which came to the High Court at Edinburgh where the accused was represented by a lawyer appeared to have had a higher rate of acquittal than those which were tried on local commissions, and on the fact that in the 1670s and 1680s there was a long series of acquittals after which the supply of cases more or less dried up.

While some lawyers had ill-concealed doubts about the possibility of witchcraft in general, and many felt increasingly that particular injustices were being done, not one lawyer was explicit about his general doubts at any point prior to the abolition of the offence by the

Witchcraft Act 1735. While this was partly due to a structural con-
servatism in the legal profession (their task is defined as the interpretation of the law as it is), it was also related to the fact that, although
famous individual sceptical treatises were written about witchcraft,
in no country was the belief argued away. It simply ceased to have
political vitality. The proportion of acquittals to convictions increased
and the number of prosecutions declined while the witch theory was
largely intact and its general possibility still widely accepted.

The legal commentary of William Forbes, Professor of Law at the
University of Aberdeen, who was unfortunate enough to publish in
1730 just five years before the Witchcraft Act, demonstrates both the
unease felt by lawyers about the crime and their reluctance to criticize
an existing statute. He drew on George Mackenzie's account of
the criminal law published in 1678 for definitions of witchcraft, but
emphasized the aspect of simple malefice:

> Witches are chiefly employed in plain Mischeif by hurting persons
> or their goods . . . But they sometimes work Mischeif under a
> pretence or colour of doing Good; as when they cure diseases,
> loose enchantments and discover other witches. All their designs
> are brought about by Charmes or ceremonious Rites instituted by
> the Devil, which are in themselves of no Efficacy, and serve only
> as Signals and Watchwords, to admonish Satan, as it were, when,
> where, and upon whom to do Mischeif or perform Cures,
> according to his Compact with the witches.[1]

Forbes's distinction between the actions of the witch and the power
of the Devil who actually causes the malefice to occur, was traditional.
The witch's actions merely pull strings for the Devil to perform
supernatural actions. 'Injuries done by witches are not occasioned by
any inherent Virtue or Efficacy in the Means used by them but only by
the Devil's influence; and that there is no natural Cause of the
Mischeif done is the Reason of ascribing it to Witchcraft.'[2]

Forbes, however, acting on precedent, was more ready than
Mackenzie to accept as proof of witchcraft a threat by a witch followed
by a misfortune which could be shown to have no other cause.

> It hath been sustained, to bring in a Woman guilty of Witchcraft,
> that she threatened to do some Mischeif to a Person, who immedi-
> ately or not long after suffered a grievous Harm in his Body or
> Goods by Sorcery or Witchcraft, without any apparent or
> natural Cause, tho' the Manner, or Inchantment used to work
> such Mischeif, was not particularly expressed, and the threat was
> only general and did not specify the Ill Turn to be done.[3]

Proofs of witchcraft, according to Forbes, are the general 'bad fame'
of being a witch, the fact of being the child, close friend, or servant of a

convicted witch, being unable to shed tears, inability to say the Lord's Prayer, and possession of the Devil's mark. These 'presumptions of witchcraft', he admits to be slender, and suggests that other 'presumptions' are in fact unlawful: those of pricking the witch, swimming the witch, and that of bringing the accused in to the bewitched person in order to see how that person will react. Ordinary proof of witchcraft is by the confession of the accused or the testimony of witnesses. About confession he said:

> Many Persons have been convicted of Witchcraft upon their own Confession. But such Confession ought (1) To be free and voluntary and no way extorted. Nor should it contain anything impossible or improbable. (2) Care must be taken to notice that the Confessor is not opprest with Melancholy, or hath taken Guilt upon him or her purely from being weary of life.[4]

In this he is quoting almost directly from Mackenzie. Forbes exemplifies the difficulty lawyers find in criticizing directly anything which is still part of the law of the land. He exhibits his unease about his own performance in an appendix in which he partially, but not entirely, repudiates his commentary in the main text:

> Only one thing is sure, that such matters of Fact have been laid in indictments and given in Evidence; which is all my business with them; and if any Man, upon reading what I have said of Witchcraft be of opinion, that I am no Witch myself, I shall be satisfied.[5]

It would be an exaggeration, therefore, to say that there was *no* development in the attitude of lawyers to the crime of witchcraft during the period it was a capital offence; but there was certainly very little, and Forbes was in fact writing outside the crucial period. Witch-prosecutions had actually died out before he wrote and he himself probably never had to defend, let alone prosecute, a witch.

Lawyers argued in court and wrote about witchcraft in terms of general contemporary assumptions. There was no question of defending a witch by attacking the position of witchcraft in the criminal law or by attacking the concept of witchcraft as such any more than a lawyer would attempt to defend a client accused of murder on the grounds that there was no such crime. The nearest that any lawyer could get to such an approach was by pouring scorn on particular details of a given set of evidence.

The authorities which lawyers could cite were the 1563 Act of Parliament, and the other later governmental pronouncements. The Act itself was extremely sceptical in its tone and belonged to a pre-witch-hunt age, in that the force of it was directed against superstition, but this in fact had the effect of covering even those who simply consulted witches although in practice very few people seem to have been executed for this. Another authority was the Canon law of the Roman Catholic Church. Lawyers in both Episcopalian and Presbyterian Scotland saw no anachronism in referring to this. Law was law. In addition to this there was precedent, which was used, but curiously seldom. The judgements reached were so diverse that precedent might have been thought useful for any lawyer.

The first way to secure the acquittal of an accused witch was on any of a number of technicalities some of which were described in Chapter 9. The accused could claim slander; she could claim that the court was not sufficiently grand to try witchcraft; insufficient witnesses could be forthcoming. The concern of this chapter is with the kind of arguments which could be used once the case had reached court, and these arguments fell into three categories. The most important of these was the argument from nature and was based on the current state of scientific understanding. The arguments were related to accusations of malefice and suggested that they had a natural rather than a supernatural cause; the second category was ridicule and was sometimes closely allied to the first; and the third was a last resort if the accused had already confessed. In that case the only hope was to suggest that the woman was simple, wandering, or of unsound mind. In the later stages of the witch-hunt, that is to say towards the end of the Restoration hunt, it became possible to complain about the use of torture to extract confessions, but in general the three weapons of scientific doubt, ridicule, and infirmity in the accused, were used throughout the period.

The trial of Isobel Young of Eastbarns near Dunbar was held on 5th February 1629 in Edinburgh.[6] Isobel was married to one George Smith who was a portioner of Eastbarns, which means he was a reasonably substantial farmer; and she was a woman of mature years. One of the articles against her claimed that she had been a witch for forty years.

She was defended by Laurence Macgill, the second son of David Macgill, the Lord Advocate, and David Primrose of Burnbrae a member of the family later to become the Earls of Rosebery. The Counsel for the prosecution was Sir Thomas Hope, and twenty four articles were offered against her in the indictment, of which twenty two were standard accusations of malefice supported by witnesses. The efforts of the lawyers were therefore principally devoted to arguing that all these occurrences were in fact natural and nothing to do with the intervention of Isobel Young. One article alleged that Isobel threatened one Thomas Carse for being with a messenger who had put a summons in the lock of her door and that subsequently Carse's 'right leg drew up and he became a cripple'. Her lawyers argued that witnesses said that the door had no lock hole, and that 'it is not libelled that she threatened either his hand or his leg but only uttered some passionate speeches which might be usual to women cited by messengers'. The argument that ill temper from women is quite normal, discussed in Chapter 8, is one that was in frequent use by defence lawyers. It was used again by Isobel's lawyers on another count: 'As to the menacing speeches they are but ordinary blasts of anger which people vent when dispossessed of their possessions.'

Hope responded to the defence against the Carse charge by urging that the lock on the door was circumstantial not material, and that the rest of the defence should be disallowed because it was contrary to the dittay (indictment). It was suggested by Black that this particular trap: that nothing contrary to what the public prosecutor put in his indictment could be allowed to the defence, was derived from the instructions in the *Malleus Maleficarum*.[7] The direct influence in Scotland of this is not very clear, but according to the eighteenth-century lawyer Arnot, 'this most incredibly absurd and iniquitous doctrine of repelling defence because contrary to the libel; this system of legal murder was till the present century a received maxim of criminal jurisprudence in Scotland'.[8] In other words it was a normal maxim for all crimes. Clearly, if it had been strictly adhered to there would have been no point in admitting defence lawyers at all, but in practice arguments against the dittay were heard in court. The argument that the dittay must stand was brought up when the prosecution case was weak or where there was for one reason or another no intention of an acquittal. In this trial, Hope, on another article, reinforced the pro-dittay argument by reference to precedent: 'The whilk form of Dittay is relevant of Law and daily sustained by the pratticqz and laws of this realm and was lately decided in the case of Margaret Wallace.'

The argument from science was used against the allegation that Isobel had taken a sickness off her own husband George Smith and put it upon her nephew 'his brother's son, by coming to the barn door where he saw the firlot (a measure of grain) running about with the stuff popling in the floor'. The defence argued that

> this article is both improbable and impossible. Because its offered to be proven that two years intervened betwixt their sicknesses. And its absurd to think that a sickness should be laid beneath a barn door: seeing a sickness cannot be inherent but in a living creature, and this is even like unto a fable reported in Ariosto— And it's clear that the person's brain who was alledged to have seen the firlot going about had been distempered.

The most serious charges against her, however, were article 10 and article 24. Article 10 cited the evidence of two executed witches, Margaret Melros and Janet Atchison, that Isobel had been with them at a meeting with the Devil at which they had procured the death of George Clerkson in Dunbar. This was the only specific charge of diabolism, though there were also two charges that she had transformed herself into the likeness of a cat and a hare, and the defence argued, as they always did in such circumstances, that infamous witnesses cannot be allowed to 'prejudge the pannel, *lege infamia*'. The prosecution replied, on very sure ground here, since the Act of 1591 made special allowance for the evidence of women and *socii criminis* in the case of witchcraft and they only had to cite it:

> That in *criminis attrocibus* as this is, the deposition of men and women who are infamous, *infamia juris*, by Conviction are ever received as violent and vehement presumptions *ad torturam vel quaestionem*, which *comuni defamatione* is libelled against this pannel and is ever received *ad convictionem et condemnationem*. Likeas this is the constant practicqz in this Justice Court, and has the warrand of a statute of Session in anno 1591 as was practised upon Euphan McAllian in her trial that same year 1591.

The most fatal of all was Article 24 which simply summed up the legal essentials for witchcraft,

> That the pannel these 40 years bygane has been a manifest witch and sorcerer, a consulter and keeper of company with witches and the Devil, for practising sorcery upon divers good people for the destruction of them and their goods, as also renuncing of her baptism and betaking her to the service of Satan and thereupon receiving from him his mark under her left pap.

Most of the argument in this trial was directed at the long list of charges of malefice. There was an implicit conflict of belief in these encounters, since the method was to say either that the alleged malefice was 'natural' and therefore no witchcraft, or that it was 'impossible' and therefore the witness was at fault. Implicit in this approach was the assumption that witchcraft in the form of the performance of unnatural miracles was impossible; or at least that witchcraft was an alternative science and followed a particular pattern of its own. Witches could transfer diseases but they could not preserve them outside a human or animal body. A suggestion that witch behaviour also followed a particular pattern which Isobel Young did not exhibit was made in relation to the charge that in order to cure her beasts she had been accustomed 'to take a quick (live) ox, with a cat and a great quantity of salt, and to bury the ox and the cat with the salt in a deep hole of the ground as a sacrifice to the Devil so that the rest of the good (animals) should be freed of sickness and diseases'. The defence argue that 'it was never heard nor read that ever salt was used by witche ffor it is a symbol of eternity and therefore abhorred by witches whos delight is in all filthy and unsavoury things as Bodin observes.' Th intrinsic difficulty of burying a live ox was not mentioned but the fact that the use of salt did not represent a standard pattern of inversion was emphasized. Part of the difficulty here for the defence was in distinguishing sorcery from counter-witchcraft in the rather ambiguous area of protection from harm.

None of these arguments were of any avail in this case. Nor was the success or failure of a case ever much dependent on the fertility of the defence. Isobel had a great deal against her in the remarkable number of attested malefices recorded, and in the fact that her own husband, George Smith, was one of her accusers. He complained that she had harboured another known witch, Christian Grintoun, in the house, and that she had come out of a hole in the roof in the likeness of a cat and then turned herself into her own shape. Husbands were themselves put at risk if their wives were accused of witchcraft: a very high proportion of men accused were married to or otherwise related to accused witches. It is scarcely surprising that they often joined with the accusers as did the husband of Elspeth Thomson of Glenshinnoch, to avoid being labelled as witches themselves or even to rid themselves of an unwanted spouse. Isobel was strangled and burnt in Edinburgh in February 1629, one of the early victims of the 1629–30 outbreak in Scotland.

Another victim later the same year was Katharine Oswald of Niddrie near Edinburgh.[9] She had been indicted by Elizabeth Steven 'who was execute and died penitent for the said crime declaring upon oath that the said Katharine Oswald was as guilty and cunning in witchcraft as the said Elizabeth Steven herself'. A list of malefices was given but more stress was laid upon her attendance at meetings with Satan at one of which she had had carnal copulation in his presence with Alexander Hamilton, who was executed the following year.

The lawyers argued again for the naturalness of the malefices Katharine was supposed to have committed. Against the accusation that she had made a cow (which John Nisbet and his wife had declined to sell to her) give red blood instead of milk for three days, the defence, familiar with mastitis and other afflictions, argued that 'there are many natural reasons that sundry times that instead of milk kyne will give blood either by unskilfullness of the milker, partly if the udder be bitten with an unbeist (monster). And if a cow ly down upon an imrock-hillock (an ant heap) the Imrocks biting her paps her milk turns blood.' The prosecution in return suggested that the fact that an event *could* be natural did not mean that on any particular occasion it must be. 'Things of a kind may both be done by nature and by witchcraft altho that one and the same they cannot be done by both.'

The defence also attempted to distinguish between non-criminal superstition and criminal witchcraft. It was alleged that Katharine cured John Niddery, servant to Patrick Hart in the Canongate of the trembling fever by instructing him to 'pluck a nettle by the root and lay it down upon the highgate and to piss upon the crop thereof three several morning before the sunrising and to be back again within his house before the sunrising.' The defence argued that this might well constitute a superstitious rite, but no witchcraft, 'for what sorcery is it to pluck up a nettle by the root and to lay it down and to stale thereupon?' They argued that no words were used for charming and that urine had a respectable medicinal value which was not necessarily associated with witchcraft.

The argument that infamous persons cannot be counted as witnesses was tried again. The defence also tried the direct argument that meetings with the Devil were actually an illusion. 'That Toppoch's Declaration' (that of the already executed Elizabeth Steven) 'cannot be respected because witches deluded by the Devil believe that they see sometimes unknown and sometimes known persons, sometimes good, sometimes bad persons, whereas all is but Imagination and pure fancy without any reality.' Here the defence gave two references to Canon Law. Turning to Alexander Hamilton who claimed to have had intercourse with her at a meeting with the Devil the defence lawyer argued: 'As for Hamilton's deposition it cannot be respected for he is known for a notorious liar' (an argument which is still being successfully used in court) 'and has often varied in his depositions. Besides before the time of his death' (he had not actually been tried, so this was something of a slip by the defence) 'God may move him to confess the verity.'

The Lord Advocate in his summing up for the prosecution, reminded the assize (jury) that the depositions of Toppoch had been ratified by her at the stake and that Alexander Hamilton had renewed his in court that day in the presence of the accused. He reminded them that the Devil's mark had been found in Katharine's shoulder and had been tested by the pricker (who in this case was a Mr. John Aird, minister). He reminded them of the oaths and declarations made by those who witnessed to her malefices and 'protests for wilfull Error against the assize if they acquit'. They did not acquit, and Katharine followed Isobel and the many others that year to the Castle hill.

In a similar case a few years later, that of Elizabeth Bathgate o Eyemouth in June 1634, whose well documented trial has been referred to more than once, the defence were more successful.[10] The difference in the verdict may have been affected by the fact that ther was no major witch panic at this time, and a consideration of each cas on its merits was made that much easier, but against that must be se the fact that minute details were similarly scrutinized during th panics. On this occasion nine people, seven women and two men were accused at Eyemouth. Three of the women, two of them sister were executed, one of the men, William Mearns, committed suicid before his trial, Elizabeth Bathgate was acquitted and the fate of th others is unknown.[11]

In some ways the predicament of Elizabeth Bathgate seemed more serious than that of either Isobel Young or Katharine Oswald. There were eighteen articles laid down in her indictment and although the substance of many of these charges was malefice, she was part of a group all of whom were accusing each other, and diabolism featured strongly in the allegations. There was a build-up of accusations of ill fame. William Mearns declared that 'the pannel (accused) was not sonsie (wholesome) in regard she had great society with Patrick Smith a notorious warlock'; Alison Wilson 'could tell strange things of the pannel if she pleased'; Margaret Bellamy declared before her conviction that the panel was 'a sicker (certain) witch'. It was further alleged under item 15

> that the pannel had a horseshoe in a secret part of her door, which she received from the Devil to make all her affairs within her house to prosper, And that the pannel and other witches held a meeting with the Devil; and also the pannel confessed several times that it was a world's wonder if Jennet Williamson were a witch, that the pannel herself were not a witch also seeing they had much private dealing together which few knew but her self. And so it is that the said Jennet Williamson confessed herself to be a witch, and therefore the pannel must be conscious to herself that she is also a witch.

Among the many malefices of which she was accused was that she had bewitched Agnes Bunkle's child so that it died.

> The pannel having threatened to do an ill turn to George Sprot, webster, in Eymouth, for keeping some cloth of the pannel's longer beside him nor she desired, came early in a sunday morning to his house and saying nothing till she came to Agnes Bunkle, his wife's bedside, she desired a sight of the said Agnes her bairn that was lying in bed with her, which, when she obtained she nipped the bairn's hough (buttocks) so as it skirled to the terror of the mother, and immediately turned to the door and went out. Which nip made a blae mark in the child's hough which never went out so long as it lived. And from that time furth the child pined pitifully for the space of three-quarters of a year and died. And the pannel having threatened the said Agnes Bunkle's child for buying two eggs from the pannel's maid without her knowledge that they should be dear eggs to those that got them. And thereupon the likeness of an egg did strike out of the child's body.

The defence argued here that there were two different and mutually incompatible accounts of the child's death, that she was not accused of any sorcery with regard to the child's death but simply of nipping it. This would infer the crime of murder and if she were accused of murder she would be able to prove at the bar by sufficient witnesses that the death of the child was occasioned by its own father. So far as the eggs were concerned 'it is not probable that the pannel would keep enchanted eggs in the house and leave them open to her servant, whereby her husband might have gotten them'.

In dealing with allegations of consultations and meetings with the Devil the defence brought in the weapon of mockery. One allegation of neighbours was that they had seen Elizabeth 'in her sark wylie coat (petticoat) and bare-legged' standing outside her own door with the Devil 'in the likeness of a man having grey cloths'. The defence argued 'that the same is altogether irrelevant For how could the bycomers have known the man to have been the Devil unless they had been sorcerers themselves seeing they saw him in a human shape, not changing his form at all nor assuming to himself an ugly shape with horns and claws as the Devil used to be painted or represented in comedies and plays as is confessed of sundry witches'. They also argued that on an occasion when they were alleged to have met by the sea shore to sink the ship of one George Holdie no-one had suggested that they 'were seen flying like Crows, Ravens, or other fowls about the ship as use is with witches'. If this *had* been alleged the defence would have argued, as Mackenzie did, for its impossibility.

The conviction of a witch at law was the last triumph of the forces of the state in the battle for minds. It was an essential element in the conviction, therefore, that the mind in question should concede guilt and sorrow and that the mind should be worth having in the first place. That is to say the accused witch should confess, not only as a necessary means of proof in a hidden and secret crime, but also as an acknowledgement of the correctness of official beliefs and values. The mind of the accused should be, as Christian Calvinist minds had to be, sentient and educated. It is a received maxim of political sociology today that ideological commitment requires a fairly high degree of ideological education: this was held very clearly by the ministers of seventeenth-century Scotland. Minimal literacy, Bible-reading, preaching and instruction, and personalized salvation were the essential ingredients in the struggle. The witch could only be a witch in the fullest possible consciousness. She had to make her pact with the Devil 'knowing him to be the Devil'. She had to confess knowing what she was confessing.

The first line of defence open to the accused then, after the legal technicalities, was to deny the allegation and refuse to confess. Although people were occasionally executed after refusing to confess this was regarded as a failure by the judiciary. Jurors were reluctant to convict without a confession, and only very strong evidence from witnesses of malefice and sorcery which would allow them to assume an implicit pact. The second line of defence was for the accused to recant any confession that she had made. A piece of half quarto dated 25 July 1661 from a box of 'precognitions' has the recantations of three accused women from Ormiston:

> Compered Marion Greinlaw and being Interogated whither or not shee was guiltie of the sine of witchcrafte she declared that she said to Whythill that about half a yere since she renounced her baptism and that thee becam the devills servant But now she denyies that it was of a truth because shee was affrayed for punishment.
>
> The same day Compered Margaret Stevinstene who being Interogat whither or not she was guiltie of the sine of witchcrafte she said she once saw the devil at the Ormistoune burne and he said to her welcom and she sayed that she renounced her Baptisme and that the devil called her Magie Spead and that she once said that the devil lay with her But now shee utterly denyes that thes things wer of truth being affrayed of punishment when shee said them.
>
> And sicklyke compered Jeane Howieson who being Interogat as aforsaid shee said that she once confessed to be the deville servant But now she denyes.[12]

Marion Greinlaw and Jeane Howieson were sent for trial on commission on the 6th of August. Their fate is not recorded, but Margaret Stevinstene does not appear again and her case may have been dropped at this stage.

Janet Blackie of Dalkeith told the court in August 1661 that 'the man who lay with her the first and second time was cold, but that the third time he was lyk another man'. Later she recanted completely. 'The devill never desyred her to be his servant, that she knew him not to be the devill bot to be onlie Henry Bear.'[13]

A further line of defence was that of appearing simple, demented, or incompetent. It was a matter of convincing the court that your mind was not worth having. The Dalkeith witches who were tried in the Court of Justiciary in August 1661 were all executed apart from Katherine Hunter. Extreme age did not help Isobel Fergussone who was seventy one, nor Beatrix Leslie who, though eighty-four, was noted as having carnal copulation with an adolescent Satan; but a very low intelligence saved Katherine. The handwriting of the scribe recording the confessions of this group one after another deteriorated when he attempted to make sense of her confession. 'Katherine Hunter Confesses that she renounced her baptisme, she knowes not baptisme' is crossed out, and starts again: 'Katharine Hunter Confesses that the divill lay with her because she was sworne. She was grosselie ignorant and could speak no further.' This formulation clearly pleased them for a further pretrial paper recorded the same day, August 3rd, gives the formal indictment for Katherine, and written in the margin is the note 'The justices passes fra this woman in respect she is grosselie ignorant.'[14]

As indicated already the most comprehensive source which we have for the methods and arguments for saving accused witches from the stake are the writings of Sir George Mackenzie. His *Laws and Customs* was actually the first comprehensive legal commentary on the Witchcraft Act of 1563. Sir James Balfour in his *Practicks*, written before the 1591 trials, merely mentions the Act in passing;[15] more surprisingly Sir Thomas Hope who acted as prosecutor in several cases during the 1629–30 hunt made no mention of witchcraft at all in either his *Minor Practicks* or his *Major Practicks*.

Mackenzie in his 'Defence of a Maevia' gives a detailed account of his defence of a particular woman indicted for witchcraft. 'Maevia' was accused of flying in the shape of a dove with two other witches to their meeting place and of putting on and then removing a disease with a charm. Mackenzie began his defence with a theological argument to prove the existence of witchcraft to undercut any attempts to discredit his defence on the grounds of atheism or 'saduceeism', but added:

> Yet I cannot think that our Saviour who came to dispossesse the devil, who wrought more Miracles in his own time upon possest persons then upon any else, at whose first appearance the oracles grew dumb, and all the devils forsook their temples; and who promised (John 12) that the Prince of this World was now to be cast out, would yet suffer him to reign like a Soveraign, as our fabulous representations would now persuade us.[16]

Having established his credentials Mackenzie went on to the charge of malefice and using the argument from science appealed for caution in the face of our ignorance of the ways of nature:

> As to the imposing or taking off diseases by Charmes, I conceive it is undenyable that there are many diseases whereof the Cures, as well as the Causes, are unknown to us: Nature is very subtile in its operations, and we very ignorant in our inquiries; from the conjunction of which two arises the many errors and mistakes we commit in our reflections upon the productions of nature: to differ then from one another because of these errors is sufferable though to be regretted; but to kill one another because we cannot comprehend the reason of what each other do, is the effect of a terrible distraction; and if this were allowed the most Learned should still be in greatest danger, because they do oftimes find mysteries which astonish the ignorant; and this should give occasion to the Learned to forbear deep searches into natural mysteries, lest they should

lose their life in gaining knowledge, and to persecute one another, but cannot comprehend what his rival doth, would immediately make him passe for a Wizard. It is natural for men to think that to be above the reach of Nature which is above theirs. If this principle had taken place amongst our predecessors, who durst have us'd the Adamant? For certainly nothing looks liker a Charm, or Spell than to see a Stone draw Iron; and men are become now so wise as to laugh at those who burnt a Bishop for alledging the World was round, so blind and cruel a thing is ignorance: And if this principle of beleiving nothing whereof we do not see a cause were admitted we may chose to doubt whether the curing of the King's Evil by the touch of a Monarch, may not be likewise called charming.[17]

The last reference was a well-placed topical allusion, for Restoration England was seeing a great revival of the belief in the magical powers of the monarch. What James VI and I had performed in England with distaste as a political necessity his grandson Charles II did with relish as a demonstration of his miraculous kingly powers.

The argument for the openness of scientific discovery was followed by a discussion about whether the mere threat by an alleged witch followed by some calamity could be held proof of witchcraft, in which Mackenzie followed all defence tradition in asserting that the threatening must be specific and the precise misfortune should follow, and after citing Canon lawyers including the Jesuit demonologist Del Rio and the English puritan William Perkins in his support he added that 'no "malefice" alone can be sufficient ground to condemn a witch, except that she either confess, or that it be proven by two famous (i.e. respectable) Witnesses, that she used means that might have produc'd that effect', adding that 'if it were otherwise, Judges might condemn upon guessing or malice, and so more would be in danger to die by injustice than by witchcraft'.[18]

The actual charge of malefice and sorcery was that 'Maevia' had quarrelled with her neighbour who had then fallen into a 'distraction' which she had then cured by applying a plantain leaf to the left side of her head and binding a paper to her wrist on which was written the name of Jesus. Mackenzie suggested that the sufferer and his client had been quite simply reconciled and that the distraction had been caused in the first place simply by their quarrel. So far as the sorcery was concerned Mackenzie pointed out, perhaps rather weakly, that 'there is nothing so cold as a Plantane Leaf and so it might have been very fit for curing a distraction, which is the most malignant and burning of all feverish distempers'. The name of Jesus he was well aware was dangerous ground, but he argued boldly that it was not likely that the Devil being an enemy of mankind would employ charms for their advantage. He admitted that such a use of the name of Jesus was improper, 'but to burn a poor ignorant woman, who knew not that to be evil which she used were to make ignorance become Witchcraft and ourselves more criminal than the person we would condemn'. He added further the familiar defence precept, which we have noted goes against all popular belief, that one witch cannot both put on and take off a disease, 'for it seems the Devil thinks that it were too much to bestow such favours upon one of his favourites'.[19]

In his refutation of the charge that his client flew like a dove with the witches to their meeting place he clearly felt far more confident. He urged the absurdity of the idea that the Devil could transport witches bodily, and the impossibility of transforming a woman into the shape of a dove, 'for how can the soul of a woman inform and actuat the body of a Dove'. He cited the *canon episcopi* (a tenth-century guide to Bishops), St Augustine, and Del Rio in support, and concluded that any confessions of witches in which they stated that they had been transformed into beasts 'is but an illusion of the fancy wroght by the Devil upon their melancholy brains whilst they sleep'.[20]

He further argued that the two women whose confessions had incriminated his client had therefore simply dreamed that she was with them: 'and were it not a horrid thing to condemn innocent persons upon meer dreams'. He would have the judge reject their evidence on the ground that they were *socii criminis* and as such ought not to be believed. Mackenzie concluded by arguing that even if the woman was in fact a witch the civil law had traditionally not always punished everything that Divines condemned. Sometimes it is more tolerant, for lawyers 'having so much more power than divines should be careful how they punish'.

It has already been noted that the 1563 Witchcraft Act under which the prosecutions took place was a sceptical, though not a liberal document. Death was the penalty even for consulting a witch. Mackenzie, unlike other defence lawyers who tended to be nervous of the Witchcraft Act for its illiberality, made frequent reference to it for its scepticism. He suggested that by the Act only arts for abusing the people were condemned, and since no such art was used in the case of his client therefore the item accusing her of causing her neighbour to fall into a distraction 'cannot be said to fall under the prohibition of the Act of Parliament'.[21]

It was of course true that the purpose of the 1563 Act bore very little relation to the purpose of the peasant when he accused his neighbour of malefice or of the Church when it pursued apostasy or of the state when it identified apostasy as a type of treason. It was an Act which dated from a period when only the elite saw a difference between superstition and religion and with paternalistic intent wished to prevent the unscrupulous from exploiting the simple through an impossible sorcery. It served the prosecution, however, throughout the seventeenth century, by its simple assertion of death for witchcraft and consulters of witches. Mackenzie's direct use of it for the defence was bold and unusual. Whether his pleading was successful he does not say.

In his chapter on witchcraft in his later *Laws and Customs of Scotland in Matters Criminal*, Mackenzie sets out much the same ground in a more formal manner, and covers some topics such as the Pact and the Mark, both of which he accepts, though he does not think much of the Mark as evidence unless there is an accompanying confession. The chapter is full of admonitions to judges concerning circumstances in which they should not prosecute, and implicit advice to defence lawyers for grounds of defence. Those who are accused are more often than not innocent. They are normally poor ignorant creatures,

> and oft-times Women who understand not the nature of what they are accused of; and many mistake their own fears and apprehensions for Witchcraft; of which I shall give you two instances, one of a poor Weaver, who after he had confessed witchcraft, being asked how he saw the Devil, he answered, like Flies dancing about the Candle. Another of a woman, who asked seriously, when she was accused, If a Woman might be a Witch and not know it? And it is dangerous that these who are of all others the most simple should be tryed for a Crime which of all others is most mysterious.[22]

He further warned that when a confession had been received it should be established that 'the person who emitted it is not weary of life, or opprest with melancholy'. Mackenzie was also well aware of the significance and effects of labelling and warned against the possibility that such labelling might have reached a point at which the accused could no longer sustain life in the community.

> I went when I was a Justice Deput to examine some Woman, who had confest judicially, and one of them who was a silly (simple) Creature, told me under Secresie, that she had not confest because she was Guilty, but being a poor Creature who wrought (begged) for her Meat, and being defamed for a Witch she knew she would Starve, for no person thereafter would either give her Meat or Lodging, and that all men would Beat her, and hound Dogs at her, and that therefore she desired to be out of the World; whereupon she wept most bitterly and upon her knees call'd God to witness to what she said.[23]

Mackenzie, who was the most acute participant–observer of the Scottish witch-hunt, argued for caution against the current beliefs and practices of Kirk sessions and secular courts in relation to the provenance of individual cases. He also argued against particular theories common in the law and theology of witchcraft which he deemed to be impossible, contrary to current scientific understanding, and based upon popular fantasy. He specifically denied, for example, that witches could penetrate walls or that the Devil could transform one species into another. He allowed no legal precedents here and quoted Del Rio with disfavour rather than, as he frequently did, as a supporting authority. At the same time he anchored his remarks firmly within the central points of current official belief concerning God and the Devil. The Devil does have certain powers through which he may manipulate human beings even if he does not actually confer this power upon them. The Devil may 'make Bruits to speak or at least speak out of them'. He can also raise storms and calm them. He can inflict diseases and cure them when he has laid them on. He may even cure 'natural' diseases 'better than Physicians can, who are not present when Diseases are contracted, and who being younger than he must have less experience'.[24] This is an echo of James VI's theory that the power of the Devil lies in his extremely long accumulation of worldly wisdom which is more considerable than the most wicked or knowledgeable of ordinary worldly men.

Mackenzie argued against the opinions of Weyer, who was still over a hundred years after his death the most notorious of the small body of witchcraft sceptics, and set his entire piece in the context not only of local theological opinion but of the body of continental legal and theological theory as expressed in Canon law and in specialist manuals on witchcraft. During the height of the Restoration witchcraft crisis he appears to have defended witches who came to court by using the kind of arguments cited here: circumstance, science, and the witch's incapacity; but in the twenty years that followed he simply did his best, by legal technicalities, to prevent them coming to trial at all, or if they came to trial to acquit on lack of evidence. A series of acquittals and dismissals with warnings in the late 1670s and early 1680s appears to have been largely due to his influence.

In 1680 Bessie Gibb, spouse to James Hunter, skipper in Bo'ness in East Lothian, sent in a petition, presumably under legal supervision, possibly Mackenzie's since the case came under him, complaining that the magistrates of Bo'ness were intending to try her for witchcraft, and that they planned

to proceed most summarlie and unjustly albeit they be nowayes judges competent thereto for the reason and cause following. In the first no inferior judges is judge competent to the tryall of the cryme of witchcraft which of all crymes is the most *difficilis causae* to tryall and probative/2[do] There is no person offers to insist against the perseuer or cause condescend on the lease malefice or prejudice done by her. There is no person has dilated her and if any dilation by the same was extracted from imprisoned and tortured witches who for their libertie or promise of favour would dare to delate persons of the greatest integritie and qualitie in the Kingdom their prosecutors could suggest. And therefore Bessie Gibb persewer is known and has been ever repute to be of a good lyff and conversar and of intire fame and repute so that (it is not fit) to ruin her good name and disgrace her husband and children.[25]

Bessie Gibb was acquitted along with five other women from Bo'ness on the 27th March 1680. Her acquittal was typical of a number in the last thirty years of the century. It was based on lack of evidence. The crime itself was never argued out of court.

CHAPTER FOURTEEN

SCOTTISH WITCHCRAFT
IN ITS COMPARATIVE SETTING

The Scottish witch-hunt spanned a period which began with the rise of the doctrine of the divine right of kings and ended with the decline of the doctrine of the godly state. The interpretation offered here both of the European hunt and of its Scottish version, while acknowledging the contribution of anthropological theory, rests essentially on themes of political sociology: power; dominance; ideology; and legitimation.

The careful distinction between the preconditions and the efficient causes of identifiable events and social changes is a respectable pursuit both among historians, who look for linear connections between them, and sociologists, who seek parallel sets of circumstances for comparisons. This distinction is not absurd and it would be impossible to make any general remarks at all about the past without some such type of analysis. Yet while preconditions are relatively easy to chart, efficient causes are elusive and their actual efficiency rarely convinces. Often they appear mere triggers which with a less substantial set of preconditions might have failed to set the event or change concerned in train. Too much emphasis on the significance of the trigger produces the 'contingent and unforeseen' school of history. Too much emphasis on the preconditions produces sociological determinism.

The view of causation which is adopted here, and which is implicit in any multiple explanation, is that both pre-conditions and triggers (sometimes identified as efficient causes because of their immediate proximity to the event to be explained) ought to be regarded as in-efficient causes. A sufficient number of inefficient causes may become an efficient cause, but the precise amount and type of inefficient causation needed to set in motion this war, that revolution, that social change, this witch-hunt, is likely to be neither firmly predictable nor totally explicable. If it were, societies would need only fortune tellers, rulers, and chroniclers; they would not need historians, no sociologists.

The 'touch and go' theory of inefficient causation outlined here is particularly appropriate when applied to the European witch-hunt. Attempts at a general explanation for all the separate witch panic tend to break down, especially those based on hunting in one area. Witch-hunts occurred in areas of peasant unrest such as France and

Germany, and peasant quiescence such as Scotland. They occurred in town as well as country, in both Catholic and Protestant areas, in areas of capitalizing agriculture and stagnant feudal or peasant economies. Obviously individual case studies can be suggestive in the development of a general theory of causation, and the Scottish case, due to the relative isolation of Scotland, perhaps particularly so. Nevertheless it is necessary to indicate the preconditions for a European hunt first, and only then turn to the variety of local conditions which increased the probability of a national or local witch-hunt.

The fundamental preconditions for the European witch-hunt were three: a peasant economy, a witch-believing peasantry, and an active belief in the Devil among the educated. These are not necessarily in chronological order, which, as the work of Cohn and Kieckhefer suggests, is still in some doubt. These preconditions are the commonplaces of European witchcraft research, but they do not in themselves necessarily produce a witch-hunt. Other factors which may bring one nearer are changes in the structure of the law and of legal organization, the growth of printing and literacy, the development of personal religion, and the rise of the nation state. All these factors are interconnected. In the days of papacy and medieval monarchy the actual beliefs of the peasantry were of little importance to the ruling class and the state of their souls was looked after by religious specialists. Heresy was attacked when it was seen to involve potential social dissidence, but the active commitment to an orthodox and educated Christianity and the responsibility of the individual for his own salvation were developments of the fifteenth and sixteenth centuries. The original enforcement of Christianity upon Europe as its official religion may have been by the sword; its lodgement in the minds of the populace was through the sermon, albeit reinforced where need be by the state. Without the concept of personal religion and personal responsibility there could be little meaning in the Demonic Pact. The growth of printing and literacy, despite the fact that literacy spread slowly and did not reach much of the peasantry of Europe directly, assisted the process of Christianization through the preaching of a more educated clergy. To what extent it so assisted is not easily measurable. The progress of literacy itself, as has recently been pointed out by Clanchy in his English study,[1] is closely connected with the development of bureaucracy. Bureaucracy brings in its wake records, the formalization of surnames and of legal procedures. It was these processes, together with the secularization of the emerging nation states, which helped to generate changes both in the form of law and in legal procedures which Cohn has suggested were important pre-conditions of the witch-hunt.[2]

Originally witchcraft was an ecclesiastical offence. Persons accused had to be processed first through a church court and then handed over to the civil power for execution. It was also a private offence against the person. Individuals had to take the initiative in bringing accusations of sorcery. If they failed to make the charges hold they were liable to suffer, under the *lex talionis*, the same penalty which the accused would otherwise have suffered. This practice was part of the pattern of inter-personal, restorative justice which was a feature of medieval Europe. It was replaced gradually over a period of at least two centuries in a process which is beginning to be known as 'the judicial revolution', by the modern system of retributive justice.[3] This was characterized by the imposition of abstract standards of justice regardless of whether there were victims to be appeased, and by management of the criminal process by state officials rather than by injured parties and feudal judges. One of its effects was to remove the element of danger in pressing charges. Counter charges of slander became the only possible recourse against accusations, and were inevitably the prerogative of the substantial citizen.

Another aspect of the judicial revolution and one which was most closely related to the rise of the nation state was the secularization of areas of law which had previously been the province of ecclesiastical courts. Statutes against witchcraft were normally parts of legislative packages which included sexual and religious offences such as bestiality, incest, and blasphemy. Under this process of secularization were passed the English Witchcraft Acts of 1542 and 1562, the Scottish Witchcraft Act of 1563, the Danish one of 1617 and the Russian one of 1592. Within the dominion of the Empire the *Constitutio Criminalis Carolina* made witchcraft a civil offence.[4] The effect of these changes was to centralize and secularize the process of social control in general and witchcraft in particular. The way was also opened for the more abstract treatment of witchcraft. Although it was helpful for the prosecution if neighbours claimed to have been offended or injured by the witchcraft of the accused this was no longer an essential part of the process.

The emergence of Christianity as a political ideology was a product of all these factors. A political ideology, by which is meant a complete set of ideas which serve as a focus for political unity, cannot flourish without a machinery for educating the populace; nor is a political ideology required unless there is a state organization in which the role of kinship and feudal ties have been eroded. So long as the only relationship of the peasant was to his lord, political ideologies were unnecessary. The Christianity of the early modern period with its emphasis on personal accountability[5] was therefore Europe's first political ideology. The split into rival versions allowed religion to function as a focus of loyalty within neighbouring hostile territories. The catch phrase *cuius regio, eius religio* (the religion of each territory shall be determined by its prince) demonstrated during the sixteenth and seventeenth centuries the significance of official beliefs for nation states and political entities like the German princedoms. Catholicism and the varieties of Protestantism represented total claims to be the whole of Christianity. Regimes acquired legitimacy through the adherence of the populace to the version of Christianity preferred there. They measured their subjects' loyalty by their religious conformity. They marked out the boundaries of their territories not with fences but with churches.

The witch-hunt lasted for as long as Christianity had political importance. It could not become rampant until personal religion had become political. It could not survive the advent of secular ideologies. In so far as the rise of secular ideologies is to be equated with the rise of rationalism, the identification of rationalism with the decline of witch-hunting is correct. But the relationship with rationalism is only partial. Right through the eighteenth and nineteenth centuries Christianity retained much of its official status and social utility. It was essentially its *political* status which was already waning in most of Europe in the late seventeenth and early eighteenth century.

In the post-medieval period regimes or princes anxious to demonstrate their legitimacy could and did pursue Catholic, Protestant or other heretics as appropriate. The peculiar utility of witches compared with these other groups is that they represented not merely erroneous beliefs about Christianity but total hostility to it. Furthermore, although the pursuit of heretics, Jews, or Moors, could serve a similar purpose, it might arouse discontent, particularly among other heretics, Jews, or Moors, and some countries were without such categories of person. The pursuit of witches could only be applauded. It was done on behalf of the community distressed by their activities. Heresy-hunting might be divisive; witch-hunting united a people.

It was also characteristic of new regimes in their search for legitimacy that they demanded a high level of social control and of conformity in behaviour as well as belief. This took the form of a punitive approach to sexual relations, drunkenness, and festivals, in addition to behaviour featured in most criminal codes: violence and theft. This pattern has been observed in recent times in China, Cuba, Vietnam, Cambodia, and Iran. In the sixteenth century it was observable throughout Europe. To punish witchcraft was a uniquely economical procedure for witchcraft was imagined as the summation of all possible forms of disorder and evil. The usefulness of witchcraft in this respect, however, was contingent on its ideological status. Witches were pursued primarily as witches, as enemies of God and the Kingdom of God, rather than as general purpose criminals, or as deviants, or as women.

If Christian political ideology is the basic context and precondition of witch-hunting in Europe this does not in itself explain why certain areas had intensive hunts, others less intensive hunts, while some had no hunts at all. A comparative study of areas which escaped witch-hunting might yield some clues, but the likelihood is that they would offer characteristics as disparate as those which had witch-hunts, and that they would also share apparently significant characteristics with witch-hunting areas. In moving on to the next layer of inefficient causes—those which might generate witch-hunts if the fundamental ideological conditions obtained—it is important to remember the extraordinarily adaptive usefulness of the idea of witchcraft. It can serve one purpose in one state and another in another. The fact that reasonable explanations for witch-hunting in Geneva cannot be applied to Essex, Finland or Denmark does not thereby invalidate them.

Among local conditions the absence of external warfare as a focus for national unity, and likewise the absence of strong heretical factions seem particularly important. The presence of internal structural unrest is a strong motive for a witch-hunt. The marxist or radical approach of Le Roy Ladurie or Harris emphasizes the role of witch-hunting in distracting peasant attention in areas of peasant revolt from the reality of oppression. But that is only one aspect of the matter. Internal unrest was as often caused by alternative ruling groups as by a dissident peasantry; and under those conditions also, a witch-hunt was a way of emphasizing the legitimacy of those currently in power.

The throwaway suggestion of Marx himself that the English stopped burning witches when they started hanging false coiners and thieves does not get us far in that the number of witches executed there was not of great significance and that the progress towards capitalism even in England was only in its earliest stages when the last witch was hanged in Exeter in 1682. The more subtle account offered recently by the Soviet scholar Chernyak, who cites this passage from *Capital*, agrees that the lowering credit of Satan coincided with the growth of the National Debt; but he also identifies secular ideology rather than nascent capitalism as ensuring the end of witch-hunting, and suggests that secular ideology was itself a precursor rather than a consequence of capitalist development.[6] It is in any case clearly only in England that the argument from 'modes of production' has very much running. In all other parts of Europe the witch-hunt both rose and declined within a period of either feudal or peasant economy.

One feature of geographical distribution is that witch-hunting tended to occur in places, especially towns and villages, where it had occurred before. While the initial outbreak may have been caused by other factors, this outbreak educated both rulers and populace in the likelihood of witch conspiracies, and tainted the friends and relatives of those who were accused with a reputation which was readily revived when required. An example of the local tenacity of witch-beliefs is given by Sebald in his account of late twentieth-century Franconian 'Switzerland', an inaccessible part of central Germany in which a subsistence peasant economy has been slightly modified by modern technology only in the last decade.[7] There have been recent cases of the attempted lynching of suspected witches, and the area is surrounded by the old witch-burning centres of Bayreuth, Nuremberg, and Bamberg. Areas of southern Italy on the other hand, which are still similarly operating a subsistence economy but which do not have a witch-hunting past, retain only a benign (in the sense of impersonal) belief in the evil eye.

The relationship of witch-hunting to the social status of women seems to have little bearing on the geographical distribution of the hunt. It cannot be argued, partly because so little is known about the changing status of women, but also because what we do know reveals no relationship to the witch-hunt, that in areas of severe witch-hunting women had higher or lower status than in areas of mild witch-hunting or no witch-hunting at all. The reasons why suspected witches were mainly women are direct and have been discussed. The reasons why suspected witches were hunted are not directly related to their being women, but to their being thought evil. It is quite possible that witch-hunting had the effect of increasing the level of misogyny rather than the other way about. The status of women can be so high that it threatens patriarchy or so low that women are peripheral property without necessarily provoking a witch-hunt. While witch-hunting involves woman-hunting the link is indirect and the two cannot be completely identified.

A more definite correlation can be drawn between those areas within and those without the sphere of Roman Law. Currie describes a spectrum of severity of inquisitorial procedure,[8] and there seems little doubt that the territories which experienced the most intensive witch-hunts were territories with a bureaucratized form of inquisition supplemented by torture and where appeal was had to the Canon Law manuals of witchcraft. Areas on the periphery of this system such as England, Russia, Denmark, and Finland, experienced milder hunts with less reference to diabolism and conspiracy. This distinction affected not so much the likelihood of a witch-hunt developing at all, as its character and intensity once established. A further factor also mentioned by Currie, the likelihood of financial gain, was of importance in some urban areas where the suspects were substantial people. It would be a reasonable estimate, however, that the prosecution of ninety per cent of witch suspects was an expense to the local though not necessarily the central government concerned.

The Scottish witch-hunt was arguably one of the major witch-hunts of Europe. During its peaks it was matched only by those of the German principalities and Lorraine. As in Germany its effects were local and highly concentrated. There were periods in 1649 and 1661 when no mature woman in Fife or East Lothian can have felt free from the fear of accusation. The Scottish hunt, however, had its own distinct characteristics.

Scotland played no part at all in the development of the educated witch theory, although echoes of incubi and succubi and references to the higher occult are to be found in early Scottish humanist writings of the sixteenth century. The educated witch theory was imported from the continent in 1591. It is clear from literary sources, however, that a lively popular belief in sorcery, in the Devil, and in a variety of fairies and demons had existed for some time prior to that. The Witchcraft Act of 1563, like other similar European acts, was part of the secularizing of the law by a new nation state.

So far as political ideology goes the Scottish witch-hunt coincided exactly with the period spanned by the doctrines of the divine right of kings and the godly state. Post-Reformation Scotland was in the hands of a new regime whose ideology primarily distinguished them from their old dominant allies and quasi-rulers, the French, and allied them with the English. By the time that James was mature and throughout the seventeenth century it was necessary to make ideological distinctions from that new friend in maintaining a Presbyterian form of Protestantism. The peculiarly Presbyterian machinery for social control, developed for a city state, was also admirably adaptable for control in rural areas. The immediate impetus to the witch-hunt after the machinery was established was given by the king whose person had been directly attacked by a conspiracy of witches. This attack on his divine person amounted to an attack on God. It demonstrated, as the contemporary pamphlet *Newes from Scotland* urged, that James was the greatest enemy that Satan had in this world. The entire process vindicated his virtue, his relationship to God, and his concern for his people. Once established witch-hunting never needed quite so specific a reason again.

With the departure of the king for England the godly state took over the position vacated by the divine king. It was less personal, but equally vulnerable and was the ideological focus of loyalty. Yet the next major hunt, that of the late 1620s, cannot be explained purely in terms of legitimizing the Scottish state. It coincided with the climax of the European hunt and was preceded by a gradual build up of cases and by a general injunction on the need for tightening up of law and order. The 1649 outbreak had no connection with events on the continent. It had a clearly ideological source in that this was a period when the Covenanting party had a stronger hold on central government than at any other time. There was much unrest and distress caused by war; the importance of demonstrating control both in terms of belief and behaviour was paramount. The last great hunt at the Restoration was under way in the closing years of the Protectorate and cannot be said to have been generated entirely by the setting up of a new regime and the need to cleanse the stables though this was partly the case. The absence of a machinery for law and order during the months before the restoration of the Privy Council seems to have engendered an anxiety among the ruling classes amounting to a 'moral panic'. This was the last national purge of God's enemies. After 1662 it was only at a local level that such cleansings were attempted. By the eighteenth century the prospect of the Union of the Parliaments had made the concept of the godly state redundant. Whatever godliness was to be retained by such of the Scottish polity as was to remain autonomous, no-one assumed that the Act of Union involved embracing anything other than Mammon.

The pattern in Scotland, then, relates as exactly as for any part of Europe to the life-time of Christianity as ideology. The peasantry were Christianized for the first time. The regime was new, keeping itself distinct first from France and then from England. It demanded a new conformity of both formal adherence and inner acceptance expressed in appropriately ordered behaviour. In other ways it reflects patterns found in some European hunts and not in others. The Scottish hunt was mainly rural. A large number of the cases said to come from Aberdeen, Dumfries, Stirling or Edinburgh were in fact merely tried there. The accused mostly came from settlements outside. There was no equivalent in Scotland to the German urban hunts in which burgomasters and substantial tradesmen and craftsmen were accused. Nor was there any trace of peasant or class unrest. It was not to distract peasants from revolt but to bind them to the aristocratic and gentry supporters of, variously, bishop, covenant, presbytery, or king, that the peat bales were heaped against the stake. Foreign war was noticeable by its absence. Only once during the century did the Scottish armies move south. There were no Turks, Jews, or Moors for the people to combine against. There were only the English, and in 1652 the English came as conquerors. They took over the administration of justice, and fearing no consequences, needing no other loyalty than respect for their swords, they let the witches free. Occupying forces do not require ideological conformity.

Recent writers on European witch-hunting have stressed the significance of border areas. That was where legitimacy was most at peril. It is a marked feature of the Scottish border that witchcraft cases occur right along its line. The Scottish cases run in a line from Berwick through Kelso, Jedburgh, Hawick, and Canonbie to Gretna. Across that border there are none. The English border was not very important to England. It was a long way to the vulnerable places. James VI had policed and pacified the Scottish border, previously an area of marauding tribes and bandits, in the last year of his Scottish residence and the first of his English reign. First the central government tamed the border men, it might be argued, and then it tamed their women; but the witch-hunting pattern is the same as in Lorraine, in the Basque country, in the Franche-Comté, on the borders of France, where the call of the centre was weakest.[9]

This pattern was partially modified for Scotland. While the border outbreaks were marked, so was the attraction of the centre. Ease of access to Edinburgh was important, and on all sides of that well-trodden path from the Scottish capital to the English border there were cases; likewise on the road from Stirling to Edinburgh and from Glasgow to Edinburgh.

The parallelism with parts of the continent are strong. The special nature of the Scottish hunt, however, can perhaps best be seen when placed alongside that of her English neighbour. The relative mildness of the English hunt can partly be explained by a lower level of religious intensity. The English do not seem to have had the same sharp break with tradition that the Scots had at the Reformation. Except for certain strongly Puritan areas changes were gradual and the intense evangelical zeal that characterized the Scottish church was largely absent in England. The struggle for legitimacy had been won earlier in England by Henry VII and the break from Rome was a mere completion of effective Tudor control. The most important differences, however, were probably in the nature of the judicial machinery. England's Witchcraft Acts of 1542 and 1563 contained detailed instructions in relation to different types of sorcery. Minor offences warranted minor penalties. The Acts knew nothing of the notion common to Roman Law countries such as Scotland that the crime was that of being a witch, that the primary act of witchcraft was the Demonic Pact, and that all witches were part of a Satanic conspiracy. Admittedly these ideas were current in Puritan writers such as Perkins and Gifford, but they did not penetrate to the law courts, which were separate and secular. The organization, too, of English law was not conducive to the creation of mass hunts or national panics. Because there was no notion of conspiracy there was no need of torture to extract the names of accomplices. Further, the crime of witchcraft was not centrally managed. The circuit judges dealt with witchcraft on site, and there was no machinery for one witch-finding judge to transmit his enthusiasm elsewhere.

In Scotland the central organization, combined with the competitive spirit of local clergy and landlords, helped to stimulate panics. Yet in one aspect Scottish witch-beliefs had more in common with English than with continental beliefs. The witches' communal occasions were relatively non-horrific. There was very little actual Devil worship or other forms of inverted Christian ceremony. Reported sexual orgies, other than private copulations with the Devil, were relatively rare, and baby-eating almost unknown. Even when a baby was believed to be eaten it was not specially murdered for the purpose. It was dug up and made into a pie to improve the consumers' powers of sorcery. On the whole Scottish witches' meetings were similar to the very few English ones which were reported. They were jollifications for eating, drinking, and dancing of which in Scotland at least peasants were in real life deprived.

The feature which Monter has shown is especially typical of

Protestant Europe is the witch's mark. He has demonstrated that it was a common feature of trials in Protestant Jura and much less common in trials in Catholic Jura.[10] Protestants laid stress on the personal relationship with the Devil; Catholics on the potency of communal worship. The dominance of the witch's mark, which provided an intellectual bridge between popular and educated belief, and the consequent role of the pricker, also appear strongly in Scotland.

There are two theological factors which seem particularly significant in Scotland. The first is that Calvinists believed that a just God rewarded sin with earthly afflictions. Misfortune was therefore not to be seen as the afflictions of Job: as a test of virtue and fidelity. They were to be seen as an indication of sin and of God's just punishment for this sin. Witchcraft was an alternative and under these circumstances particularly attractive explanation for disease, bereavement, or economic misfortune. This is a psychological factor which one would expect to be present in all Protestant, and particularly Calvinist, cultures although its actual operation is difficult to demonstrate. The second factor which is even more characteristic of Scotland is the potency and political significance of the idea of covenant. The legal records in Scotland normally referred to a pact or paction with the Devil, but they did sometimes use the actual term covenant. The central position of the Old Testament concept of the covenanted people in Scottish political thought gave the inversion of a covenant with Satan a power and an intensity which it may not have had under other regimes.

It would in some respects be true to say that Scotland offers a middle position between the witchcraft of England and that of the continent. There are similarities with England in the local functioning of witch-beliefs and in the details of the Demonic Pact, though in Scotland the Demonic Pact is more prominent. There are similarities with the continent in the operation of the law, in the inquisitorial system, and in the belief in conspiracy and witches' meetings, though in Scotland the concept of meetings was weaker and less ritualistic than on the continent. The idea of a middle position is perhaps most convincing in the practice of the Court of Justiciary where the continental inquisitorial system was uneasily juxtaposed with an emerging adversary system in which the outcome depended on a duel between prosecution and defence. It is nevertheless misleading to think of witch-beliefs and witchcraft control operating on a range from severe continental to gentle English, with Scotland in the middle. There were parts of the continent such as Denmark and Russia where witchcraft control was similar in its operation to England, and other parts where governments did not hunt witches at all. There were regions, especially in France and Switzerland, where witchcraft control was similar to, or slightly milder than in Scotland. In particular, Protestant areas of continental Europe resembled Scotland in their beliefs and practices. In the European context then, witchcraft control in Scotland should be seen as fairly severe.

There remains finally the question as to whether the prominence given to the content and autonomy of the Christian witch-belief in this study is deserved. Certainly many sociologists of both marxist and functionalist persuasions would argue that beliefs and ideologies are social or socio/economic products. They cannot affect the social or economic structure itself which can only be altered in so far as there is a change in the means of production, or through some internal strain.

There is an obvious sense in which this is true. Ideas are social products in that they are not handed down on tablets of stone from on high. They are developed by humans in a social context. There are also some social constraints, though not actually very many, on the content of any religion or ideology. However, the case for a direct relationship between the fantasies, nightmares, religions, or ideologies of a given society and its social structure seems quite unproven. Was the social structure of hell feudal or was it more likely 'hydraulic' (the term given by Wittfogel to despotic regimes organized in relation to permanent water shortage)? From what social structure comes the three-personed God?

In fact the variety of belief systems which can stem from societies with similar social structures seems haphazard and almost unlimited. What is more, the possible impact of these beliefs is considerable. It is true that beliefs are not in themselves likely to change the economic base of a society, but the effect of a belief system on the lives of those either holding it or under the control of those holding it can nevertheless be very extensive. The division of human knowledge earlier in this book into technology and speculation was not intended to imply that the social value of areas of speculation was necessarily the same for all societies. It is manifest that societies vary greatly in their capacity to invent ideas which are dysfunctional as well as dotty. There is very little doubt, for example, that the impersonal and apolitical witch-beliefs of the Highlands caused less human suffering than the witch-beliefs of central and lowland Scotland.

To what extent then does this analysis of the Scottish version of European witchcraft differ from that of Lecky who declared in 1841 that 'Scotch witchcraft was but the result of Scotch Puritanism'?[11] In two respects. In the first Lecky did not pursue the logic of this statement. For him the hunt for witches was an activity mainly of the bigoted clergy whom he saw as being in opposition to holders of other more enlightened patterns of thought and belief. This study places a stronger emphasis on the interconnectedness of different strands of belief, on the role of other sections of the ruling class and on the active cooperation of the peasantry. In the second, Lecky and other rationalist writers of the period saw punitive societies as belonging to the remote past. Dalyell, searching in 1842 for contemporary parallels to Scottish seventeenth-century barbarism, could only find rumours of such things in Turkey.[12] Today we are in the unhappy position of knowing that punitive societies are recurrent, and that the chances for any human of being born into one of those societies which have undamaging relationships with their gods are not high.

APPENDIX 1: CHRONOLOGICAL OUTLINE

Date	State	Church	Calamities	Witchcraft Control	
1560	MARY	Reformation/Gen. Assembly/Presbytery			**1560**
1563				Witchcraft Act	
1567	JAMES VI				
1570			Plague	Few cases	**1570**
1580					**1580**
1590				**National panic** (1590–91)	**1590**
1591	Marriage to and coronation of Q. Anne				
1594			Famine (1594–8)		
1597		Episcopal Commissions Modified Episcopacy with Presbytery		**National panic** Witchcraft Commissions revoked Numbers fall to a few per year	
1600			Plague		**1600**
1603	James departs to England Admin. by Privy Council thereafter				
1607			Plague		
1610	Administration by Privy Council	Modified Episcopacy			**1610**
1620					**1620**
1623			Famine	Numbers rise	
1624			Plague (Edinburgh)		
1625	CHARLES I				
1629				**National panic** (1629–30)	
1630			Plague	Numbers fall	**1630**
1635		Laud's Prayer Book/Gen.	General plague & Famine		

Year	Witchcraft	Plague & Famine	Church	Political events
		Plague & Famine		
		frequent until 1652		
1644				
1645				Montrose ascendant/KilsythX/PhiliphaughX
1646				Charles I surrenders to Scottish army; handed over to English army commissioners
1648		Scarcity		
1649				CHARLES II
1650	**National panic**			Execution of Montrose/DunbarX
1651	English occupation			CROMWELL
1652	Many witches acquitted			
1653	Increase		Assembly meets last time until 1690	
1658				
1660	**National panic** (1661–2)		Episcopacy	RESTORATION
1661	Small local panics & isolated cases			CHARLES II Middleton/Lauderdale
1666				(Covenanters)/Pentland Rising/Rullion GreenX
1670	Local panic (E. Lothian)	Famine		
1675				
1678				
1679			Murder of Archbishop Sharpe	James, Duke of York
				DrumclogX/'The Killing Times' (until 1684)
1680	Isolated cases/many acquittals			
1685				JAMES VII
1688				WILLIAM & MARY
1689				KilliecrankieX
1690			Abolition of episcopacy Gen. Assembly meets Presbytery	
1692				Darien Scheme
1695		Famine 'Seven Lean Years'		
1697	Local panic (Paisley)			
1700				ANNE
1702	Isolated cases until 1727			
1707				Act of Union

COMMISSIONS

The following are a typical sample of the membership of Parliamentary and Privy Council Commissions for the trial of cases of witchcraft. 'Of' or 'of that ilk' indicates a landowner.

1. Commission 'in ordinary form' to try Jonet Murry, Elspeth Ranaldson, and Agnes Waterston, of Burntisland, Fife, given to
   Sir Jas. Melvill
   Robert Aytoun of Inchderny
   Alexander Orroch of that ilk
   Robert Ged of Baldrig
   The baillies of Burntisland
   Burntisland, 27th September 1649
   RPC, 2nd Ser., Vol. 8, p. 200

2. Presbytery of Paisley asked the Committee of Estates to grant a commission for the trial and punishment of Margaret Finlayson and requested the
   Lairds of Houston
           Nether Pollock
           Craigends
           Ralstoun
           Glanderstoun
           Southbarr
           Westland
           John Spreull, Provost of Renfrew
   Paisley, 21st March 1650
   RPC, 2nd Ser., Vol. 8, p. 211

3. Commission to try Euphaim Adair issued to
   Sir W. Murray of Neatoune
   Alexander Borthwick of Johnstonburn
   Jas Scott of Lockquarrat
   William Scott, bailie of Dalkeith
   Andro Borthwick of Sachlan
   Martin Grinlaw of Costertoun
   Crichton, East Lothian, 7th November 1661
   RPC, 3rd Ser., Vol. 1, p. 74

4. For Duddingston and Liberton the Justice Deputes were sent out because of the proximity to Edinburgh.
   Alexander Colvill of Blair

Sir George Mackenzie }
John Cunninghame   } Justice Deputes
to attend and the heritors (land owners) and their prisoners were to appear.
The heritors were to produce the evidence.
Duddingston, 1st August 1661
RPC, 3rd Ser., Vol. 1, pp. 16–17

5. Commission to try Anna Kemp, Isobel Smith, and Margaret Kerr of
   Belston, East Lothian, given to
       Sir R. Hepburn of Keith
           [legally qualified RPC, 3rd Ser., Vol. 1, p. 57.]
       *Patrik Broun of Colston
       Alexander Cockburne of Letham
           [on commission to try accidental homicide RPC, 5th Ser., p. 10.]
       Alexander Hay of Baro
       *Thos Haliburton of Eglincarno
       *John Butler of Kirkland
       *Doctor Hepburn of Monkrig
   Belston 7th June 1661
   APS, Vol. 7, p. 247.
   * On a commission to try eight witches at Carriden in 1649.

6. Commission to try Barbara Hood and Helen Belshes in Eyemouth granted to
       Col. John Horne of Plendergaist
       Arch. Douglas of Lumsden
       George Craw of Netherbyre
       William Craw of Henchheid
       Robert Ruell, Peilwalls
       Samuel Lauder, bailie of Eyemouth
       Jon Curry Merchant in Eyemouth
       Jon Robison Merchant in Eyemouth
       Thos. Robison Merchant in Eyemouth
       Thos. Gray, Portioner of Eyemouth
   7th November 1661
   RPC, 3rd Ser., Vol. 1, p. 73.

7. Commission to try Elspeth Seaton, Elspeth Bruce, and Margaret Bell in
   Abdie, Fife, granted to
       Sir John Aytoun of that ilk
       David McGill of Rankzillour
       Robt. Paterson of Dinruin
       James Arnot of Woodmilne
       Mitchell Balfour of Pitmedden
       Robt. Barclay of Collairnie
       Mitchell Ramsey, Portioner of Berriehill
       Gavin Adamson }
       George Orme   } Portioners of Newburgh
   23rd January 1662
   RPC, 3rd Ser., Vol. 1, p. 141.
In 1661 Aytoun and McGill had fallen out over who was to have the be
seats in Abdie Kirk. The Presbytery had supported Aytoun.

8. Commission to try Isobel Gowdie of Auldearn (Nairn) given to
    William Dallas of Cantry, Sheriff Depute of Nairn
    Thomas Dunbar of Grange
    Master Harry Forbes, Minister of Auldearn
    Alexander Brodie, younger of Leathin
    Alexander Dunbar of Brath
    James Dunbar, younger thereof
    Henry Hay of Brightmanney
    Hew Hay of Newtoune
    William Dunbar of Clune
    David Smith ⎱
    John Weir   ⎰ in Auldearn
13th August 1662
Pitcairn, *Criminal Trials*, Vol. III, p. 602.

NOTES

INTRODUCTION

1 Bruce Lenman and Geoffrey Parker, 'Crime in Early Modern Scotland: a Preliminary Report on Sources and Problems', SSRC Final Report No. HR 4373/2. See also their article 'Crime and Control in Scotland 1500–1800'. *History Today*, Vol. 30, Jan. 1980.

2 Keith Thomas, *Religion and the Decline of Magic*, London 1971.

3 Alan Macfarlane, *Witchcraft in Tudor and Stuart England*, London 1970.

4 Norman Cohn, *Europe's Inner Demons*, London 1975.

5 H. C. Erik Midelfort, *Witchhunting in Southwestern Germany 1562–1684*, Stanford, 1972; G. Schormann, *Hexenprozesse in Nordwestdeutschland*, Hildesheim, 1977; Thomas, *op. cit.*: Macfarlane, *op. cit.*; E. William Monter, *Witchcraft in France and Switzerland*, Ithaca, 1976; Marie-Sylvie Dupont-Bouchat, Willem Frijhoff, and R. Muchembled, *Prophètes et Sorciers dans les Pays-Bas*, Paris, 1978; Paul Boyer and Stephen Nissenbaum, *Salem Possessed: The Social Origins of Witchcraft*, Cambridge, Mass., 1974; and A. Heikkinen, 'Paholaisen Liittolaiset: Noita-Ja Magiakäsityksia ja-Oikendenkäyntejä Suomessa 1600—Luvun Jälkipuoliskolla' in *Historiallisia Tutkimuksia Julkaissut Suomen Historiallinen Seura* (with English summary), Helsinki, 1969, pp. 374–94; Russell Zguta, 'Witchcraft Trials in Seventeenth-Century Russia' in *American Historical Review*, Vol. 82², 1977, pp. 1187–1207.

CHAPTER ONE

1 Philip Mayer, 'Witches' in Max Marwick (ed.) *Witchcraft and Sorcery*, Harmondsworth, 1970, pp. 45–6.

2 E. E. Evans-Pritchard, *Witchcraft, Oracles, and Magic among the Azande*, Oxford, 1937, p. 21.

3 J. G. Campbell, *Witchcraft and Second Sight in the Highlands and Islands of Scotland*, Glasgow, 1902; A. Macgregor, *Highland Superstitions*, Stirling, 1922.

4 Barbara Littlewood, 'The Evil Eye in Southern Italy', unpublished paper.

5 See A. Richards, 'A modern Movement of Witch-finders', *Africa*, Vol. 8, 1935; J. R. Crawford, *Witchcraft and Sorcery in Rhodesia*, Oxford, 1967, pp. 278–90; M. G. Marwick, 'Another Modern Anti-witchcraft Movement in East Central Africa', *Africa*, Vol. 20, 1950; L. Mair, *Witchcraft*, London, 1969, pp. 172–9.

6 See Evans-Pritchard, *Witchcraft, Oracles, and Magic*; M. Wilson, *Communal Rituals of the Nyakyusa*, London, 1959; C. Kluckhohn, *Navaho Witchcraft*, Cambridge, Mass., 1944.

7 Evans-Pritchard, *Witchcraft, Oracles, and Magic*, p. 21.

8 *Corpus Iuris Civilis*, Codex 9, Tit. 18.

9 *APS*, Vol. II, p. 539.

10 E.g. Mair, *Witchcraft*, p. 22; A. Richards, 'A Modern Movement of Witch-finders', *Africa*, Vol. 8, 1935, pp. 56–7.

11 J. F. M. Middleton, 'Witchcraft and Sorcery in Lugbara', in J. F. M. Middleton and E. H. Winter (eds.), *Witchcraft and Sorcery in East Africa*, London, 1963.

12 Evans-Pritchard, *op. cit.*, pp. 31–2.

13 Kluckhohn, *op. cit.*, p. 60.

14 Middleton, *loc. cit.*, p. 262.

15 E. Goody, 'Legitimate and Illegitimate Aggression in a West African State', in Mary Douglas (ed.), *Witchcraft Confessions and Accusations*, London, 1970, p. 240

16 M. Wilson, 'Witch Beliefs and Social Structure', *American Journal of Sociology*, 1951, 56, No. 4, p. 309; R. F. Gray in Middleton and Winter (eds.), *op. cit.*, p. 166.

17 Macfarlane, *op. cit.*, p. 214.

18 Cohn, *op. cit.*, pp. 206–24; Macfarlane, *op. cit.*, p. 214.

19 J. M. McPherson, *Primitive Beliefs in the North-East of Scotland*, London, 1929, pp. 159–61; Isaac Shapera, 'Sorcery and Witchcraft in Bechuanaland', *African Affairs*, Vol. 51, 1951, excerpt in Marwick (ed.), *Witchcraft and Sorcery*, p. 112.

20 J. H. Langbein, *Prosecuting Crime in the Renaissance*, Cambridge, Mass., 1974, p. 134; Midelfort, *op. cit.*, pp. 22–3.

21 See for example Evans-Pritchard, *op. cit.*, p. 63; J. D. Y. Peel, 'Understanding Alien Belief Systems', *British Journal of Sociology*, 20, 1969; J. Beattie, *Other Cultures*, London, 1964; W. R. G. Horton, 'African Traditional Thought and Western Science', *Africa*, XXXVII, No. 1 and 2; P. Winch, *The Idea of a Social Science and its Relation to Philosophy*, London, 1958, and 'Understanding a Primitive Society', *American Philosophical Quarterly*, 1964; Steven Lukes, 'Some Problems About Rationality', and 'On the Social Determination of Truth', in *Essays in Social Theory*, London, 1977; E. Gellner, 'The Savage and the Modern Mind', in R. Horton and R. Finnegan (eds.), *Modes of Thought*, London, 1973, 'The New Idealism: Cause and Meaning in the Social Sciences', in A. Giddens (ed.), *Positivism and Sociology*, London, 1974, and *Legitimation of Belief*, Cambridge, 1974.

22 Gellner, 'The Savage and the Modern Mind', *loc. cit.*, pp. 162–3; *Legitimation of Belief*, p. 153.

23 Winch, 'Understanding a Primitive Society', *loc. cit.*

24 Gellner, 'The New Idealism', *Positivism and Sociology*, p. 149.

25 *SRO*, JC2/16 25, April 1684.

CHAPTER TWO

1 Parts of this chapter draw on my article 'Crimen exceptum' in B. Lenman, G. Parker, V. Gatrell (eds.), *Crime and the Law: the social history of crime in western Europe since 1500*, London, 1980, pp. 49–75.

2 Mair, *Witchcraft*, p. 222.

3 H. R. Trevor-Roper, *The European Witch-Craze of the Sixteenth and Seventeenth Centuries*, Harmondsworth, 1969.

4 Thomas, Macfarlane, Midelfort, Monter, Schormann, Dupont-Bouchat, and Muchembled, *op. cit.* A. Soman, 'Les procès de sorcellerie au Parlement de Paris', in *Annales*, 4, 1977, pp. 790–814, and 'The Parliament of Paris and the Great Witch Hunt 1565–1640', *Sixteenth Century Journal*, IX, 2, 1978.

5 Conversation with Professor Cohn.

6 In particular the work of members of the International Association for the History of Crime.

7 Cohn, *Europe's Inner Demons*, pp. 126–46.

8 R. Kieckhefer, *European Witch Trials*, London, 1976, pp. 11–26.

9 *Ibid.*, p. 19.

10 *Ibid.*, pp. 18–26.

11 Trevor-Roper, *op. cit.*, pp. 63 ff.

12 Monter, *op. cit.*, pp. 72–3.

13 Trevor-Roper, *op. cit.*, p. 83.

14 Monter, *op. cit.*, p. 81.

15 Julio Caro Baroja, *The World of Witches*, London, 1964, pp. 207–8, and Heikkinen, 'Paholaisen Liittolaiset', *loc. cit.*, pp. 375–7.

16 The Salem trials have an extensive literature of their own. See Boyer and Nissenbaum, *op. cit.*

17 French summary of B. Baranowski, *Procesy czarownic w Polsce w XVII i XVIII wieku*, Lódź, 1952, pp. 178–81; Trevor-Roper, *op. cit.*, p. 98.

18 Margaret Murray, *The Witch Cult in Western Europe*, Oxford, 1921 (reprinted 1962).

19 For example J. B. Russell, *Witchcraft in the Middle Ages*, Cornell, 1972. See the discussion of this literature in Cohn, *op. cit.*, pp. 99–125.

20 Trevor-Roper, *op. cit.*, pp. 55–96.

21 Kai Erikson, *Wayward Puritans*, New York, 1966, pp. 3–29 *et passim*.

22 *Ibid.*, p. 64.

23 Elliot P. Currie, 'The Control of Witchcraft in Renaissance Europe', in *Law and Society Review*, Vol. 3, No. 1, 1968, and in D. Black (ed.) *The Social Organisation of Law*, New York, 1973.

24 Thomas, *op. cit.*; Macfarlane, *op. cit.*

25 Macfarlane, *op. cit.*, pp. 168–76.

26 Max Marwick, *Sorcery in its Social Setting*, Manchester, 1965, and 'Witchcraft as a social strain-gauge', *The Australian Journal of Science*, Vol. 26, No. 9, 1964.

27 Macfarlane, *The Origins of English Individualism*, Oxford, 1978, pp. 1–2, 59.

28 Thomas, *op. cit.*, p. 461.

29 Lenman & Parker, 'The State, the Community and the Criminal Law in Early Modern Europe', in *Crime and the Law*.

30 Russell Zguta, *loc. cit.*

31 *Ibid.*, pp. 1205–6.

32 Muchembled, *La Sorcière au Village*, Paris, 1979.

33 Cohn, *op. cit.*, p. 255.

34 Kieckhefer, *op. cit.*, pp. 4 and 8.

35 Midelfort, *op. cit.*, p. 71.

36 Monter, *op. cit.*, pp. 88–113.

37 Soman, 'Criminal Jurisprudence in Ancien-Regime France: the Parlement of Paris in the Sixteenth and Seventeenth Centuries' in *Crime and Justice in Europe and Canada*, ed. L. A. Knafla, Montreal, 1980.

38 Jean Delumeau, *Catholicism between Luther and Voltaire*, London, 1977, pp. 170–72.
39 Muchembled, *Culture Populaire et Culture des élites*, Paris, 1978, p. 295, and in Dupont-Bouchat *et al.*, *op. cit.*, pp. 27–9.
40 Monter, *op. cit.*, pp. 10–11.
41 Marvin Harris, *Cows, Pigs, Wars, and Witches*, London, 1974, pp. 236–40.
42 E. Le Roy Ladurie, *Les Paysans de Languedoc*, Paris, 1966, pp. 407–13. Extract in E. W. Monter (ed.), *European Witchcraft*, New York, 1969, p. 165.

CHAPTER THREE

1 See H. G. Aldis, *List of Books Printed in Scotland Before 1700*, Edinburgh, 1904; John Ferguson, 'Bibliographical Notes on the Witchcraft Literature of Scotland', in *Proceedings of the Edinburgh Bibliographical Society*, Edinburgh, 1899; C. Larner, 'Two Late Scottish Witchcraft Tracts', in Sydney Anglo (ed.), *The Damned Art*, London, 1977.
2 See Bernard Capp, *Astrology and the Popular Press*, London, 1979, esp. pp. 274–5.
3 *Newes from Scotland*, London, 1591, reprinted in D. Webster (ed.), *Collection of Rare and Curious Tracts on Witchcraft*, Edinburgh, 1820.
4 James VI of Scotland, *Daemonologie*, Edinburgh, 1597 and London, 1603. See the commentary by Stuart Clark, 'King James's Daemonologie: Witchcraft and Kingship', in Anglo *loc. cit.* and Rhodes Dunlap, 'King James and Some Witches: the date and text of the Daemonologie', *Philological Quarterly, 54*, 1975.
5 *Trial, Confession, and Execution of Isobel Inch, John Stewart, Margaret Barclay, and Isobel Crawford for Witchcraft at Irvine, Anno 1618*, N.P. N.D.; reprinted N.P., 1855.
6 Sir George Mackenzie, *Pleadings in some Remarkable Cases*, Edinburgh, 1872, and *Laws and Customs of Scotland in Matters Criminal*, Edinburgh, 1678.
7 *RPC*, Vol. X., Third Ser., p. 161.
8 George Sinclair, *Satan's Invisible World Discovered*, Edinburgh, 1685.
9 It was republished in Edinburgh in 1746, 1764, 1769, 1779, 1789, 1808, 1831, and 1871, and in London in 1814 and 1815.
10 *A Relation of the diabolical practice of above Twenty Wizards and Witches of the Sheriffdom of Renfrew*, London, 1697, was followed by a Scottish account: *A True Narration of the Sufferings and Relief of a Young Girl*, Edinburgh, 1698, which contained an abstract of the London tract and was itself republished as *Sadducismus Debellatus*, London, 1698. Other pamphlets of this period were Alexander Telfair's *True Relation of an Apparition*, Edinburgh 1696 which was republished as *A New Confutation of Sadducism*, London, 1696 and the Pittenweem pamphlets, *A True and Full Relation of the Witches of Pittenweem*, Edinburgh, 1704, and *Letters Concerning the Witches of Pittenweem, Fifeshire*, Edinburgh, 1705.
11 *Witchcraft Proven, Arreigned and Condemn'd in its Professors Professions and Marks by diverse pungent and convincing Arguments excerpted forth of the most Authentick Authors, Divine and humane, Ancient and Modern*, by a Lover of the Truth, Glasgow, 1697; *The Tryal of Witchcraft or Witchcraft arraigned and Condemned*, Anon, Glasgow, 1705, and *An Ingenious and Scientific Discourse*

of Witchcraft, Anon., N.P., 1705. See C. Larner, *Two Late Scottish Witchcraft Tracts*, Anglo (ed.), *loc. cit.*, 1977, for a discussion of these.

12 William Forbes, *The Institutes of the Law of Scotland*, Edinburgh, 1730.

13 John Erskine, *The Principles of the Law of Scotland*, Edinburgh, 1764 (Third edition), and *An Institute of the Law of Scotland*, Edinburgh, 1773; Hugo Arnot, History of Edinburgh, Edinburgh, 1779; David Hume, *Commentaries on the Law of Scotland*, Edinburgh, 1819 (2nd ed.).

14 Hugo Arnot, *A Collection and Abridgement of Celebrated Criminal Trials in Scotland from 1536 to 1784*, Edinburgh, 1785.

15 John Millar (ed.), *A History of the Witches of Renfrewshire*, Paisley, 1809, and Webster (ed.), *Collection of Rare and Curious Tracts*.

16 Robert Pitcairn, *Criminal Trials in Scotland 1488–1624*, Edinburgh, 1833.

17 Robert Law, *Memorialls*, Edinburgh, 1818, with introduction by Charles Kirkpatrick Sharpe published in an extended version as *Historical Account of the Belief in Witchcraft in Scotland*, Glasgow, 1884.

18 J. G. Dalyell, *The Darker Superstitions of Scotland*, Edinburgh, 1834.

19 Walter Scott, *Letters on Demonology and Witchcraft*, London, 1830; M. C. Boatright, 'Witchcraft in the Novels of Sir Walter Scott', *University of Texas Studies in English*, XIII, 1933; C. O. Parson, *Witchcraft and Demonology in Scott's Fiction*, Edinburgh, 1964.

20 Robert Kirk, *The Secret Commonwealth*, Edinburgh, 1815, 1893, and 1933. The 1815 edition says that it was 'reprinted' from the 1691 edition but this is an error. It was printed from one of two known manuscripts of which the second is the only survivor. (Edinburgh University Library La. III 551). See M. M. Rossi, 'Text Criticism of Robert Kirk's *Secret Commonwealth*', *Edinburgh Bibliographical Society Transactions*, Vol. III, Part 4, 1957.

21 Charles Mackay, *Memoirs of Extraordinary Popular Delusions*, London, 1841; W. E. H. Lecky, *Rise and Influence of the Spirit of Rationalism in Europe*, London, 1865.

22 Lecky, *op. cit.*, pp. 126–9.

23 H. T. Buckle, *History of Civilisation in England*, London, 1861.

24 F. Legge, 'Witchcraft in Scotland', in *The Scottish Review*, 1891.

25 Ferguson, *loc. cit.*

26 Margaret Murray, *op. cit.*, pp. 98 ff, 139 ff.

27 Cohn, *op. cit.*, pp. 110–15.

28 Alex Keiller, *The Personnel of the Aberdeenshire Witchcraft Covens*, London, 1922.

29 J. M. McPherson, *op. cit.*, pp. 134–74.

30 Helen Stafford, 'Notes on Scottish Witchcraft Cases 1590–1591', in Norton Downes (ed.), *Essays in Honour of Conyers Read*, Chicago, 1953.

31 See for example Thomas Davidson, *Rowan Tree and Red Thread*, Edinburgh, 1949; Ronald Seth, *In the Name of the Devil*, London, 1969; Nicholas A. MacLeod, *Scottish Witchcraft*, St. Ives, 1975.

32 G. F. Black, *Calendar of Cases of Witchcraft in Scotland 1510–1727*, New York, 1938, and *Some Unpublished Scottish Witchcraft Trials*, New York, 1941.

33 Clark, *loc. cit.* Also C. Larner, 'James VI and I and Witchcraft', in A. G. R. Smith (ed.), *The Reign of James VI and I*, London, 1973.

34 Wallace Notestein, *History of Witchcraft in England*, Washington, 1911; G. L. Kittredge, *Witchcraft in Old and New England*, Cambridge, Mass., 1929; C. L'Estrange Ewen, *Witch-hunting and Witch Trials*, London, 1929.

5 T. C. Smout, *A History of the Scottish People*, London, 1969, pp. 198–207;

Rosalind Mitchison, *A History of Scotland*, London, 1970, pp. 143, 150–51.
36 Davidson, *op. cit.*; Seth, *op. cit.*; Macleod, *op. cit.* Angus Black (ed.), *The Devil's Coven*, London, 1972. Interesting fictional accounts of real trials include Elizabeth Sutherland, *The Eye of God*, London, 1977, and Isobel Adam, *Witch Hunt*, London, 1978. John Buchan's *Witchwood*, London, 1929, while pure fiction, is unrivalled in its evocation of the period.
37 *RPC*, Vol. IV, p. 680.
38 *RPC*, Vol. V, pp. 409–10.
39 Pitcairn, *op. cit.*; Black, *Unpublished Witchcraft Trials*; R. Scott-Moncrieff, *Records of Proceedings of the Justiciary Court, Edinburgh 1661–1678*, Scottish Historical Society, Vol. 48.
40 J. M. Thomson, *The Public Records of Scotland*, Glasgow, 1922; Lenman and Parker, 'Crime in Early Modern Scotland', *loc. cit.*
41 One set of questions and answers for the trial of Isobel Haldane (987/991) has been published in Rossell Hope Robbins, *The Encyclopedia of Witchcraft and Demonology*, Feltham, 1959, ppl 382–4. No reference is given but the question and answer form has been extracted from the questions implicit in the formal record of the trial in *RPC*, 2nd ser., Vol. 8, pp. 352–4.
42 Maureen Anderson, 'Calendar of Witchcraft in Moray', undergraduate dissertation, University of St. Andrew 1976; A. E. Truckell, Dumfries Burgh Museum; unpublished list of witchcraft cases in Galloway and Dumfriesshire. See also his 'Unpublished Witchcraft Trials' in *Transactions of the Dumfriesshire and Galloway Natural History and Antiquarian Society 1975 and 1976–1977*; Brian Levack, unpublished paper on 'The Great Scottish Witch Hunt of 1661–2'; Ben Benson, unpublished list of cases of witchcraft in Fife.
43 For example, *Diurnal of Remarkable Occurents*, Maitland Club, Edinburgh, 1833; J. Lamont, *Diary*, Maitland Club, Edinburgh, 1830; J. Nicoll, *A Diary of Public Transactions*, Bannatyne Club, Edinburgh, 1836; D. Laing (ed.), *The Diary of Alexander Brodie*, Spalding Club, Aberdeen, 1863; R. Birrell, *Diary*, Edinburgh, 1795.
44 See *SBSW*, pp. 288–302.

CHAPTER FOUR

1 See for example W. L. Mathieson, *Politics and Religion*, Glasgow, 1902; Gordon Donaldson, *The Scottish Reformation*, Cambridge, 1960, and *Scotland, James V—James VII*, Edinburgh, 1965; H. Trevor-Roper in *Religion, the Reformation and Social Change*, London, 1967; G. D. Henderson, *Religious Life in Seventeenth Century Scotland*, Cambridge, 1937.
2 David Stevenson, *The Scottish Revolution*, Newton Abbot, 1973, p. 325.
3 John Foster, 'Capitalism and the Scottish Nation', in G. Brown (ed.), *The Red Paper on Scotland*, Edinburgh, 1975.
4 See Ian Whyte, *Agriculture and Society in Seventeenth-Century Scotland*, Edinburgh, 1979.
5 Whyte, *op. cit.*, p. 131.
6 David Thorner, 'Peasant Economy as a Category in Economic History', in T. Shanin (ed.), *Peasants and Peasant Societies*, Harmondsworth, 1971, p. 202
7 Thorner, *ibid.*, p. 205.
8 Thorner, *ibid.*, p. 205.

9 Smout, *A History of the Scottish People*, p. 144.
10 Smout, *ibid.*, pp. 157-9, and S. G. E. Lythe & J. Bott, *An Economic History of Scotland*, Glasgow, 1975, pp. 28-34.
11 J. E. Handley, *Scottish Farming in the Eighteenth Century*, London, 1953, p. 48.
12 Thorner, *ibid.*, p. 205.
13 Ian Carter, *Farm Life in North East Scotland 1840-1914*, Edinburgh, 1979.
14 J. Foster, *loc. cit.*, p. 143.
15 J. M. Wormald (J. M. Brown), 'The Exercise of Power', in J. M. Brown (ed.), *Scottish Society in the Fifteenth Century*, London, 1977, pp. 54-5.
16 I. F. Grant, *Social and Economic Development of Scotland Before 1603*, Edinburgh, 1930, p. 183.
17 Smout, *op. cit.*, p. 135.
18 *Ibid.*
19 *Ibid.*, p. 136.
20 Grant, *op. cit.*, p. 204.
21 See Smout, *op. cit.*, p. 145.
22 Donaldson, *op. cit.*, p. 238.
23 G. S. Pryde, *Scotland from 1603 to the Present Day*, London, 1962, pp. 26-27
24 Christopher Hyde Lee, 'Jurisdictions in Early Seventeenth-Century Scot-. land', unpublished paper.
25 S.G.E. Lythe, *The Economy of Scotland in its European Setting 1550-1627*, Edinburgh, 1960.
26 H. Hamilton, *An Economic History of Scotland in the Eighteenth Century*, 1963.
27 Smout, *op. cit.*
28 Smout in M. Flinn (ed.), *Scottish Population History*, Cambridge, 1977.
29 K. J. Logue, *Popular Disturbances in Scotland 1780-1815*, Edinburgh, 1979.
30 Tom Johnson, *History of the Working Classes in Scotland*, London, 1946.
31 Christopher Hill, *The World Turned Upside Down*, 1972 (Penguin, 1975), p. 19.
32 Smout, *op. cit.*, pp. 177-8, 226-7.
33 Donaldson, *op. cit.*, p. 241.
34 Lythe, 'The Economy of Scotland under James VI and I' in A. J. R. Smith (ed.), *The Reign of James VI and I*, p. 60.
35 *Ibid.*
36 Whyte, *op. cit.*, p. 63.
37 H. Hamilton, *Economic History of Scotland*, p. xiv.
38 Donaldson, *op. cit.*, p. 239.
39 Wormald, *loc. cit.*, p. 59.
40 Whyte, *op. cit.*, *passim*.
41 Hugo Arnot, *History of Edinburgh*, 1826, p. 374.
42 Stair Society, *Introduction to Scottish Legal History*, Stair Society Vol. 20, Edinburgh, 1958. See also Donaldson, 'The legal profession in Scottish society in the sixteenth and seventeenth centuries', *Juridical Review*, v. XXI, 1976.
43 Christopher Hyde Lee, 'Jurisdictions in Early Seventeenth Century Scotland'. The following paragraphs draw extensively on this paper.
44 Peter McIntyre, 'The Franchise Courts', in *Introduction to Scottish Legal History*, p. 376.
45 See David Robertson, 'Burgh Court Records', in *An Introductory Survey of the Sources and Literature of Scots Law*, Stair Society Vol. 1, Edinburgh, 1936.
46 Arnot, *History of Edinburgh*, p. 371.

47 See Erving Goffman, *Asylums*, Harmondsworth, 1968, pp. 24 ff.
48 R. Mitchison, 'A Parish and its Poor' in *Transactions of the East Lothian Antiquarian and Field Naturalists' Society*, Vol. 14, 1974, pp. 15–16.
49 W. R. Foster, *The Church Before the Covenants*, Edinburgh, 1975, pp. 69–70.
50 Brian Manning, 'The Nobles, the People and the Constitution', in *Crisis in Europe*, ed. Trevor Aston, London, 1965, pp. 251–2.
51 W. Ross, *Aberdour and Inchcolme*, Edinburgh, 1885, pp. 325–8.
52 W. Makey, *The Church of the Covenant, 1637–1651*, Edinburgh, 1979, p. 117.
53 T. Morris, *Deviance and Control: the secular heresy*, London, 1976, p. 24.

CHAPTER FIVE

1 *SBSW, passim.*
2 Midelfort, *op. cit.*, p. 9.
3 Monter, *op. cit.*, p. 89.
4 Black, *op. cit.*, pp. 23–4; *SBSW*, pp. 5–9 and 173.
5 Black, *op. cit.*, pp. 26–9; *SBSW*, pp. 9–10, 16, 175–80.
6 *SBSW*, p. 237.
7 Black, *op. cit.*, p. 18; Legge, *op. cit.*, p. 274.
8 Jason Ditton, *Controlology*, London, 1979, pp. 8–37.
9 See Thomas, *op. cit.*, p. 450, for a discussion of C. L'Estrange Ewen's estimate of under 1,000. My lower estimate is based on the low incidence of witchcraft cases found in criminal archives outside Essex in recent research. See articles by J. S. Cockburn and T. C. Curtis in J. S. Cockburn (ed.), *Crime in England 1550–1800*, London, 1977.
10 *SBSW*, pp. 158–71.
11 C. K. Sharpe, *The History of Witchcraft in Scotland*, London, 1884, p. 34.
12 R. Pitcairn, *Criminal Trials in Scotland*, Vol. 1, p. 66.
13 Ed. G. Donaldson, *St. Andrews Formulare*, Stair Society, Edinburgh, 1944, Vol. II, p. 365; ed. R. K. Hannay, *Rentale Sancti Andree*, Scottish History Society, Edinburgh, 1915, p. 139.
14 Larner, 'Crimen Exceptum', *loc. cit.*, pp. 68–9.
15 J. L. Teall, 'Witchcraft and Calvinism in Elizabethan England: Divine Power and Human Agency', *Journal of the History of Ideas* 23 (1962), pp. 21–36; E. W. Monter, 'Witchcraft in Geneva 1537–1662', *The Journal of Modern History*, Vol. 43, No. 2, 1971, pp. 179–204.
16 *The Book of the Universall Kirk of Scotland*, Maitland Club, Edinburgh, 1839, pp. 1, 19.
17 *APS*, Vol. 2, p. 539.
18 *Ibid.*
19 J. Knox, *The History of the Reformation*, in *The Works of John Knox*, ed D. Laing, Edinburgh, 1848, Vol. II, p. 383.
20 *Ibid.*, p. 484.
21 *APS*, Vol. 3, p. 44.
22 *RPC*, Vol. 2, p. 198. See Larner, 'Crimen Exceptum', *loc. cit.*
23 *RPC*, Vol. 2, p. 318.
24 *Ibid.*
25 *Book of the Universall Kirk*, Vol. 1, pp. 343–4.
26 *Ibid.*, Vol. 2, p. 632.

CHAPTER SIX

1 See H. Stafford, 'Notes on Scottish Witchcraft Cases 1590–1591', in *Essays in Honor of Conyers Read*, Chicago, 1953, pp. 96–118; C. Larner, 'James VI and I and Witchcraft', *loc. cit.*, pp. 74–90; S. Clark, 'King James's *Daemonologie*: Witchcraft and Kingship', *loc. cit.*, pp. 156–81.
2 *Warrender Papers*, Edinburgh 1932, Vol. II, p. 167.
3 *Calendar of State Papers*, Vol. 2, p. 697.
4 *Ibid.*, Vol. 2, p. 739.
5 *Ibid.*, Vol. 2, p. 740.
6 *RPC*, Vol. 4, p. 680.
7 Spottiswoode, *History of the Church of Scotland* (1655), Edinburgh, 1851, Vol. 3, p. 66.
8 *Ibid.*, pp. 66–7.
9 *Ibid.*, p. 67.
10 *BUK*, Pt. 3, p. 393.
11 *Calendar of State Papers*, Vol. 2, p. 739; Spottiswoode, *op. cit.*, p. 67; *RPC*, Vol. 5, introduction p. lxiv.
12 *RPC*, Vol. 5, pp. 409–10.
13 *Maitland Club Miscellany*, Vol. 1, p. 89.
14 J. Row, *Historie of the Kirk of Scotland*, p. 449.
15 Dalyell, *The Darker Superstitions of Scotland*, p. 624.
16 *SBSW*, pp. 77–9.
17 *RPC*, 2 Ser., Vol. 2, p. 437.
18 *SBSW*, pp. 11–12, 77–107, 185–6.
19 *Acts of the General Assembly*, pp. 19, 63.
20 *Ibid.*, 1642.
21 *Ibid.*, 1643, p. 27; *APS*, Vol. 6, pt. 1, p. 197.
22 *AGA*, 1643, p. 28; *APS*, Vol. 6, pt. 1, p. 197.
23 *APS*, Vol. 6, Pt. 1, p. 197.
24 *Records of Commissions of the General Assemblies 1646–1647*, p. 123.
25 *APS*, Vol. 6, pt. 1, p. 197.
26 *SBSW*, pp. 158–71.
27 *APS*, Vol. 6, Pt. 2, p. 490.
28 *APS*, Vol. 6, Pt. 2, pp. 563, 564, and 566.
29 *APS*, Vol. 6, Pt. 2, p. 546.
30 B. Whitelocke, *Memorials of the English Affairs*, London, 1682, p. 545.
31 *Mercurius Politicus*, 1652, quoted in Black, *Calendar*, p. 63.
32 *Spottiswoode Miscellany*, Vol. 2, pp. 90–91.
33 *SBSW*, pp. 17–24, 55–7
34 *APS*, Vol. 7; Appendix, p. 31. I am grateful to Professor B. Levack for allowing me to see his unpublished paper on 'The Origins of the Great Scottish Witch Hunt'.
35 *SBSW*, pp. 25–39, 120–42, 214–18.
36 *RPC*, 3rd Ser., Vol. 1, p. 48.
37 *SBSW*, p. 272, Mary Somervail (591).
38 *RPC*, 3rd Ser., Vol. 1, p. 14.
39 *SBSW*, p. 279, Mary Morrison (690).
40 *SBSW*, p. 150 (1928, 1929).
41 E. Burt, *Letters from the North of Scotland*, ed. 1876, Vol. 1, pp. 242–3.

42 Janet Cornfoot (2990, 3001), D. Cook (ed.), *Notes and Extracts from the Ancient Records of the Burgh of Pittenweem*, Anstruther, 1867, pp. 109 ff.

CHAPTER SEVEN

1 *SBSW*, p. 81 (1112) and p. 138 (1785).
2 Cook, *Ancient Records of the Burgh of Pittenweem*, p. 53.
3 M. Flinn (ed.), *Scottish Population History*, pp. 109–200. The possible relation between ergot poisoning and outbreaks of hysteria which could be interpreted as diabolism has been raised as an explanation for witch-hunting in Scotland in M. L. Parry, *Climatic Change, Agriculture and Settlement*, Folkestone, 1978, p. 142. Such an explanation, however, would depend on further evidence that the poor weather conditions of 1591–98 and of 1647–49 did produce ergot poisoning and that this generated hysterical symptoms selectively in middle-aged women. There are no accounts of non-selective hysteria for which witches could have been blamed, nor were witches accused of generating collective hysteria. I am grateful to Leslie Alcock for drawing my attention to this reference.
4 *RPC*, Vol. XIII, p. 192.
5 *RPC*, Vol. XIII, p. 230.
6 *SBSW*, pp. 20–21 and pp. 24–5 (where they feature under Stirling).
7 Buckle, *op. cit.*, ed. H. J. Hanham as *On Scotland and the Scotch Intellect*, London, 1970, pp. 47–50; Lecky, *op. cit.*, pp. 132 ff.
8 *Book of the Universall Kirk* III, p. 993.
9 *RPC*, Vol. XIII, pp. 612–14; Vol. VIII, pp. 328–9.
10 *RPC*, Vol. IX, p. 191; Vol. V, pp. 76, 231, 329.
11 *RPC*, Vol. XIII, p. 620.
12 *APS*, Vol. VI, Pt. 1, p. 197.
13 One pound Scots was equal to one-twelfth of an English pound. A boll of oatmeal (140 lbs.), the price of which varied greatly, was valued at £6 13s 4d Scots in 1643. Flinn (ed.), *Scottish Population History*, p. 490.
14 *Acts of the General Assembly*, pp. 7, 37.
15 B. Levack, 'The Great Scottish Witch Hunt of 1661–2', unpublished paper.
16 *RPC*, 3rd Ser., Vol. VI, p. 162.
17 *SRO*, PA 11/8, p. 143.

CHAPTER EIGHT

1 *SBSW*, pp. 242–7.
2 Such internal evidence is found for example for the Jedburgh suspects of 1649 (*SRO*, RCE PA 11/8); the Stirling suspects of 1659 (*SRO*, JC 10); the Samuelston suspects of 1662 (*SRO*, JC 26/28); and the Paiston suspects of 1678 (*SRO*, JC 2/15).
3 Macfarlane, *Witchcraft in Tudor and Stuart England*, p. 160.
4 (671) *SRO*, JC 2/81 D9.
5 (678) *SRO*, JC 26/81 D9, JC 3 D1 89.
6 (2063/2208) *SRO*, RCE PA 11/8, p. 135.
7 (2938) Lord Fountainhall, *Historical Notices*, Edinburgh, 1848, p. 561.

8 H. Paton, *The Session Book of Rothesay 1658–1750*, 1931, pp. 200–1.

9 Extracted from computerized material collected for *SBSW* but not presented there in that form.

10 A. Soman, 'Les procès de sorcellerie au Parlement de Paris', *Annales* No. 4, 1977, pp. 790–814.

11 Midelfort, *op. cit.*, p. 179.

12 Monter, *op. cit.*, pp. 22–4.

13 P. Shuttle and P. Redgrove, *The Wise Wound*, London, 1978, pp. 221–2.

14 Pliny the Younger, *Naturalis Historia*, Book VII, XV, Loeb edition, 1842, Vol. II, p. 548.

15 James VI, *Daemonologie*, pp. 43–4.

16 See M. G. Dickson, 'Patterns of European Sanctity: the Cult of Saints in the Later Middle Ages', Ph.D. thesis, University of Edinburgh, 1974; P. Delooz, *Sociologie et Canonisation*, Liège, 1969; M. Goodich, 'A Profile of Thirteenth-century Sainthood'; *Comparative Studies in Society and History*, 1976.

17 Zguta, *loc. cit.*, p. 1189.

18 Kieckhefer, *op. cit.*, p. 145.

19 Monter, *op. cit.*, pp. 118–20.

20 Midelfort, *op. cit.*, p. 95.

21 Thomas, *op. cit.*, pp. 520–22.

22 *Ibid.*, pp. 524–6.

23 *Ibid.*, p. 520.

24 Dalyell, *op. cit.*, p. 577.

25 (400) *SRO*, JC 2/11; JC 26/27.

26 Thomas, *op. cit.*, p. 520.

27 (378) *SRO*, JC 26/27.

28 E. Goody, 'Legitimate and Illegitimate Aggression in a West African State', in M. Douglas, *Witchcraft Confessions and Accusations*, p. 240.

29 S. Townsend Warner, *Lolly Willowes*, London, 1926 (reprinted 1978).

30 *SBSW*, p. 241.

31 Macfarlane, *op. cit.*, p. 158.

32 Thomas, *op. cit.*, pp. 567–8.

33 Sir George Mackenzie, *Pleadings in Some Remarkable Cases*, p. 196.

34 P. J. Heine, *Personality and Social Theory*, Harmondsworth, 1972, p. 45.

35 G. F. Black, *Some Unpublished Scottish Witchcraft Trials*, New York, 1941. Elizabeth Bathgate (2414/155/1424/1427).

36 Helen Thomson, *SRO*, Kirk Session Records, Dumfries, August 1657. A. E. Truckell, Unpublished List and transcripts of Witchcraft Cases in Galloway and Dumfriesshire.

37 Helen Cursetter (2384), Dalyell, *Darker Superstitions*, p. 33.

38 Issobel Grierson (122), *SRO*, JC 2/4, Dalyell, *op. cit.*, p. 33.

39 Agnes Finnie (165/1466), Black, *Scottish Witchcraft Trials*, p. 21.

40 Bathgate, (2414), Black, *ibid.*, p. 14.

41 E. M. Schur, *Labeling Deviant Behaviour*, New York, 1971, pp. 8–13.

42 Margaret Bigland (1861), Suna Voe (1864), *RPC*, 3rd Ser., Vol. 4, p. 5.

43 Helen Stewart (2901), G. Sinclair, *Satan's Invisible World Discovered*, Edinburgh, 1685, p. 231.

44 Bessie, Thomas, and John Carfa (1256, 1629, and 1259), *RPC*, 2nd Ser., Vol. 3, p. 269.

45 *Ibid.*

46 Elspet Paris (992), David Langlandis (993), *RPC*, Vol. 13, p. 422.

47 William Falconner (1008), Isobel Falconner (1006), Marioun Symsoun (1009), *RPC*, Vol. 13, pp. 460–64.
48 William Barton and wife (2744/2745), G. Sinclair, *Satan's Invisible World Discovered*, Edinburgh, 1685, pp. 160–64.
49 Elizabeth Maxwell (199), *SRO*, JC 26/26.
50 Agnes Finnie (165/1466)
51 Walker (2396), *The Presbytery Book of Strathbogie*, Aberdeen, 1843, p. 5.
52 Janet Taylor (2413), Ronald, *Landmarks of Old Stirling*, p. 354.
53 Deiff Meg (Margaret Anderson), *RPC*, 2nd Ser., Vol. 3, p. 110.
54 Archibald Watt (2630), R. Chambers, *Domestic Annals of Scotland*, Edinburgh, 1861, Vol. 2, p. 195.
55 Janet Wright (1090), *RPC*, 2nd Ser., Vol. 2, p. 444.
56 William Chrichtoun (2535), E. Henderson, *Annals of Dunfermline*, Glasgow, 1879, p. 317.
57 E. Nadel, *Nupe Religion*, London, 1954, pp. 163–81.
58 B. Ehrenreich and D. English, *Witches, Midwives and Nurses*, Compendium, 1974; A. Oakley, 'Wise Woman and Medicine Man', in J. Mitchell and A. Oakley, *The Rights and Wrongs of Women*, Harmondsworth, 1976, pp. 25–30.
59 James Williams, 'Women', in *Encyclopedia Britannica*, 9th Ed.
60 See A. Clark, *The Working Life of Women in the Seventeenth Century*, London, 1919; R. McDonough and R. Harrison, 'Patriarchy and Relations of Production', in A. Kuhn and A. M. Wolpe (eds.), *Women and Modes of Production*, London, 1978; Sheila Rowbotham, *Hidden from History*, London, 1973.
61 James Williams, *loc. cit.*
62 A. Anderson and R. Gordon, 'Witchcraft and the Status of Women', *British Journal of Sociology*, 1978; J. K. Swales & H. V. McLachlan, 'Witchcraft and the Status of Women', *BJS*, 1979; Anderson & Gordon, 'The Uniqueness of English Witchcraft', *BJS*, 1979.

CHAPTER NINE

1 Mackenzie, *Pleadings in Some Remarkable Cases*, p. 195.
2 Arnot, *A Collection and Abridgement of Celebrated Criminal Trials in Scotland*, p. 367.
3 Janet Thomson (330) and Marioun Yool (350), *SRO*, JC 26/26.
4 George Guidlet (592/842), *SRO*, JC 2/13.
5 Goodaile (2879).
6 G. Sinclair, *Satan's Invisible World*, p. 211.
7 Tranent witches, *SBSW*, pp. 22–5, *SRO*, JC 26/26.
8 *Ibid.*
9 Catherine Rowan (2437), Culross Kirk Session Records, *SRO* CH 2/77/1. I am indebted to Ben Benson for material from Fife Kirk Sessions.
10 A. L. Lowell, 'The Judicial Use of Torture', in *The Harvard Law Review*, Vol. 2, 1897, pp. 290–300; R. D. Melville, 'The Use and Forms of Judicial Torture in England and Scotland', *Scottish Historical Review*, Vol. 2, No. 7, 1905, pp. 225–48.
11 Lowell, *loc. cit.*, pp. 220–33.
12 Culross Kirk Session Records, *SRO*, CH 2/77/1.
13 Dunfermline Kirk Session Records, *SRO*, CH 2/592/1.

14 Presbytery of Dunfermline, *SRO*, CH 2/105/1.
15 Margaret Thomsone (1465), *RPC*, 2nd Ser., Vol. 8, pp. 37, 108–9, 117–19, 138.
16 *RPC*, 3rd Ser., Vol. 5, p. 171.
17 Melville, 'The Use and Forms of Judicial Torture', p. 239.
18 Melville, *loc. cit.*, p. 245.
19 *RPC*, Vol. 13, p. 363.
20 Marion Hardie (1137), *RPC*, 2nd Ser., Vol. 3, pp. 15, 41–2.
21 Alison Balfour (108), R. Pitcairn, *Criminal Trials*, Vol. 1, pp. 375–7.
22 Committee of Estates, *SRO*, PA U/8 p. 187.
23 Black, *Calendar*, p. 63.
24 *RPC*, 3rd Ser., Vol. 1, p. 48.
25 Max Gluckman, *Custom and Conflict in Africa*, Oxford, 1956 (1970 edition), p. 89.
26 Dalyell, *Darker Superstitions*, pp. 635–6.
27 See Black, *Calendar*, p. 26.
28 Black, *Calendar*, p. 81.
29 Dalyell, *op. cit.*, pp. 639–40, Janet Barker (163/2456), *SRO*, JC 2/8, p. 345.
30 R. Renwick (ed.), *Extracts from the Records of the Royal Burgh of Lanark*, Glasgow, 1893, p. 143.
31 Dalyell, *op. cit.*, p. 640, Jonet Paiston (396), *SRO*, JC 26/27/1.
32 Dalyell, *op. cit.*, p. 641.
33 W. Penfield & T. Rasmussen, *The Cerebral Cortex of Man*, New York, 1950.
34 Dalyell, *op. cit.*, p. 643, John Dicksone *SRO*, JC 26/28; Black, *Calendar*, p. 72.
35 Black, *Calendar*, p. 72.
36 Elizabeth Maxwell (199), *SRO*, JC 26/26; Truckell, *Transactions of Dumfriesshire and Galloway Natural History Society*, 1975–6.
37 Alison Patersone (193), *SRO*, JC 26/26.
38 Bessie Graham (194), *SRO*, JC 26/26.
39 Dalyell, *op. cit.*, p. 642.
40 Black, *Calendar*, p. 47.
41 Sharpe, *History of the Belief in Witchcraft in Scotland*, pp. 193–4.
42 *RPC*, 1st Ser., Vol. 8, p. 20.
43 *Spalding Club Miscellany*, Aberdeen, 1841, Vol. 5, p. 67.
44 J. Buchan, *History of Peeblesshire*, Glasgow, 1925–27, Vol. 2, pp. 177–8.
45 Black, *Calendar*, p. 31.
46 John Dicksone, *SRO*, JC 26/28.
47 Margaret Dunham (2552); Arnot, *Celebrated Criminal Trials*, p. 393.
48 A. Lang, *Sir George Mackenzie*, London, 1909, pp. 39–40.
49 Arnot, *loc. cit.*, p. 393.
50 Black, *Calendar*, p. 55.
51 Cook, *Records of Pittenweem*, pp. 49–50.
52 *Ibid.*
53 *Ibid.*
54 *SRO*, CH 2/105/1
55 Culross Kirk Session Records, *SRO*, CH 2/77/1.
56 *Selections from the Records of the Kirk Session of Aberdeen*, Spalding Club, 1846, pp. 38–9.
57 Register of Convictions of Delinquents for forestalling regretting, etc., October 1645–Sept. 1688. MS in Aberdeen Town House, Charter Room.
58 Lord Fountainhall, *Decisions*, p. 14.

59 *SRO*, Porteous Roll of Ayr 1658, JC 26/25.
60 *RPC*, 2nd Ser., Vol. 1, pp. 297–8.
61 *RPC*, 2nd Ser., Vol. 2, p. 489.
62 H. B. McCall, *History of Mid Calder*, Edinburgh, 1894, p. 33.
63 *SRO* Committee of Estates, RCE PA 11/8 Marion Durie (2063/2208), pp. 135, 157.
64 (602/603/604) *SBSW*, pp. 273–4.
65 Dunfermline Kirk Session Records, *SRO*, CH 2/592/1.
66 *RPC*, Vol. 13, pp. 460–61.
67 Black, *Calendar*, p. 63; Whitelocke, *Memorialls of the English Affairs*, London, 1682.
68 *SBSW*, p. 237.
69 Elizabeth Fouller (328), *SRO*, JC 26/26/13.
70 Janet Hill (1183), *RPC*, 2nd Ser., Vol. 3, p. 156; Black, *Calendar*, p. 44.
71 Janet Smellie (2666), J. Paterson, *History of Ayr and Wigton*, Edinburgh, 1863–66, p. 101.
72 Presbytery of Dunfermline, *SRO*, CH 2/105/1, Margaret Henderson, Lady Pittathrow (2600).
73 Fountainhall, *Historical Notices*, Edinburgh, 1848, Vol. 1, p. 144.

CHAPTER TEN

1 The cases are found in *SRO*, JC 10/3 and JC 26/38. All direct quotations in this chapter are taken from these documents, some of which are transcribed in A. E. Truckell, *loc. cit.*, 1976, pp. 95–108.
2 Dalyell, *op. cit.*, pp. 455 ff., 568, 627.
3 Peter Laslett, *Family Life and Illicit Love in Earlier Generations*, Cambridge, 1977, p. 45.
4 Macfarlane, *Witchcraft in Tudor and Stuart England*, p. 234.
5 *Ibid.*, p. 232.
6 E. M. Lemert, *Social Pathology*, New York, 1951, pp. 76–7.
7 Other examples are given by Dalyell, *op. cit.*, pp. 38–9, and McPherson, *op. cit.*, pp. 274–5.
8 William Perkins, *A Discourse of the Damned Art of Witchcraft*, Cambridge, 1608, p. 206; Macfarlane, *op. cit.*, p. 109.
9 *SBSW*, p. 213; W. McDowall, *History of the Burgh of Dumfries*, Edinburgh, 1867, p. 376.
10 See Dalyell, *op. cit.*, pp. 106–7; McPherson, *op. cit.*, pp. 227–34.

CHAPTER ELEVEN

1 *SBSW*, pp. 261–8.
2 *SBSW*, p. 252.
3 Cohn, *op. cit.*, pp. 110 ff.
4 Monter, *op. cit.*, pp. 10–11.
5 Kieckhefer, *op. cit.*
6 Cohn, *op. cit.*
7 *Ibid.*, p. 255.
8 *Ibid.*, p. 237.

9 Thomas, *op. cit.*, p. 185.
10 McPherson, *Primitive Beliefs*, p. 246.
11 R. Chambers, *Domestic Annals of Scotland*, Vol. 2, p. 153.
12 McPherson, *op. cit.*, p. 141.
13 *Ibid.*, pp. 250 ff.
14 Mackenzie, *Remarkable Cases*, p. 193.
15 *SBSW*, p. 253.
16 Isobel Bennet (301/804), *SRO*, JC 26/26.
17 Bessie Pain (599/2889), *SBSW*, pp. 269–71.
18 A. E. Truckell, 'Unpublished Witchcraft Trials' in *The Dumfriesshire and Galloway Natural History and Antiquarian Society*, LI, 1975, p. 53.
19 Bessie Paine, *SBSW*, pp. 269–71.
20 *A Cloud of Witnesses for the Royal Prerogatives of Jesus Christ*, Glasgow, 1796.
21 J. L. Austin, *Philosophical Papers*, Oxford, 1970 (2nd ed.), p. 138.
22 *SBSW*, pp. 276–7.
23 Truckell, *loc. cit.*
24 Margaret Wallace (138) *SRO* JC 2/6.
25 *SBSW*, p. 253.
26 *Ibid.*, p. 276.
27 Christian Wilson (553), *SRO*, JC 26/28.
28 Janet Miller (273), *SBSW*, p. 250.
29 Black, *Some Unpublished Scottish Witchcraft Trials*, pp. 15–16.
30 Truckell, *loc. cit.*, p. 50.
31 Jonet Dempstar, *RPC*, 2nd Ser., Vol. 1, p. 309.
32 Janet Daill (360), *SRO*, JC 26/27.
33 *SRO*, JC 26/27 1,661 cases Liberton; *SBSW*, pp. 256–8.
34 Jonet Boyman (7), *SRO*, JC 26/1.
35 1590 cases, Catherine Wallace (55), Janet Straton (86), Donald Robinson (87), *SRO*, JC 26/2.
36 Elene Case (391), *SRO*, JC 26/278–9; JC 2.
37 Janet Paxton or Paiston (369), *SRO*, JC 26/27/1.
38 Donald Mair (1906), *Reliquae Scoticae*, Edinburgh, 1828, p. 2.
39 Beatrix Lesley (377), *SRO*, JC 26/27.
40 Agnes Pegavie (378), *SRO*, JC 26/27.
41 Bessie Flinkar (396), *SBSW*, p. 258.
42 A. G. Reid, *Annals of Auchterarder*, Crieff, 1899, pp. 218 ff.
43 Janet Man (304), *SRO*, JC 26/26.
44 Mackenzie, *Laws and Customs of Scotland*, p. 51.
45 Margaret Watson (1470), *RPC*, 2nd Ser., Vol. 8, pp. 146 ff.
46 Thomas Black (381), *SRO*, JC 26/27.
47 John Scott (593/857), *SRO*, JC 26/27, Bundle 1, Item 4.
48 James Welsh (432), *SRO*, JC 26/28.
49 Patrick Lowrie (121), *SRO*, JC 2/4, p. 56.
50 Robert Wilson (1681), Reid, *Annals of Auchterarder*, p. 230.
51 Elspeth Blackie (380), *SBSW*, p. 256. Janet Paiston (369), *SRO*, JC 26/27/1, Janet Man (304), *SRO*, JC 36/26, Bessie Lacost (298), *SRO*, JC 26/26/C.
52 Isobel Rutherford (1147), *RPC*, 2nd Ser., Bessie Henderson (1676), Reid, *Annals of Auchterarder*, p. 227. Thomas Roy (Unnumbered), *SRO*, JC 2/2. Stenton Witches 1659, *SRO*, JC 26/26C.
53 Stenton Witches, *SRO*, JC 26/26C.
54 *Ibid.*

55 Reid, *Annals of Auchterarder*, p. 227.
56 G. R. Kinloch, *Reliquae Antiquae*, Edinburgh, 1848, p. 114.
57 *Ibid.*
58 Agnes Spark (2829), Kinloch *Reliquae Antiquae*, p. 115.
59 Isobel Gowdie (1756), *RPC*, 3rd Ser., Vol. VI, p. 243.
60 Elspet Bruice (1812), Kinloch *Reliquae Antiquae*, p. 122.
61 Bessie Lacost (298), *SRO*, JC 26/26/C
62 Marion Angus (269), *SRO*, JC 26/26.
63 Bessie Flinkar (396), *SBSW*, p. 258.
64 John Douglas (333), *SRO*, JC 26/26.
65 G. Turreff, *Antiquarian Gleanings*, Aberdeen, 1859, p. 21.
66 Maxwell, *History of Galloway*, p. 93.
67 Black, *Calendar*, p. 26.
68 Elspeth Blackie (380).
69 Black, *Unpublished Cases*, p. 17.
70 *RPC*, 2nd Ser., Vol. 8, p. 150.
71 Bessie Henderson (1676), Reid *Annals of Auchterarder*, p. 227.
72 Black, *Unpublished Cases*, p. 16.
73 *Ibid.*
74 Alison Fermer (295), *SRO*, JC 26/26.
75 Marion Angus, (269) *SRO*, JC 26/26.
76 Janet Wood (299), *SRO*, 26/26/C.

CHAPTER TWELVE

1 See Delumeau, *Catholicism Between Luther and Voltaire*, pp. 1–21; Much-embled, *Culture Populaire et Culture des Elites*, Paris, 1978, pp. 154–201.
2 R. Mitchison, *Life in Scotland*, London, 1978, pp. 40 ff; Smout, *History of the Scottish People*, pp. 62 ff.
3 See e.g. Lecky, *History of Rationalism*, 1910, pp. 126 ff; Black, *Calendar*, p. 14; R. Trevor Davies, *Four Centuries of Witch Belief*, London, 1947, pp. 5–12.
4 J. L. Teall, 'Witchcraft and Calvinism in Elizabethan England: Divine Power and Human Agency', *Journal of the History of Ideas* (23), 1962.
5 E. W. Monter, 'Witchcraft in Geneva, 1537–1662', *The Journal of Modern History*, Vol. 43, No. 2, 1971.
6 J. Calvin, *Harmony of the Pentateuch* (Geneva 1563), Edinburgh, 1853, Vol. II, p. 90.
7 W. M. Campbell, *The Triumph of Presbyterianism*, Edinburgh, 1958, pp. 136 ff.
8 *Ibid.*, pp. 1–12 *et passim*.
9 See e.g. *Funeral Sermons on the Death of Patrick Forbes*, ed. C. F. Shand, Edinburgh, 1845.
10 Andrew Gray, *Twelve Select Sermons*, Gisborne, N. 2. 1961, p. 63.
11 *Ibid.*, pp. 64–76.
12 Robert Bruce, *Sermons in the Kirk of Edinburgh*, Edinburgh, 1591, unpaginated
13 Robert Leighton, *Sermons*, London, 1828, p. 156.
14 *Ibid.*, p. 153.
15 Campbell, *op. cit.*, pp. 18–19.
16 Delumeau, *op. cit.*, pp. 154 ff.

17 T. G. Law (ed.), *The Catechism of Archbishop Hamilton*, Oxford, 1884, pp. 50–51.
18 *Ibid.*
19 *Ibid.*
20 *Dictionary of National Biography*; H. Scott, *Fasti Ecclesiae Scoticanae*, Edinburgh, 1866–71.
21 Transcribed G. Neilson in *Scottish Historical Review*, Vol. 7, 1910, pp. 391 ff.
22 James VI, *Daemonologie*, p. 7.
23 *Dictionary of National Biography*; Scott, *Fasti Ecclesiae Scoticanae*.
24 *The Witches of Renfrewshire*, pp. 165–81.
25 See Larner, 'Two Late Scottish Witchcraft Tracts' in Anglo (ed.), *The Black Art*.
26 *Witchcraft Proven*, p. 4.
27 Robert Law, *Memorialls*, pp. 145–6.
28 *Ibid.*, p. 146. Note by C. K. Sharpe.
29 *Tryal of Witchcraft*, p. 18.
30 *Malleus Maleficarum*, Trans. M. Summers, London, 1948, p. 1.
31 *Witchcraft Proven*, pp. 4–5.
32 *Tryal of Witchcraft*, p. 9.
33 Mair, *Witchcraft*, pp. 12, 30, and 103.
34 Leighton, *Sermons*, p. 279.
35 G. Sinclair, *Satan's Invisible World* (ed. Edinburgh, 1871), p. 47. Robert (Hob) Grieve (2111/2599), SRO, RCE PA 11/8.
36 Janet Man (304), SRO, JC 26/26.
37 Janet Saers (257/798), SRO, JC 26/25, Porteous Roll, Ayr; JC 10/2.

CHAPTER THIRTEEN

1 William Forbes, *The Institutes of the Law of Scotland*, p. 32.
2 *Ibid.*, p. 36.
3 *Ibid.*, p. 35.
4 *Ibid.*, p. 40.
5 *Ibid.*, p. 371.
6 Isobel Young (1148), Black, *Unpublished Cases*, pp. 4–10.
7 Black, *loc. cit.*, p. 5 n.
8 Arnot, *Criminal Trials*, p. 354.
9 Katharine Oswald (144/1176), Black, *Unpublished Cases*, pp. 10–14.
10 Elizabeth Bathgate (155/1424/2414), Black, *Unpublished Cases*, pp. 14–19.
11 *SBSW*, p. 109.
12 *SRO*, JC 26/27.
13 Janet Blackie (398), SRO, JC 26/27/1.
14 Katherine Hunter (371/1591), SRO, JC 26/27/1.
15 J. Balfour, *Practicks* (1675), Edinburgh, 1854, p. 357.
16 Mackenzie, *Remarkable Cases*, p. 185.
17 *Ibid.*
18 *Ibid.*, p. 188.
19 *Ibid.*, pp. 190–91.
20 *Ibid.*, pp. 193–4.
21 *Ibid.*, p. 189.
22 Mackenzie, *Laws and Customs of Scotland in Matters Criminal*, p. 45.

23 *Ibid.*, pp. 45–6.
24 *Ibid.*, pp. 52–3.
25 Bessie Gibb (646), *SRO*, JC 2/15.

CHAPTER FOURTEEN

1 M. T. Clanchy, *From Memory to Written Record*, London, 1979, pp. 46–7, 258 ff.
2 Cohn, *op. cit.*, pp. 161–3.
3 Lenman & Parker, 'The State, the Community, and the Criminal Law in Europe', in Lenman, Parker & Gatrell, *Crime and the Law*.
4 Langbein, *op. cit.*, p. 134.
5 On this see P. Paravy, 'À propos de la genese médiévale des chasses aux sorcières: le traité de Claude Tholosan juge dauphinois (vers 1436)' in *Mélanges de L'École Française de Rome*, Vol. 91, 1979, p. 349.
6 E. Chernyak, 'Demonologiya i okhota na ved'm v XVI–XVII vekakh' (Demonology and the Witch Hunt in the 15th–17th Centuries) in *Voprosy Istorii*, No. 10, 1979, pp. 99–111. I am grateful to Alec Nove for drawing my attention to this and translating it for me.
7 H. Sebald, *Witchcraft: The Heritage of a Heresy*, New York, 1978, pp. 1–33.
8 Currie, *loc. cit.*, pp. 251 ff.
9 Muchembled, in Dupont-Bouchat *et al.*, *Prophètes et Sorciers*, p. 30; *Culture Populaire et Culture des Élites*, p. 294.
10 Monter, *op. cit.*, p. 159.
11 Lecky, *op. cit.*, Vol. 1, p. 133.
12 Dalyell, *op. cit.*, p. 645.

BIBLIOGRAPHY

Acts of the General Assembly 1638–1842, Edinburgh, 1943.

Adam, Isobel, Witch Hunt, London, 1978.

Aldis, H. G., List of Books Printed in Scotland Before 1700, Edinburgh, 1904.

Anderson, A. & Gordon, S., 'Witchcraft and the Status of Women', British Journal of Sociology, 1978.

Anderson, A. & Gordon, S., 'The Uniqueness of English Witchcraft', British Journal of Sociology, 1979.

Anderson, Maureen, 'A Calendar of Witchcraft in Angus', Undergraduate Dissertation, University of St. Andrews, 1976.

Anon, Diurnal of Remarkable Occurents, Edinburgh, 1833.

Anon, An Ingenious and Scientific Discourse of Witchcraft, N.P., 1705.

Anon, Letters Concerning the Witches of Pittenweem, Edinburgh, 1705.

Anon, A New Confutation of Sadducism, London, 1696.

Anon, Newes from Scotland, Edinburgh, 1591.

Anon, A Relation of the diabolical Practice . . . London, 1697.

Anon, Sadducismus Debellatus, London, 1698.

Anon, Trial, Confession, and Execution of Isobel Inch, John Stewart, Margaret Barclay and Isobel Crawfurd for witchcraft at Irvine Anno 1618, N.P., 1855.

Anon, True and Full Relation of the Witches of Pittenweem, Edinburgh, 1704.

Anon, A True Narration of the Sufferings and Relief of a Young Girl, Edinburgh, 1698.

Anon, The Tryal of Witchcraft Glasgow, 1705.

Anon, Witchcraft Proven, Glasgow, 1697.

Arnot, Hugo, Collection and Abridgement of Celebrated Criminal Trials in Scotland, Edinburgh, 1785.

Arnot, Hugo, History of Edinburgh, Edinburgh, 1779.

Austin, J. L., Philosophical Papers, Oxford, 1970.

Balfour, J., Practicks (1675), Edinburgh, 1854.

Baranowski, B., Procesy czarnownic w Poland w XVII i XVIII wieku, Lódź 1952.

Baroja, Julio Caro, The World of Witches, London, 1964.

Beattie, J., Other Cultures, London, 1964.

Birrell, R., Diary, Edinburgh, 1795.

Black, Angus (ed.), The Devil's Coven, London, 1972.

Black, G. F., Calendar of Cases of Witchcraft in Scotland 1510–1727, New York, 1938.

Black, G. F., Some Unpublished Scottish Witchcraft Trials, New York, 1941.

Boatright, M. C., 'Witchcraft in the Novels of Sir Walter Scott', University of Texas Studies in English XIII, 1933.

Book of the Universall Kirk of Scotland, Maitland Club, Edinburgh, 1839.

Box, S., Deviance, Reality and Society, London, 1971.

Boyer, Paul & Nissenbaum, Stephen, Salem Processed: the Social Origins of Witchcraft, Cambridge, Mass., 1974.

Brodie, Alexander, *The Diary of Alexander Brodie*, Ed. D. Laing, Spalding Club, Aberdeen, 1863.

Bruce, Robert, *Sermons in the Kirk of Edinburgh*, Edinburgh, 1591.

Buckle, H. T., *History of Civilisation in England*, London, 1861.

Buchan, John, *Witchwood*, London, 1929.

Buchan, J., *History of Peeblesshire*, Glasgow, 1925–27.

Burt, Edward, *Letters from the North of Scotland*, London, 1876.

Calendar of State Papers Relating to Scotland, Edinburgh, 1936.

Calvin, J., *Harmony of the Pentateuch* (Geneva, 1563), Edinburgh, 1853.

Campbell, J. G., *Witchcraft and Second Sight in the Highlands and Islands of Scotland*, Glasgow, 1902.

Campbell, W. M., *The Triumph of Presbyterianism*, Edinburgh, 1958.

Capp, Bernard, *Astrology and the Popular Press*, London, 1979.

Carter, Ian, *Farm Life in Northeast Scotland 1840–1914*, Edinburgh, 1979.

Chambers, Robert, *Domestic Annals of Scotland*, Edinburgh, 1861.

Chernyak, E., 'Demonologiya i okhota na ved'm v XVI–XVII vekakh' (Demonology and the Witch Hunt in the 15th–17th Centuries), *Voprosy Istorii* No. 10, 1979.

Clanchy, M. T., *From Memory to Written Record: England 1066–1307*, London, 1979.

Clark, Alice, *The Working Life of Women in the Seventeenth Century*, London, 1919.

Clark, Stuart, 'King James's *Daemonologie*: Witchcraft and Kingship', in S. Anglo, ed., *The Damned Art*, London, 1977.

A Cloud of Witnesses for the Royal Prerogatives of Jesus Christ, Glasgow, 1796.

Cockburn, J. S., *Crime in England 1550–1800*, London, 1977.

Cohn, Norman, *Europe's Inner Demons*, London, 1975.

Cook, David, *Notes and Extracts from the Ancient Records of the Burgh of Pittenweem*, Anstruther, 1867.

Corpus Iuris Civilis

Crawford, J. R., *Witchcraft and Sorcery in Rhodesia*, Oxford, 1967.

Currie, Elliot P., 'The Control of Witchcraft in Renaissance Europe' in D. Black, *The Social Organisation of Law*, New York, 1973.

Dalyell, J. G., *The Darker Superstitions of Scotland*, Edinburgh, 1834.

Davidson, Thomas, *Rowan Tree and Red Thread*, Edinburgh, 1949.

Davies, R. Trevor, *Four Centuries of Witch Belief*, London, 1947.

Delumeau, Jean, *Catholicism between Luther and Voltaire*, London, 1977.

Delooz, P., *Sociologie et Canonisation*, Liège, 1969.

Dickson, M. G., 'Patterns of European Sanctity: the Cult of Saints in the Later Middle Ages', Unpublished Ph.D. thesis, Edinburgh, 1974.

Ditton, Jason, *Contrology*, London, 1979.

Donaldson, G., 'The legal profession in Scottish Society in the sixteenth and seventeenth centuries', *Juridical Review*, Vol. XXI, 1976.

Donaldson, G., *Scotland: James V–James VII*, Edinburgh, 1965.

Donaldson, G., *The Scottish Reformation*, 1960.

Donaldson, G. (ed.), *St. Andrews Formulare*, Stair Society, Edinburgh, 1944.

Douglas, Mary (ed.), *Witchcraft Confessions and Accusations*, London, 1970.

Dunlap, Rhodes, 'King James and some Witches: the Date and Text of the *Daemonologie*', *Philological Quarterly* 54, 1975.

Dupont-Bouchat, Marie Sylvie, Frijhoff, Willem, & Muchembled, R. (eds.), *Prophètes et Sorciers dans les Pays-Bas*, Paris, 1978.

Ehrenreich, B. & English, D., *Witches, Midwives and Nurses*, London, 1974.

Erikson, Kai, *Wayward Puritans*, New York, 1966.

Erskine, John, *An Institute of the Law of Scotland*, Edinburgh, 1773.

Erskine, John, *The Principles of the Law of Scotland*, Edinburgh, 1764 (3rd ed.).

Evans-Pritchard, E. E., *Witchcraft, Oracles and Magic among the Azande*, Oxford, 1937.

Ewen, C. L'Estrange, *Witch-hunting and Witch Trials*, London, 1929.

Ferguson, John, 'Bibliographical Notes on the Witchcraft Literature of Scotland', in *Proceedings of the Edinburgh Bibliographical Society*, Edinburgh, 1899.

Flinn, M. (ed.), *Scottish Population History*, Cambridge, 1977.

Forbes, William, *The Institutes of the Law of Scotland*, Edinburgh, 1730.

Foster, J., 'Capitalism and the Scottish Nation', in G. Brown (ed.), *The Red Paper on Scotland*, Edinburgh, 1975.

Foster, W. R., *The Church Before the Covenants*, Edinburgh, 1975.

Fountainhall, Lord, *The Decisions of the Lords of Council and Session*, Edinburgh, 1759–1761.

Fountainhall, Lord, *Historical Notices*, Edinburgh, 1848.

Gellner, E., 'The Savage and the Modern Mind', in R. Horton & R. Finnegan (eds.) *Modes of Thought*, London, 1973.

Gellner, E., 'The New Idealism', in A. Giddens, *Positivism and Sociology*, London, 1974.

Gellner, E., *Legitimation of Belief*, Cambridge, 1974.

Gluckman, Max, *Custom and Conflict in Africa*, Oxford (1956), 1970.

Goffman, Erving, *Asylums*, Harmondsworth, 1970.

Grant, I. F., *Social and Economic Development of Scotland Before 1603*, Edinburgh, 1930.

Gray, Andrew, *Twelve Select Sermons*, Gisborne N.Z., 1961.

Gray, R. F., in Middleton & Winter, *Witchcraft and Sorcery in East Africa*, London, 1963.

Goodich, M., 'A Profile of Thirteenth Century Sainthood', *Comparative Studies in Society and History*, 1976.

Goody, E., 'Legitimate and Illegitimate Aggression in a West African State', in M. Douglas (ed.), *Witchcraft Confessions and Accusations*, London, 1970.

Hamilton, Henry, *An Economic History of Scotland in the Eighteenth Century*, Oxford, 1963.

Handley, J. E., *Scottish Farming in the Eighteenth Century*, London, 1953.

Hannay, R. K., *Rentale Sancti Andree*, Scottish History Society, Edinburgh, 1915.

Harris, Marvin, *Cows, Pigs, Wars, and Witches*, London, 1974.

Heikkinen, Antero, *Paholaisen Liittolaiset* (Allies of the Devil), Helsinki, 1969.

Heine, P. J., *Personality and Social Theory*, Harmondsworth, 1972.

Henderson, E., *Annals of Dunfermline*, Glasgow, 1879.

Henderson, G. D., *Religious Life in Seventeenth-Century Scotland*, Cambridge, 1937.

Hill, Christopher, *The World Turned Upside Down*, 1972 (Penguin 1975).

Horton, W. R. G., 'African Traditional Thought and Western Science', *Africa* XXXVII, No. 1 and 2.

Hume, David, *Commentaries on the Law of Scotland*, Edinburgh, 1819 (2nd ed.).

James VI of Scotland, *Daemonologie*, Edinburgh, 1597.

Johnson, Tom, *History of the Working Classes in Scotland*, London, 1946.

Keiller, Alex, *The Personnel of the Aberdeenshire Witchcraft Covens*, London, 1922.

Kieckhefer, R., *European Witch Trials*, London, 1976.

Kinloch, G. R., *Reliquae Antiquae*, Edinburgh, 1848.
Kittredge, G. L., *Witchcraft in Old and New England*, Cambridge, Mass., 1929.
Kluckhohn, Clyde, *Navaho Witchcraft*, Cambridge, Mass., 1944.
Knox, John, *History of the Reformation* in *The Works of John Knox*, ed. D. Laing, Edinburgh, 1848.
Lamont, J., *Diary*, Maitland Club, Edinburgh, 1830.
Lang, A., *Sir George Mackenzie*, London, 1909.
Langbein, J. H., *Prosecuting Crime in the Renaissance*, Cambridge, Mass., 1974.
Larner, C., 'James VI and I and Witchcraft', in *The Reign of James VI and I*, ed. A. G. R. Smith, London, 1973.
Larner, C., 'Crimen Exceptum' in Lenman, Parker & Gatrell (eds.), *Crime and the Law: the Social History of Crime in Western Europe since 1500*, London, 1980.
Larner, C., 'Two Late Scottish Witchcraft Tracts', in Sydney Anglo (ed.), *The Damned Art*, London, 1977.
Larner, C., Lee, Christopher Hyde, & McLachlan, Hugh, *A Source Book of Scottish Witchcraft*, Glasgow, 1977.
Laslett, Peter, *Family Life and Illicit Love in Earlier Generations*, Cambridge, 1977.
Law, Robert, *Memorialls*, Edinburgh, 1818.
Law, T. G. (ed.), *The Catechism of Archbishop Hamilton*, Oxford, 1884.
Lecky, W. E. H., *History of the Rise and Influence of the Spirit of Rationalism in Europe*, London, 1865.
Lee, C. H., 'Jurisdiction in Early Seventeenth Century Scotland', Unpublished paper, 1974.
Legge, F., 'Witchcraft in Scotland', *The Scottish Review*, 1891.
Leighton, Robert, *Sermons*, London, 1828.
Lemert, E. M., *Social Pathology*, New York, 1951.
Lenman, B., Parker, G. & Gatrell, V. (eds.), *Crime and the Law: the Social History of Crime in Western Europe since 1500*, London, 1980.
Lenman, B. & Parker, G., 'Crime and Control in Scotland 1500–1800', *History Today*, 1980.
Lenman, B. & Parker, G., 'Sources for the History of Crime in Early Modern Scotland', SSRC Final Report No. HR 4373/2.
Le Roy Ladurie, E., *Les Paysans de Languedoc*, Paris, 1966.
Levack, Brian, 'The Great Scottish Witch Hunt of 1661–2', Unpublished paper, 1979.
Littlewood, Barbara, 'The Evil Eye in Southern Italy', Unpublished paper, 1975.
Logue, K. J., *Popular Disturbance in Scotland 1780–1815*, Edinburgh, 1979.
Lowell, A. L., 'The Judicial Use of Torture', *Harvard Law Review*, Vol. 2, 1897.
Lukes, Steven, *Essays in Social Theory*, London, 1977.
Lythe, S. G. E., *The Economy of Scotland in its European Setting 1550–1627*, Edinburgh, 1960.
Lythe, S. G. E., 'The Economy of Scotland under James VI and I', in A. G. R. Smith (ed.), *The Reign of James VI and I*, London, 1973.
Lythe, S. G. E. & Bott, J., *An Economic History of Scotland*, Glasgow, 1975.
McCall, H. B., *History of Mid Calder*, Edinburgh, 1894.
McDonough, R. & Harrison, R., 'Patriarchy and the Relations of Production', in A. Kuhn & A. M. Wolpe (eds.), *Women and Modes of Production*, London, 1978.
McDowall, *History of the Burgh of Dumfries*, Edinburgh, 1867.
Macfarlane, A., *The Origins of English Individualism*, Oxford, 1978.
Macfarlane, A., *Witchcraft in Tudor and Stuart England*, London, 1970.

MacGregor, A., *Highlands Superstitions*, Stirling, 1922.

McIntyre, Peter, 'The Franchise Courts', in Stair Society *Introduction to Scottish Legal History*, Edinburgh, 1958.

MacKay, Charles, *Memoirs of Extraordinary Popular Delusions*, London, 1841.

Mackenzie, George, *Laws and Customs of Scotland in Matters Criminal*, Edinburgh, 1678.

Mackenzie, George, *Pleadings in Some Remarkable Cases*, Edinburgh, 1672.

MacLeod, Nicholas A., *Scottish Witchcraft*, St. Ives, 1975.

McPherson, J. M., *Primitive Beliefs in the North-East of Scotland*, London, 1929.

Mair, Lucy, *Witchcraft*, London, 1969.

Maitland Club Miscellany, Edinburgh, 1833.

Makey, Walter, *The Church of the Covenant 1637–1651*, Edinburgh, 1979.

Manning, Brian, 'The Nobles and People and the Constitution', in *Crisis in Europe*, ed. T. Aston, London, 1965.

Marwick, M. G., 'Another Modern Anti-witchcraft Movement in East Central Africa', *Africa*, Vol. 20, 1950.

Marwick, M. G., *Sorcery in its Social Setting*, Manchester, 1965.

Marwick, M. G. (ed.), *Witchcraft and Sorcery*, Harmondsworth, 1970.

Marwick, M. G., 'Witchcraft as a Social Strain-Gauge' in *Australian Journal of Science*, Vol. 26, 1964.

Mathieson, W. L., *Politics and Religion*, Glasgow, 1902.

Maxwell, W., *History of Dumfries and Galloway*, Edinburgh, N.D.

Mayer, Philip, 'Witches', in M. G. Marwick, *Witchcraft and Sorcery*, Harmondsworth, 1970.

Melville, R. D., 'The Use and Forms of Judicial Torture in England and Scotland', *Scottish Historical Review*, Vol. 2, No. 7, 1905.

Middleton, J. F. M. & Winter, E. H. (eds.), *Witchcraft and Sorcery in East Africa*, London, 1963.

Midelfort, H. C. Erik, *Witchhunting in Southwestern Germany 1562–1684*, Stanford, 1972.

Millar, John, *A History of the Witches of Renfrewshire*, Paisley, 1809.

Mitchison, R., *A History of Scotland*, London, 1970.

Mitchison, R., *Life in Scotland*, London, 1978.

Mitchison, R., 'A Parish and its Poor', in *Trans. of the East Lothian Antiquarian and Field Naturalists' Society*, Vol. 14, 1974.

Monter, E. W., 'Witchcraft in Geneva 1537–1662', *The Journal of Modern History*, Vol. 43, No. 2, 1971.

Monter, E. W., *Witchcraft in France and Switzerland*, Ithaca, 1976.

Morris, Terence, *Deviance and Control: the Secular Heresy*, London, 1976.

Muchembled, R., *Culture Populaire et Culture des élites*, Paris, 1978.

Muchembled, R., *La Sorcière au village*, Paris, 1979.

Murray, Margaret, *The Witch Cult in Western Europe*, Oxford, 1921, reprinted, 1962.

Nadel, E., *Nupe Religion*, London, 1954.

Neilson, G., 'Transcription of Sermon by James Hutchison', *Scottish Historical Review*, Vol. 7, 1910.

Nicoll, J., *A Diary of Public Transactions*, Bannatyne Club, Edinburgh, 1836.

Notestein, Wallace, *History of Witchcraft in England*, Washington, 1911.

Oakley, A., 'Wise Woman and Medicine Man' in J. Mitchell & A. Oakley (eds.), *The Rights and Wrongs of Women*, Harmondsworth, 1976.

Parsons, C. O., *Witchcraft and Demonology in Scott's Fiction*, Edinburgh, 1964.

Paterson, J., *History of Ayr and Wigton*, Edinburgh, 1863–66.
Paton, H. (ed.), *The Session Book of Rothesay 1658–1750*.
Peel, J. D. Y., 'Understanding Alien Belief Systems', *British Journal of Sociology* 20, 1969.
Penfield, W. & Rasmussen, T., *The Cerebral Cortex of Man*, New York, 1950.
Perkins, William, *A Discourse of the Damned Art of Witchcraft*, Cambridge, 1608.
Pitcairn, Robert, *Criminal Trials in Scotland 1488–1624*, Edinburgh, 1833.
Pliny the Younger, *Naturalis Historia*, Loeb translation, 1842.
Presbytery Book of Strathbogie, Aberdeen, 1843.
Records of Commissions of the General Assemblies 1646–1647, Edinburgh, 1842.
Reid, A. G., *Annals of Auchterarder*, Crieff, 1899.
Reliquae Scoticae, Edinburgh, 1828.
Renwick, R., *Extracts from the Records of the Royal Burgh of Lanark*, Glasgow, 1893.
Richards, Audrey, 'A Modern Movement of Witch-finders', *Africa*, Vol. 8, 1935.
Robbins, Rossell Hope, *The Encyclopaedia of Witchcraft and Demonology*, Feltham, 1959.
Robertson, David, 'Burgh Court Records', in *An Introductory Survey of the Sources and Literature of Scots Law*, Stair Society, Vol. 1, Edinburgh, 1936.
Ross, W., *Aberdour and Inchcolme*, Edinburgh, 1885.
Row, John, *Historie of the Kirk of Scotland 1558–1637*, Wodrow Society, Edinburgh, 1842.
Rowbotham, Sheila, *Hidden from History*, London, 1973.
Russell, Jeffrey, *Witchcraft in the Middle Ages*, Cornell, 1972.
Schormann, G., *Hexenprozesse in Nordwestdeutschland*, Hildersheim, 1977.
Schur, E. M., *Labeling Deviant Behaviour*, New York, 1971.
Scott, Hew, *Fasti Ecclesianae Scotticanae*, Edinburgh, 1866–71.
Scott, Walter, *Letters on Demonology and Witchcraft*, London, 1830.
Scott-Moncrieff, R., *Records of the Proceedings of the Justiciary Court, Edinburgh 1661–1678*, Scottish Historical Society, Vol. 42, Edinburgh.
Sebald, Hans, *Witchcraft: the Heritage of a Heresy*, New York, 1978.
Selections from the Records of the Kirk Session of Aberdeen, Spalding Club, Edinburgh, 1846.
Seth, Ronald, *In the Name of the Devil*, London, 1969.
Shand, C. F. (ed.), *Funeral Sermons on the Death of Patrick Forbes*, Edinburgh, 1845.
Shapera, Isaac, 'Sorcery and Witchcraft in Bechuanaland', *African Affairs*, Vol. 51, 1951, and in Marwick *Witchcraft and Sorcery*.
Sharpe, Charles K., *Historical Account of the Belief in Witchcraft in Scotland*, Glasgow, 1884.
Shuttle, P. & Redgrove, P., *The Wise Wound*, 1978.
Sinclair, George, *Satan's Invisible World Discovered*, Edinburgh, 1685.
Smout, T. C., *A History of the Scottish People*, London, 1969.
Soman, A., 'Criminal Jurisprudence in Ancien-Regime France: The Parlement of Paris in the Sixteenth and Seventeenth Centuries', in *Crime and Justice in Europe and Canada*, ed. Louis A. Knafla, Montreal, 1980.
Soman, A., 'Les procès de sorcellerie au Parlement de Paris', *Annales* 4, 1977.
Soman, A., 'The Parliament of Paris and the Great Witch Hunt (1565–1640)', *Sixteenth Century Journal*, IX, 2, 1978.
Spalding Club Miscellany, Vol. 5, Aberdeen, 1841.

Spottiswoode, Archbishop, *History of the Church of Scotland* (1655), Edinburgh, 1851.

Spottiswoode Miscellany, Edinburgh, 1844.

Sprenger, J. & Kramer, H., *Malleus Maleficarum* (Trans. M. Summers), London, 1948.

Stafford, Helen, 'Notes on Scottish Witchcraft Cases 1590–1591', in Norton Downes (ed.), *Essays in Honour of Conyers Read*, Chicago, 1953.

Stair Society, *Introduction to Scottish Legal History*, Edinburgh, 1958.

Stair Society, *Sources and Literature of Scots Law*, Edinburgh, 1936.

Stevenson, D., *The Scottish Revolution*, Newton Abbot, 1973.

Sutherland, Elizabeth, *The Eye of God*, London, 1977.

Swales, J. K. & McLachlan, H. V., 'Witchcraft and the Status of Women', *British Journal of Sociology*, 1979.

Teall, J. L., 'Witchcraft and Calvinism in Elizabethan England: Divine Power and Human Agency', *Journal of the History of Ideas*, 23, 1962.

Telfair, Alexander, *True Relation of an Apparition*, Edinburgh, 1696.

Thomas, Keith, *Religion and the Decline of Magic*, London, 1971.

Thomson, J. M., *The Public Records of Scotland*, Glasgow, 1922.

Thorner, D., 'Peasant Economy as a Category in Economic History', in T. Shanin (ed.), *Peasants and Peasant Societies*, Harmondsworth, 1971.

Trevor-Roper, H. R., *The European Witch-Craze of the Sixteenth and Seventeenth Centuries*, Harmondsworth, 1969.

Trevor-Roper, H. R., *Religion, the Reformation and Social Change*, London, 1967.

Truckell, A. E., 'Unpublished Witchcraft Trials', *Transactions of the Dumfriesshire and Galloway Natural History and Antiquarian Society*, 1975 and 1976.

Turreff, G., *Antiquarian Gleanings*, Aberdeen, 1859.

Warner, Sylvia Townsend, *Lolly Willowes*, London, 1926.

Warrender Papers, Edinburgh, 1932.

Webster, D. (ed.), *Collection of Rare and Curious Tracts on Witchcraft*, Edinburgh, 1820.

Whitelocke, B., *Memorials of the English Affairs*, London, 1682.

Whyte, Ian, *Agriculture and Society in Seventeenth Century Scotland*, Edinburgh, 1979.

Williams, James, 'Women' in *Encyclopedia Britannica*, 9th ed., Edinburgh, 1880.

Wilson, Monica, 'Witch Beliefs and Social Structure', *American Journal of Sociology*, 1951, 56, No. 4.

Wilson, Monica, *Communal Rituals of the Nyakyusa*, London, 1959.

Winch, P., *The Idea of a Social Science and its Relation to Philosophy*, London, 1958.

Winch, P., 'Understanding a Primitive Society', *American Philosophical Quarterly*, 1964.

Wormald, J. M., (J. M. Brown), 'The Exercise of Power' in J. M. Brown (ed.), *Scottish Society in the Fifteenth Century*, London, 1977.

Zguta, Russell, 'Witchcraft Trials in Seventeenth Century Russia', *American Historical Review*, Vol. 82², 1977.

INDEX

Over 250 individual accused witches, spouses of witches, accusers, and jurors mentioned in the text have not been indexed unless referred to more than once. References to accused witches can be found in the Notes.